Kindergarten JUMBO Workbook

This book belongs to:

....

US Editors Nancy Ellwood, Margaret Parrish, Allison Singer
Editors Fran Baines, Rohini Deb, Tanya Desai,
Camilla Gersh, Jolyon Goddard, Nandini Gupta,
Nishtha Kapil, Shahwar Kibria, Cécile Landau,
Deborah Lock, Monica Saigal
Art Editors Dheeraj Arora, Jyotsna Julka,
Rashika Kachroo, Kanika Kalra, Radhika Kapoor,
Pallavi Narain, Tanvi Nathyal, Yamini Panwar, Marisa Renzullo
Managing Editor Soma B. Chowdhury
Managing Art Editors Richard Czapnik, Ahlawat Gunjan
Production Editor Gillian Reid
Production Controller Mandy Inness
Jacket Designer Jomin Johny
Publisher Andrew Macintyre
Associate Publishing Director Liz Wheeler
Publishing Director Jonathan Metcalf

Content previously published in *Extra Math Practice K*
and *DK Workbooks: Math, Science, Geography,
Language Arts, Spelling K*

This Edition published in 2020
First American Edition, 2015
Published in the United States by DK Publishing
1450 Broadway, Suite 801, New York, NY 10018

A catalog record for this book
is available from the Library of Congress.

ISBN 978-0-7440-3297-0

DK books are available at special discounts when purchased
in bulk for sales promotions, premiums, fund-raising,
or educational use. For details, contact:
DK Publishing Special Markets,
1450 Broadway, Suite 801, New York, NY 10018
SpecialSales@dk.com

Printed in Canada

All images © Dorling Kindersley Limited
For further information see: www.dkimages.com

For the curious
www.dk.com

Contents

This chart lists all the topics in the book.

Letter to Parents

This book is intended to assist children in kindergarten. By working through the book, your child will learn all the key concepts taught at this level in a fun and informative way. The exercises and activities will help reinforce his or her understanding of the basic concepts taught in kindergarten in the following subjects:

- math;
- science;
- geography;
- language arts;
- spelling.

All the activities in the book are intended to be completed by a child with adult support. As you work through the pages with your child, make sure he or she understands what each activity requires. Read the facts and instructions aloud. Encourage questions and reinforce observations that will build confidence and increase active participation in classes at school.

By working with your child, you will understand how he or she thinks and learns. When appropriate, use props and objects from daily life to help your child make connections with the world outside.

In addition, try to help your child connect the content to specific personal experiences. For example, as you read a book together, explore the book cover. Ask your child to retell a story you have read, using temporal words such as "first," "next," "then," and "finally." Encourage your child to practice math, letters, and writing on the practice pages given at the end of the book.

Be sure to praise your child as he or she completes a page, gives a correct answer, or makes progress. This will help build your child's confidence and increase his or her interest in the subjects being studied.

Good luck and remember to have fun!

K Math

Authors Sean McArdle, Linda Ruggieri

Educational Consultant Alison Tribley

Contents

This chart lists all the topics in the Math section.

Write the number.

1 ⋮

Write the word.

one oｎｅ

Write the number.

2 2

Write the word.

two ｔｗo

Write the number.

3 3

Write the word.

three ｔｈｒｅｅ

Write the number.

4 4

Write the word.

four four

Write the number.

5 5

Write the word.

five five

How many?

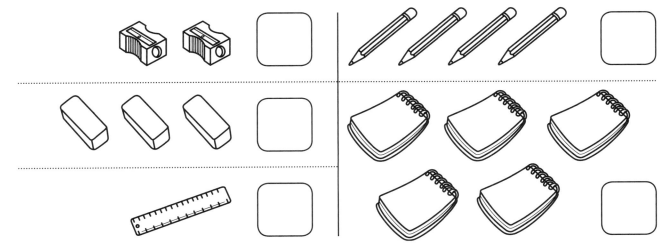

This is a circle.

Draw a circle around each object.

Draw some circles of your own.

These are ovals. An oval is egg-shaped.
An oval is like a squashed circle.

Draw an oval around each object.

Draw some ovals of your own.

Circle the animal that is the same.

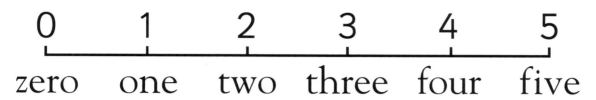

Count the objects in each group. Then write down the number that is **one more** than the group. Write the number and the word.

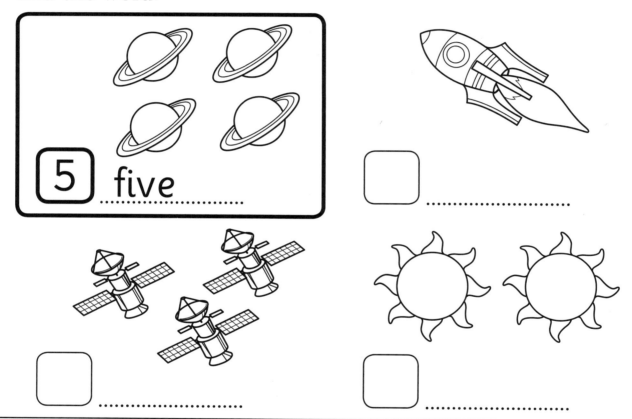

5 five ....

☐ ....

☐ ....

☐ ....

Draw **one more** in each group.

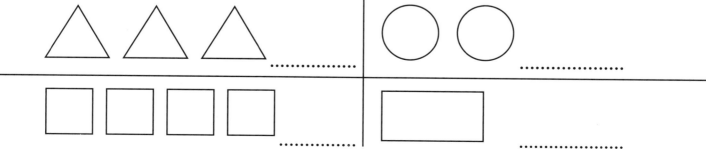

....

....

How many objects are there in each group or set?
Write the number in the box.

Triangles have three straight sides and three corners.

Circle the triangles.

Connect the triangles that are exactly the same.

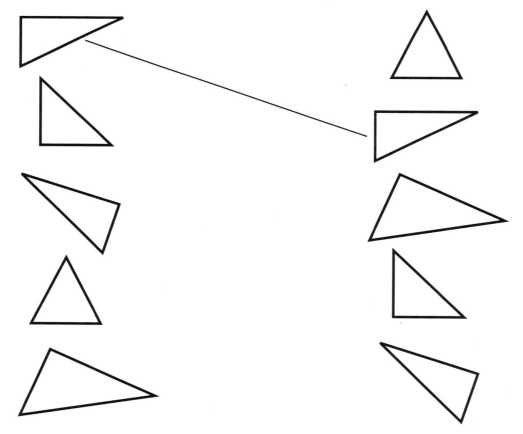

Circle the fruit that is **not the same**.

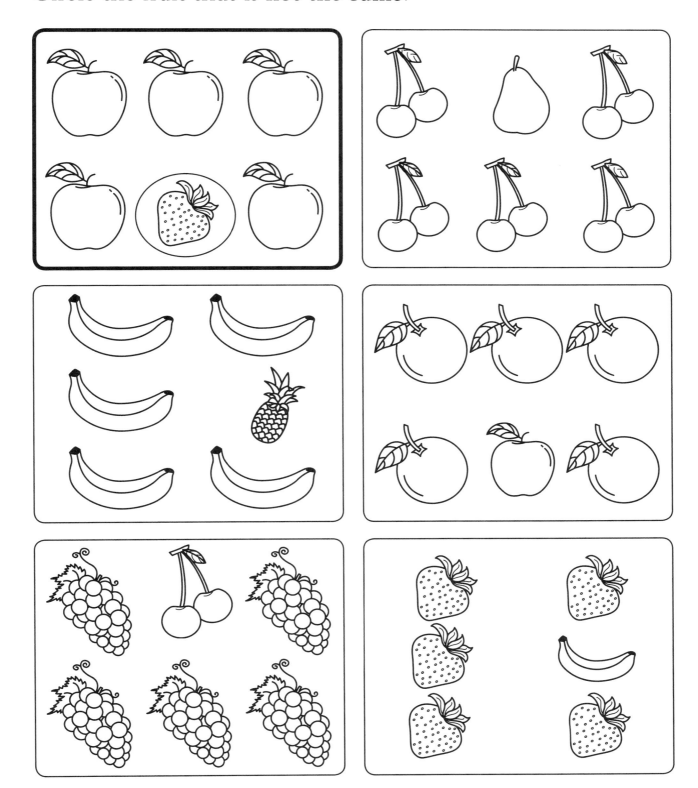

Color the ovals green.　Color the triangles blue.

Draw the next shape.

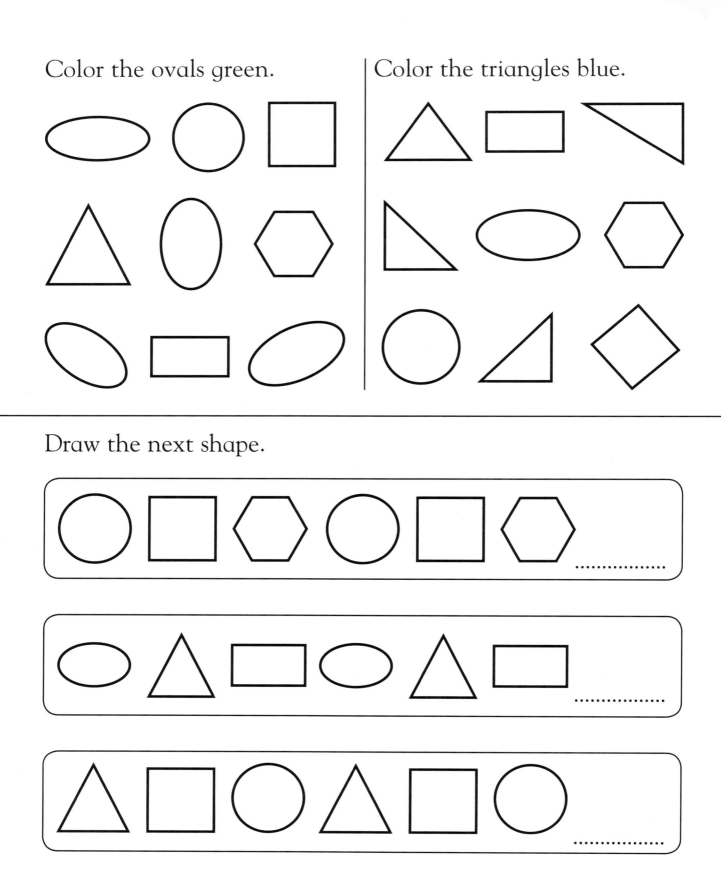

Connect the matching numbers, pictures, and words.

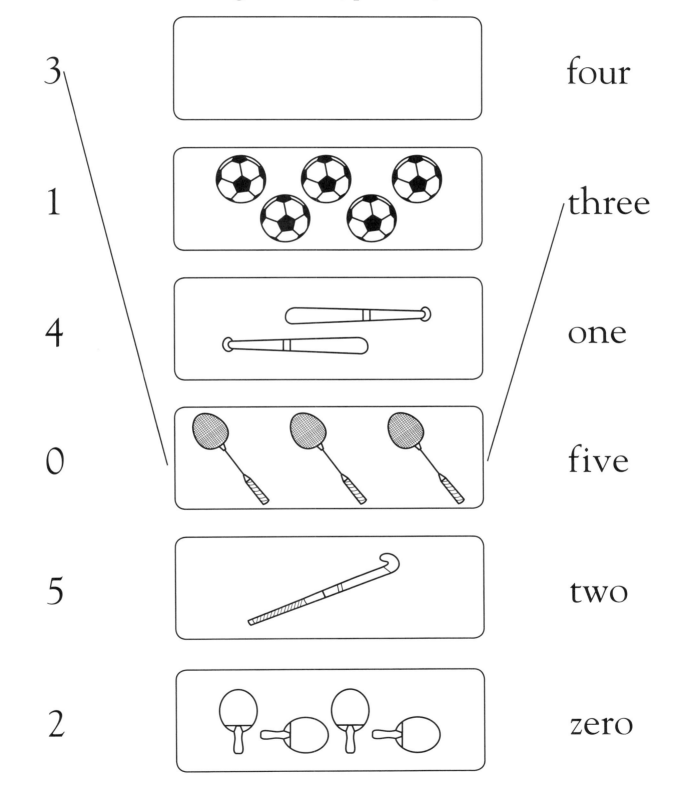

3

1

4

0

5

2

four

three

one

five

two

zero

In each row, cross out (**X**) the group that has more.

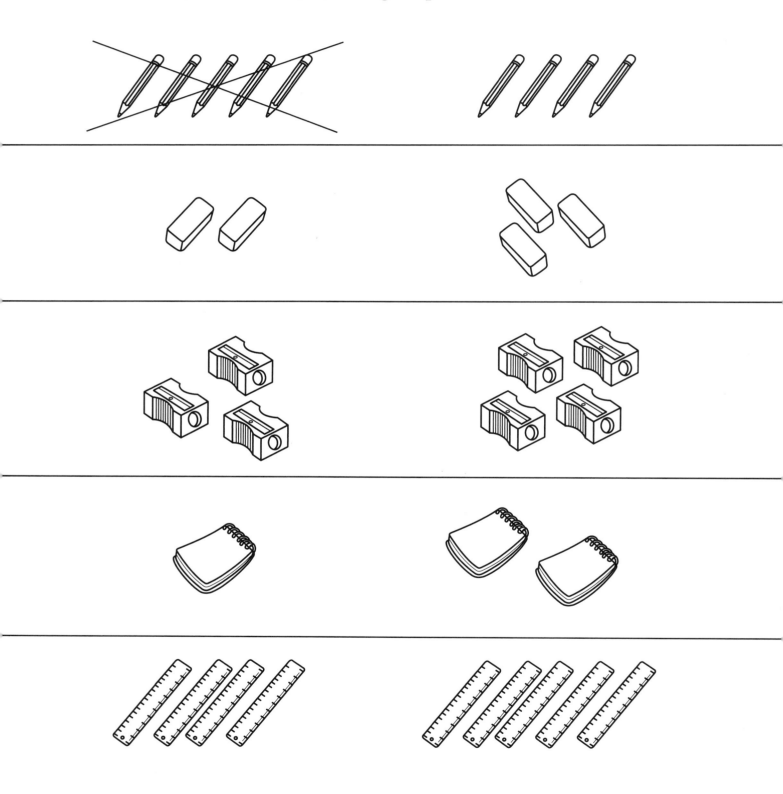

Draw the flowers and write the numbers to complete each sentence.

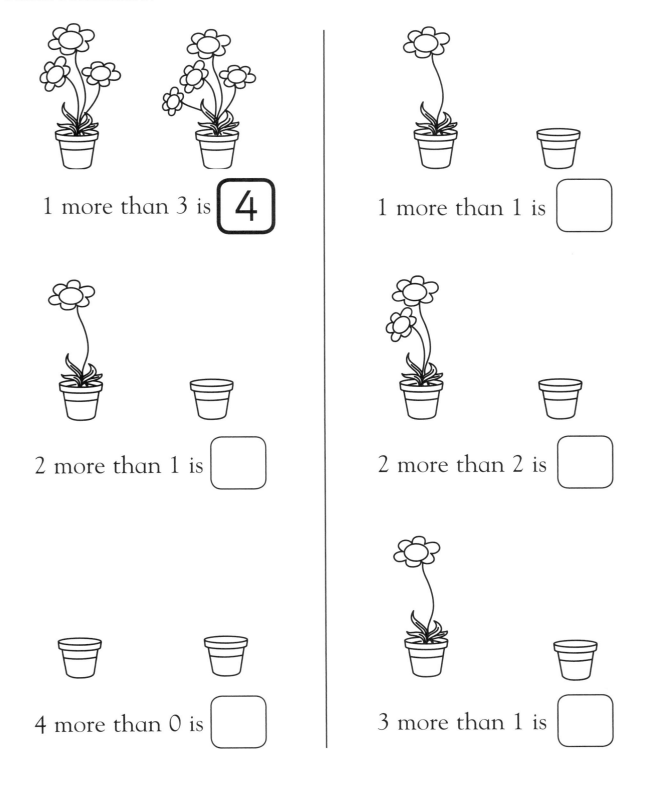

1 more than 3 is 4

1 more than 1 is ☐

2 more than 1 is ☐

2 more than 2 is ☐

4 more than 0 is ☐

3 more than 1 is ☐

Cross out (**X**) all the triangles below.

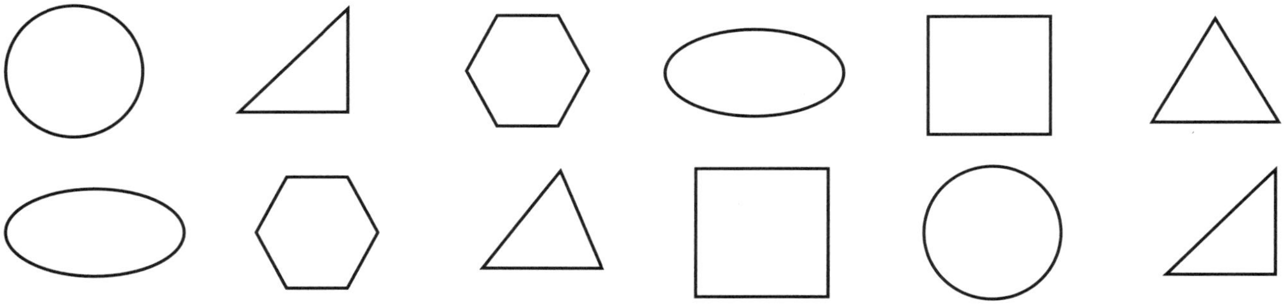

Write 1 more than each number.

4 [ ]   3 [ ]   1 [ ]

0 [ ]   2 [ ]

How many?

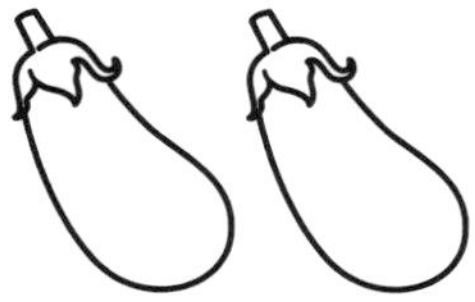

[ ] eggplants    [ ] tomatoes

Connect the word to the number.

one   3

three   5

five   1

Connect the name to the shape.

oval

circle

triangle

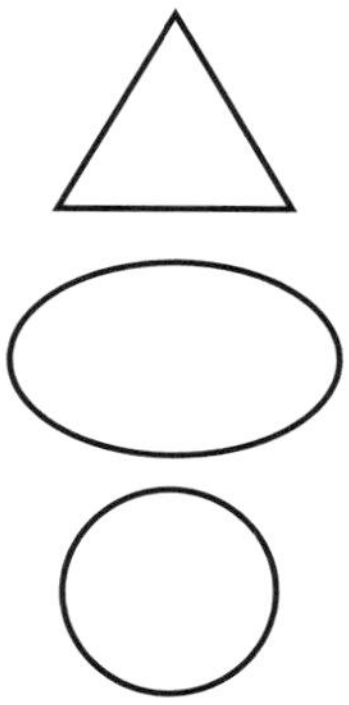

Circle the vegetables that are **not the same** as the carrot.

Draw a smiley face ☺ next to the group that has more.

What is 1 more than each number?

Write the answer.

1 more than 3 is

2 is one more than

Write the number.

6 6

Write the word.

six six

Draw 6 circles.

Draw six ovals.

Draw 6 squares.

Draw six triangles.

Write the number.

7

Write the word.

seven   seven

Cross out (**X**) the groups with 7 animals.

This is a square. A square has four sides of the same length and four corners.

Complete these squares. Use a ruler. | Cross out (**X**) all the squares.

Draw six squares.

Draw the other half of each object.

Write the number.

8 8

Write the word.

eight eight

Count the objects and write the answers in numbers and words.

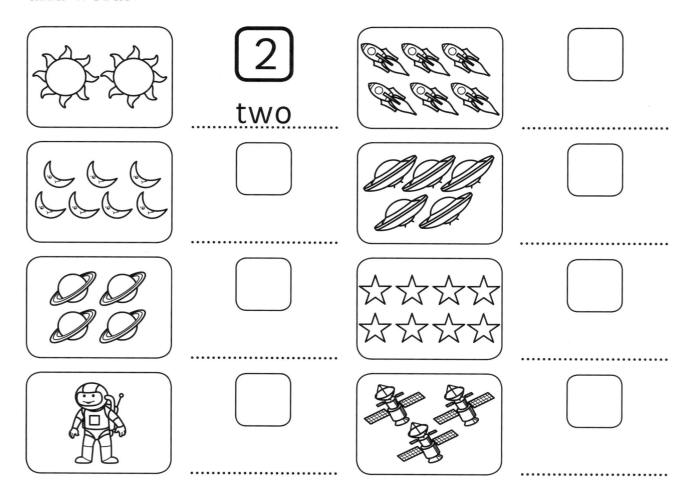

2

two

Write the number.

9 9

Write the word.

nine nine

Circle the groups with 9 items.

Write the number.

10 10

Write the word.

ten ten

Draw 10 circles.

Draw 10 triangles.

How many toes are on two feet?

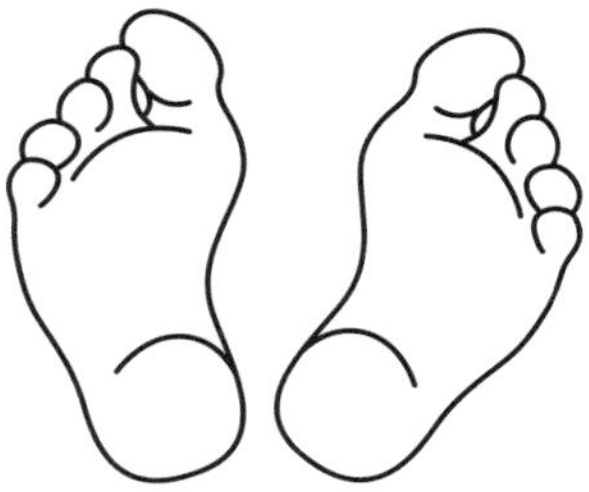

Draw two hands.

This is a special sign **+**. It means **add**.
We can also say **plus**.

What is the answer?

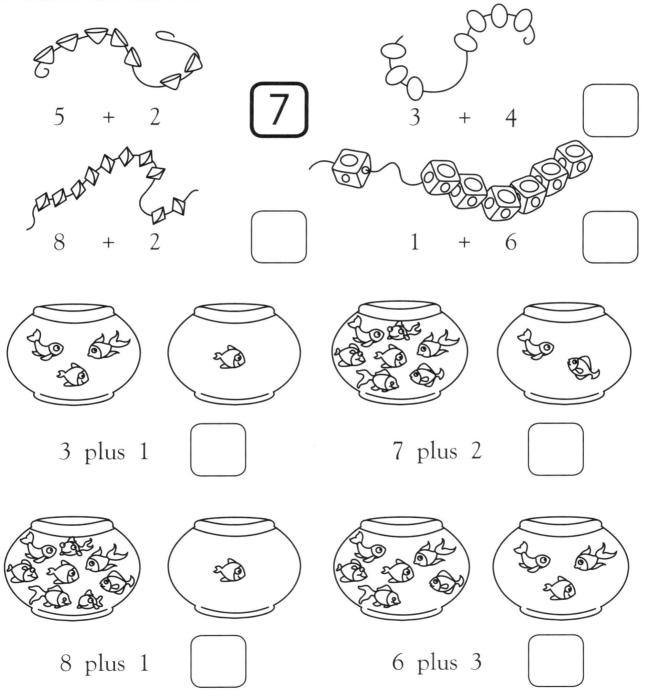

5 + 2   [7]   3 + 4   ☐

8 + 2   ☐   1 + 6   ☐

3 plus 1   ☐   7 plus 2   ☐

8 plus 1   ☐   6 plus 3   ☐

This is a special sign −. It means **minus**, **subtract**, and **take away**.

Draw the apples and write the numbers that make each sentence true.

4 is one less than ......**5**......

7 is one less than ....

8 is one less than ....

3 is one less than ....

What is the answer?

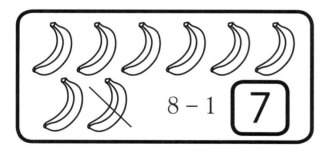
8 − 1 [7]

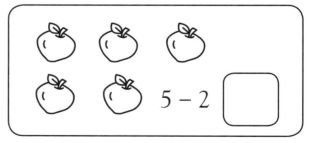
5 − 2 ☐

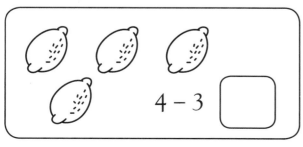
4 − 3 ☐

9 − 4 ☐

Count up.

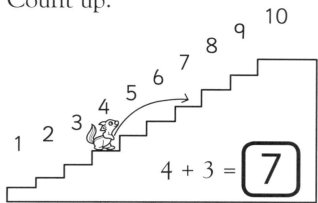

$4 + 3 = \boxed{7}$

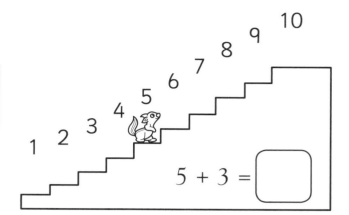

$5 + 3 = \square$

Count down.

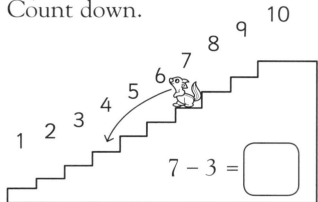

$7 - 3 = \square$

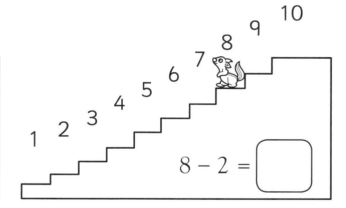

$8 - 2 = \square$

Write the missing numbers in the boxes.
Use the number line below to help you.

$5 + 5 = \boxed{10}$ $9 - 4 = \square$

$10 - 1 = \square$ $6 + 4 = \square$

$9 + 1 = \square$ $8 - 6 = \square$

0 1 2 3 4 5 6 7 8 9 10

Here are some 4-sided shapes.

Square   Rectangle   Kite

Cross out (**X**) the squares.

Cross out (**X**) the rectangles.

Cross out (**X**) the kites.

Cross out (**X**) the rectangle shapes.

Connect the dots to make a number or shape.

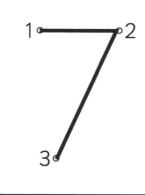

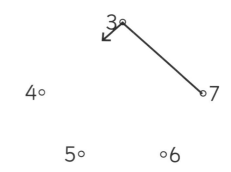

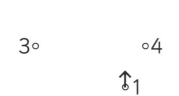

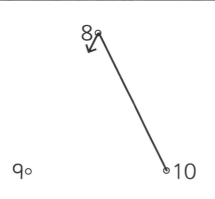

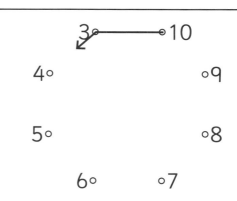

Connect the word to the number.

seven	6
nine	10
eight	9
six	7
ten	8

Draw the other half.

Write the answers.

How many candies? Draw the candies in the jar.

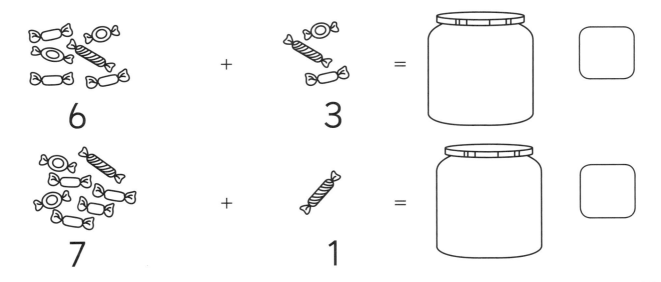

6   +   3   =   [ ]

7   +   1   =   [ ]

Write the answers. Use the number line below to help you.

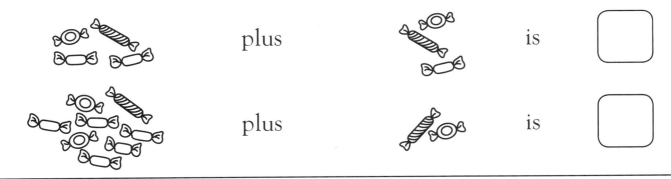

plus   is   [ ]

plus   is   [ ]

Write the answers. Use the number line below to help you.

Four add four is   [ ]   Nine plus one is   [ ]

Eight plus one is   [ ]   Two add three is   [ ]

0   1   2   3   4   5   6   7   8   9   10

Write the number.

11 11

Write the word.

eleven eleven

Write the number.

12 12

Write the word.

twelve twelve

Write the number.

13 13

Write the word.

thirteen thirteen

Write the number.

14   14

Write the word.

fourteen   fourteen

Write the number.

15   15

Write the word.

fifteen   fifteen

How many?

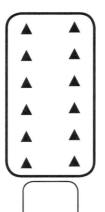 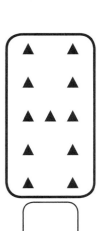   

Connect all the animals that are the same.

Connect all the shapes that are the same.

Connect all the fruits that are the same.

Continue each pattern.

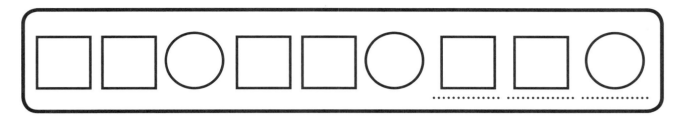

2 4 1 1 2 4 1 1 ....

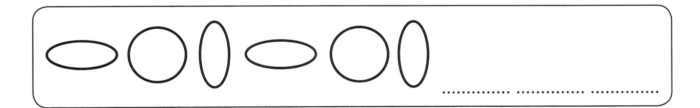

3 5 7 3 5 7 ....

$$0 \quad 1 \quad 2 \quad 3 \quad 4 \quad 5 \quad 6 \quad 7 \quad 8 \quad 9 \quad 10$$

What is 2 less and 2 more than each number?

−2

+2

Less

More

Write the answer. Use the number line.

12 + 2 ☐   6 add 2 ☐   14 plus 2 ☐

15 − 2 ☐   14 subtract 2 ☐   8 minus 2 ☐

11 12 13 14 15 16 17 18 19 20

What makes 5?

3 + [2]   9 − ☐

0 + ☐   5 − ☐

What makes 6?

2 + ☐   8 − ☐

5 + ☐   9 − ☐

What makes 7?

4 + ☐   8 − ☐

5 + ☐   10 − ☐

What makes 8?

3 + ☐   9 − ☐

2 + ☐   10 − ☐

What makes 9?

3 + ☐   10 − ☐

6 + ☐   9 − ☐

What makes 10?

6 + ☐   13 − ☐

1 + ☐   15 − ☐

Write the number.

16 16

Write the word.

sixteen sixteen

Write the number.

17 17

Write the word.

seventeen seventeen

Write the number.

18 18

Write the word.

eighteen eighteen

Write the number.

19   *9*

Write the word.

nineteen *nineteen*

Write the number.

20 *20*

Write the word.

twenty *twenty*

How many?

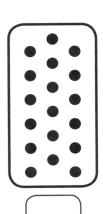

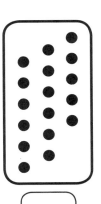

Connect the matching numbers, picture sets, and words.

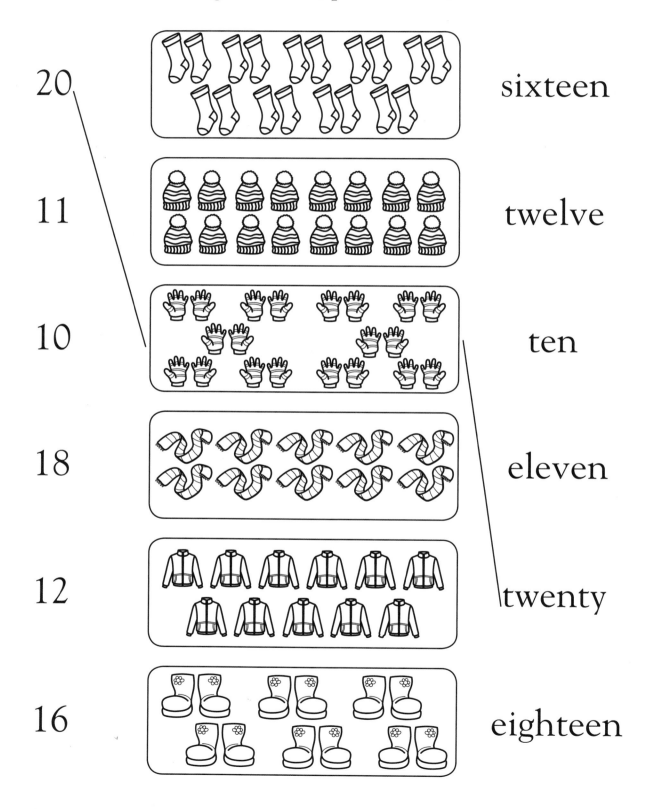

20

11

10

18

12

16

sixteen

twelve

ten

eleven

twenty

eighteen

Draw a taller giraffe.

Draw a larger elephant.

Draw a longer snake.

Draw a thinner cat.

Circle the longest vine.

Circle the skinniest bench.

 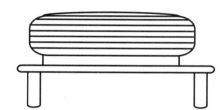 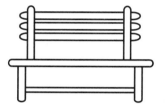

Circle the longest bush.

Circle the skinniest fence.

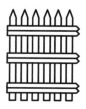   

Draw a circle...

next to the cat.

above the dog.

below the owl.

beneath the monkey.

beside the donkey.

on top of the cow.

What is in the middle of the park?

....

What is on the tree?

....

What is in the pond?

....

What is beneath the tree?

....

What is beside the pond?

....

Draw a dog next to the tree.

Write the days of the week in the right order.

| Sunday | Monday | Thursday | Friday |

| Tuesday | Saturday | Wednesday |

..........Sunday.......... ....

....

What day comes before Tuesday?

....

What is two days after Monday?

....

How many days are there in a week?

....

How many days are there in two weeks?

....

The numbers below go from eleven to twenty, in order.
Write the missing numbers.

| ☐ | 12 | 13 | ☐ | ☐ |

| ☐ | 17 | ☐ | ☐ | 20 |

How many are there in each group?

☐ mice

☐ chicks

Connect the shapes to their correct set.

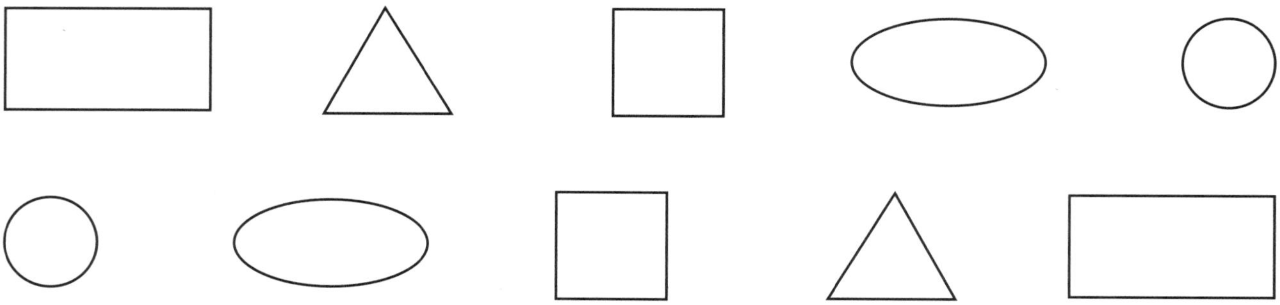

4-sided   Curved   3-sided

Write the answers.

12 – 2 = ☐   17 – 7 = ☐   20 – 2 = ☐

14 – 4 = ☐   11 – 2 = ☐   18 – 8 = ☐

Write 2 more than each number.

18 ☐   12 ☐   15 ☐   11 ☐

Write 2 less than each number.

19 ☐   14 ☐   20 ☐   17 ☐

Draw a snake that is shorter than the one shown.

Fill in the missing days.

Monday   ....   Wednesday   ....

....   Sunday

Practice counting from 1 to 5.

How many stars are there in each row?
Circle the correct number.

   2   3   4

★ ★ ★ ★   2   3   4

   1   2   3

   3   4   5

Write the two missing numbers on each line.

1   2   4

     2   3   5

1   □   3   4   □

1234567891234567891 2

Practice counting
from 6 to 10.

6 7 8 9 10

How many apples are there in each row?
Circle the correct number.

 5 6 7

 6 7 8

 5 8 9

 6 8 10

Circle any ten flowers below.

Practice counting from 10 to 15.

10 11 12 13 14 15

How many objects are there in each box?
Write the correct number.

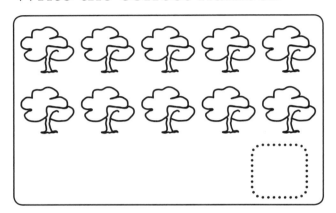

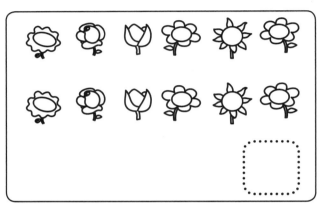

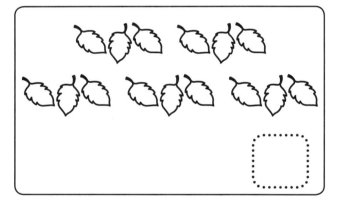

Write the missing numbers in the boxes.

1 ⬚ 3   4 ⬚ 6

7 ⬚ 9   10 ⬚ 12

13 ⬚ 15

1234567891234567891 2

Practice counting up to 20.

15 16 17 18 19 20

Look at the twenty houses along the trail. Write the numbers that are missing in the circle next to each house.

Count twenty doors. Cross out (**X**) extra doors.
Then write the number 20 in the box.

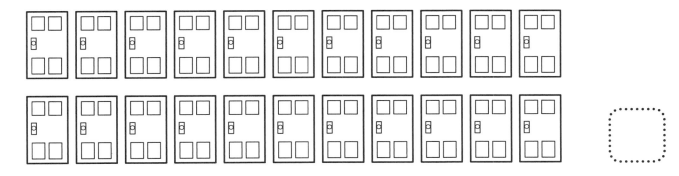

Add different numbers from 1 to 9 to make 10.

Count each group of toys. Write the correct number
of toys in the box.

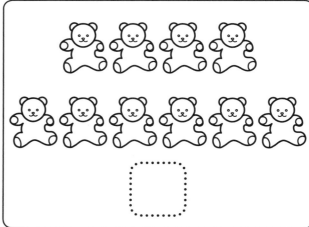

Copy the pattern of dots on the other side of the domino.

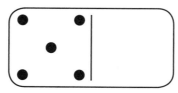

Now count all the dots on the domino,
and write the correct number.

1 2 3 4 5 6 7 8 9 1 2 3 4 5 6 7 8 9 1 2

Review how to make 10.

Write the numbers from 1 to 10 in the circles next to each car on the path below.

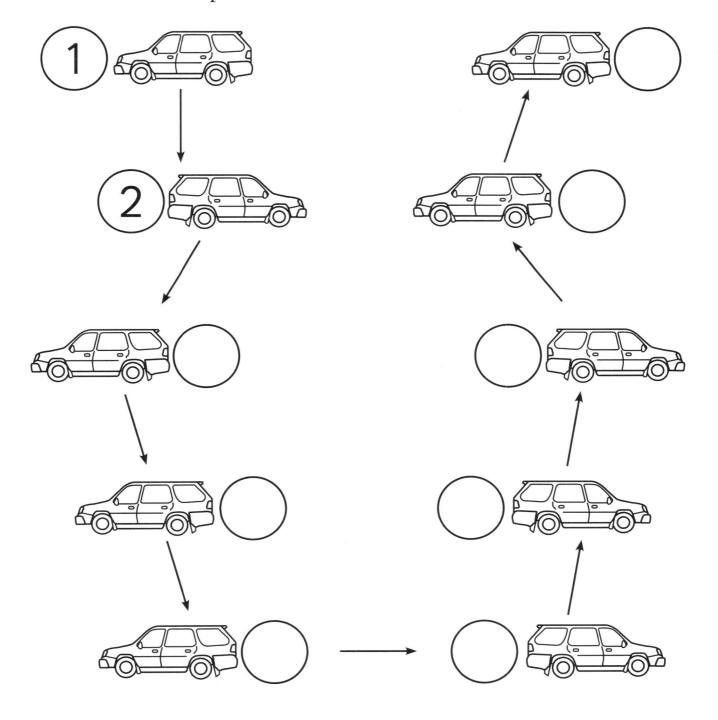

Learn about items in groups that make 20.

Count the objects in each box and answer the questions below.

How many boats are there?

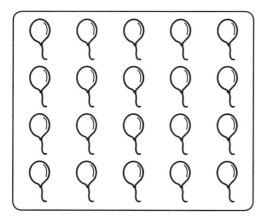

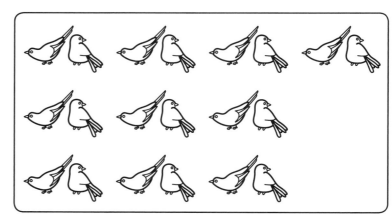

How many balloons are there?

How many birds are there?

Review ways to make 20, such as 10 + 10.

Solve these equations.

6 + 14 =	9 + 11 =	8 + 12 =
5 + 15 =	3 + 17 =	16 + 4 =
13 + 7 =	18 + 2 =	19 + 1 =

Circle the equation that adds up to 20.

12 + 4 + 6   5 + 5 + 10   4 + 4 + 9

Follow the path to the castle and write the missing numbers on each stone.

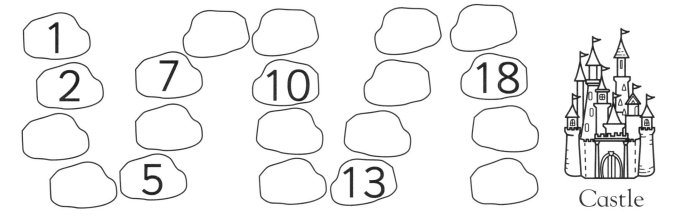

Castle

Learn that objects have shapes, and shapes have names.

Look at the objects. Circle the correct shape of the object in each row.

The cookie has the shape of a   square   circle

The door has the shape of a   rectangle   triangle

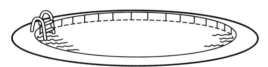 

The pool has the shape of an   square   oval

The tree has the shape of a   circle   triangle

Circle the word to describe the shape of this ball.

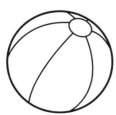

square   circle   triangle

Learn to identify different shapes.

Look at the shapes in each row. Circle the shape that is different.

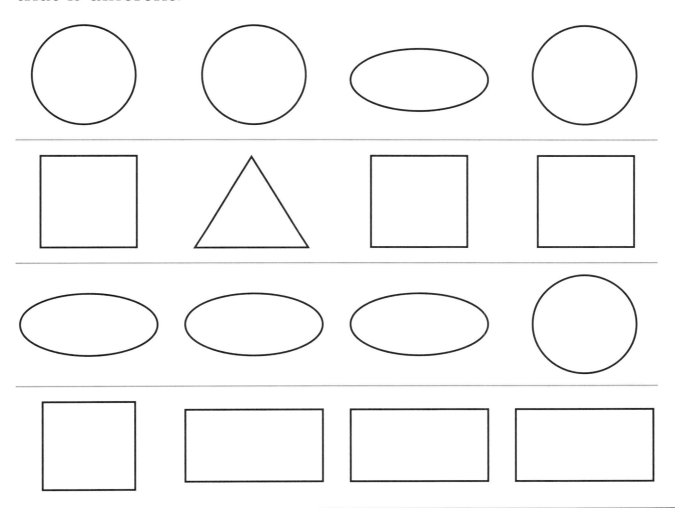

Draw five triangles below. Then draw a silly face on each one.

Describe shapes by the number of sides and corners.

Circle the word that correctly completes each sentence.

A square has four corners and .... sides.

three   four

A circle is ....

round   straight

A rectangle has four corners and is ....

round   long

A triangle has three corners and .... sides.

two   three

Circle the triangle that is larger than the others.

 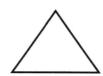 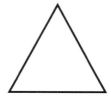

Shapes can vary in size. Learn to find the shapes that are larger.

Look at the shapes in each box. Color in the largest shape.

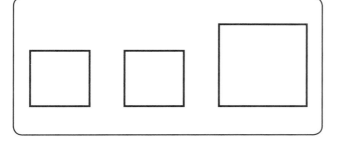

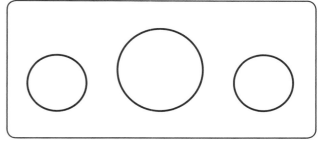

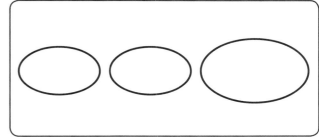

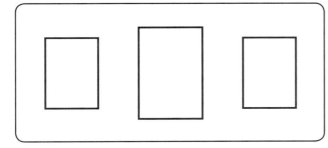

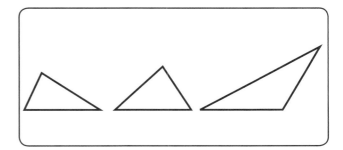

Circle the shape that has four sides.

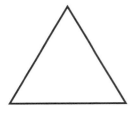

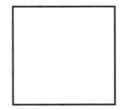

Learn to draw shapes.

Look at each shape and make it into an object.

Draw a circle
and make it
into the sun.

Draw a square
and make it
into a present.

Draw a triangle
and make it
into a hat.

Draw an oval
and make it
into a face.

Practice finding and counting shapes.

Color the circles red. ◯ Color the rectangles yellow. ▭

Color the squares blue. ☐ Color the triangles green. △

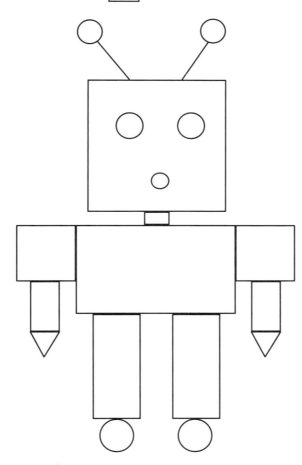

How many of each shape is there in the robot?
Write the correct numbers in the boxes below.

☐ squares   ☐ circles

☐ triangles   ☐ rectangles

Learn to draw shapes and continue patterns.
Patterns are repeated sets of objects.

Draw the shape to continue the pattern in each row.

....

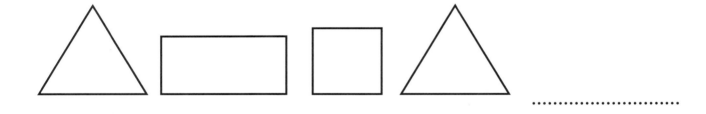

....

....

....

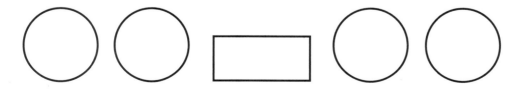

....

Practice continuing patterns.

Look at the cupcakes below. In each row, follow the pattern and decorate the tops of the undecorated cupcakes with the correct design.

Look at the pattern of the cookies below. Draw two more cookies to continue the pattern.

....

Learn to identify objects that are the same.

Look at each row of animals. Circle the two animals that are the same.

Circle the two fish that have the same number on them.

1234567891234567891 2

Learn to compare characteristics, such as numbers and letters.

Put the balls into the correct boxes: Draw a line from each ball with a number on it to the number box. Draw a line from each ball with a letter on it to the letter box.

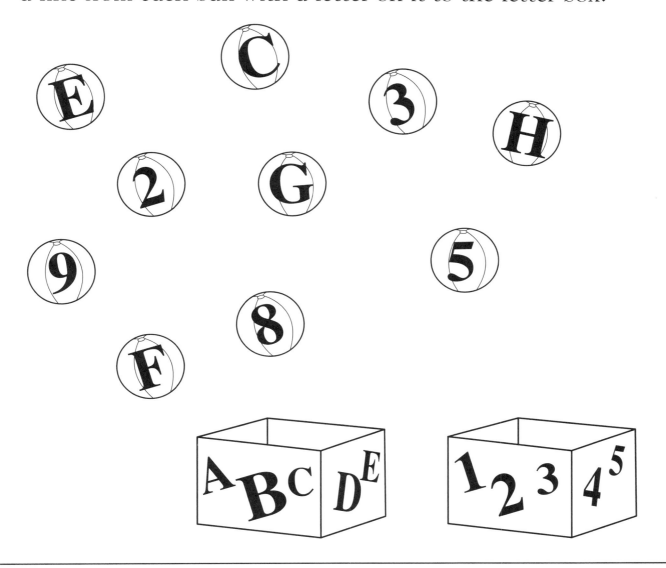

How many balls are there altogether?

Learn to find things that are not the same, or different.

Circle the leaf in each row that is different.

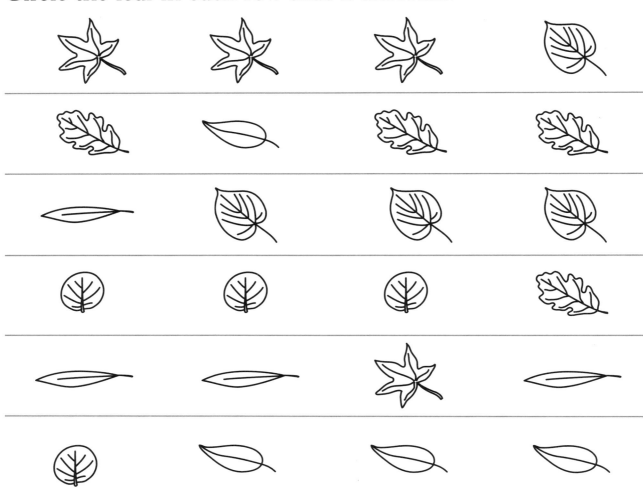

Circle the six flowers that are the same.

Learn to identify (spot) which is different.

Circle the animal in each row that is different.

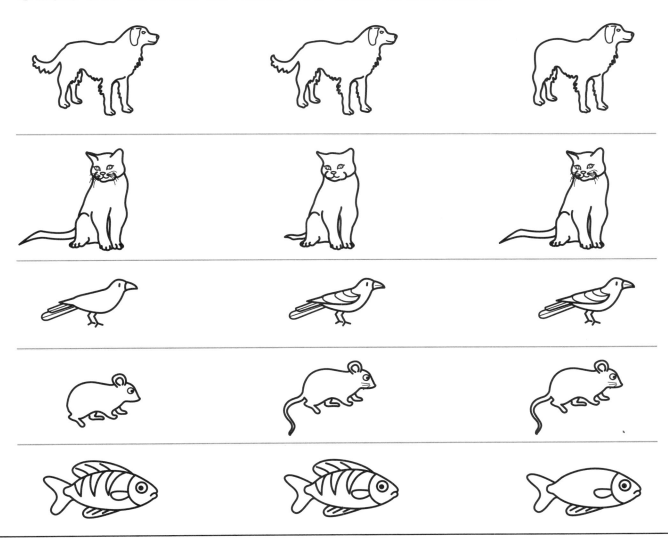

Add spots to the frog on the right to make the two frogs look the same.

Count the objects to find out which set has more.

Write the letter **M** on the line under the box that
has more objects.

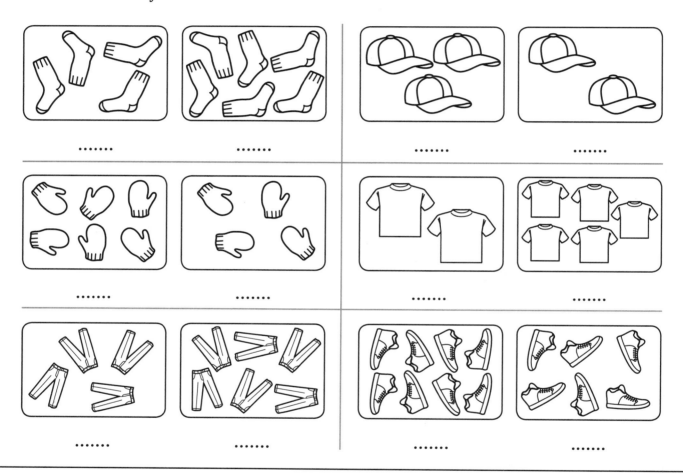

....

....

....

How many sneakers are there below? To find out, count
how many are in each pair, then add up the numbers.

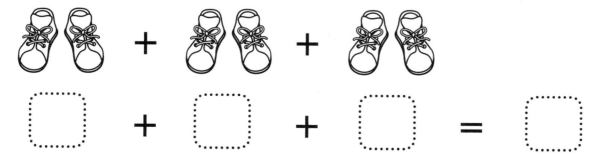

1234567891234567891 2

Learn to add one more.

Add one more to each group in the boxes. Then count the total items in the group and write the correct number.

Draw one more balloon, then count the balloons.
How many are there altogether?

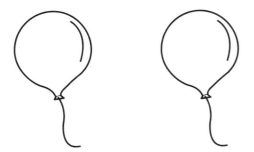

Draw more shapes to add to the group. The + sign means to add.

$\bigcirc + \bigcirc\bigcirc = \boxed{3}$

Draw two more of the same shape in each box. Then add all the shapes and write the correct number.

How many triangles are there on this page? Circle the answer.

7   9   11

123456789123456789 12

Find the total, which is the answer you get when you add things together.  = 6

Draw a + sign between the boxes in each row. Then count all the items in both of the boxes and write the total number.

 = ⬚

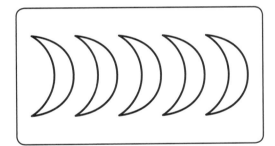 = ⬚

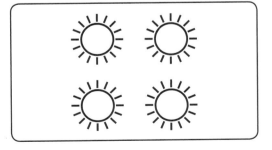 = ⬚

In total, how many moons and stars are there on this page? Circle the answer.

12   14   17

Find the group that
has fewer objects.

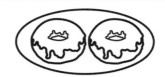 

Look at the baked goods below. For each treat, circle
the group that has fewer objects than the other.

cakes

cupcakes

cookies

pies

Count all the cupcakes above. How many are there?

1 2 3 4 5 6 7 8 9 1 2 3 4 5 6 7 8 9 1 2

Take away one object so that a group has one fewer.  2

Look at the pictures in each row. Cross out (**X**) one of the pictures. Then count the remaining pictures and write the correct number in the box.
Remember: Do not count the picture with the **X** on it.

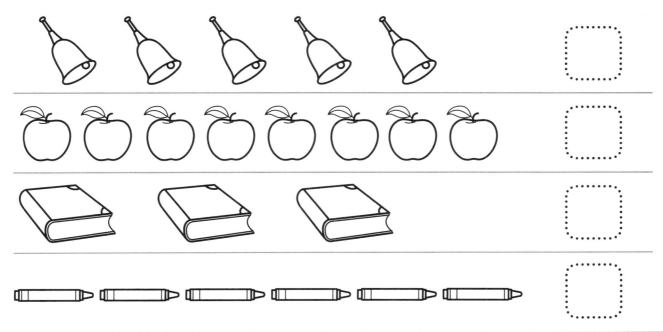

Count the cups below that are not crossed out.
Circle the correct number.

9   15   19

1 2 3 4 5 6 7 8 9 1 2 3 4 5 6 7 8 9 1 2

Cross out to show taking away more than one. Count to find how many are left.  1

Cross out (**X**) two vegetables in each row. Then count how many are left. Write the correct number in the box.
Remember: Do not count the vegetables you crossed out.

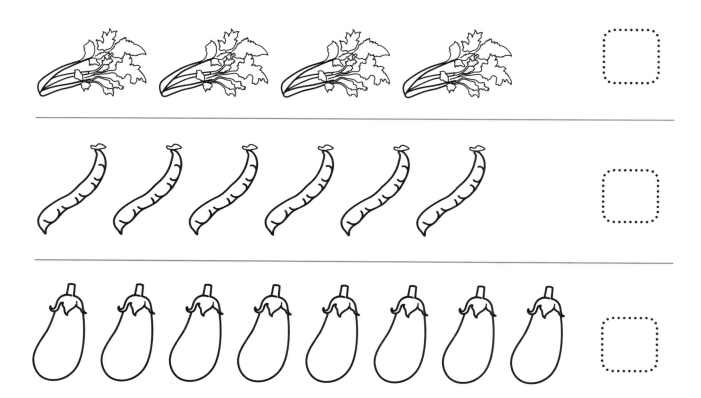

Read the counting poem below. Write the words to complete the poem.

One potato, two potato, ... potato, four!

Five potato, ... potato, seven potato, more!

Practice subtracting, which means to take away. Then count how many are left.

Cross out (**X**) three of the animals in each box to subtract them. Then count the animals left in the box.
Remember: Do not count the animals that have an **X**.

bear

How many bears are left?

rabbit

How many rabbits are left?

Read the poem below. Then write the word to finish the poem.

I saw four birds in a tree.
One flew away, and then there were ....

Add together groups to make sets of ten.

Draw a line from the group in the first column to the group in the second column that makes a set of ten.

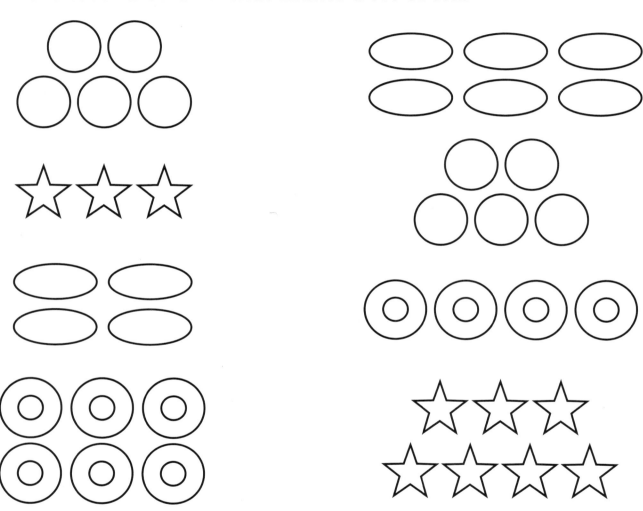

Circle a set of ten crayons below.

123456789123456789

Learn to sort items into groups that are the same.

Draw a line to match the number on each child's shirt to the numbers on the flags below.

Count all of the children on this page. How many are there?

Learn to match sets and find pairs.

Look at these socks. Find and match the correct pairs.

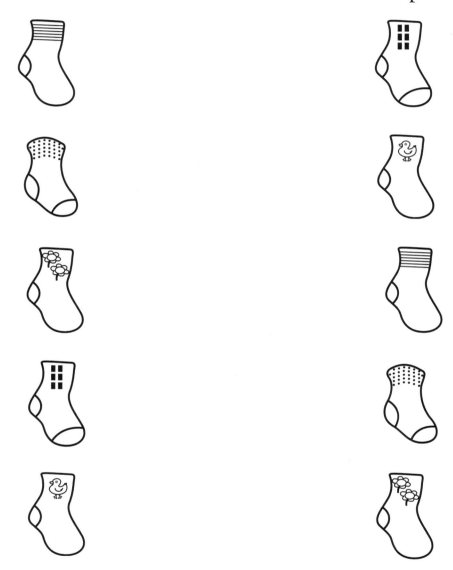

How many sets, or pairs, of socks are there above?
Circle the correct number.

5   6   8

123456789123456789 12

GOAL

Count to find the number of things in each set.

Count the farm animals in each box below. Then write the correct number of animals next to each box.

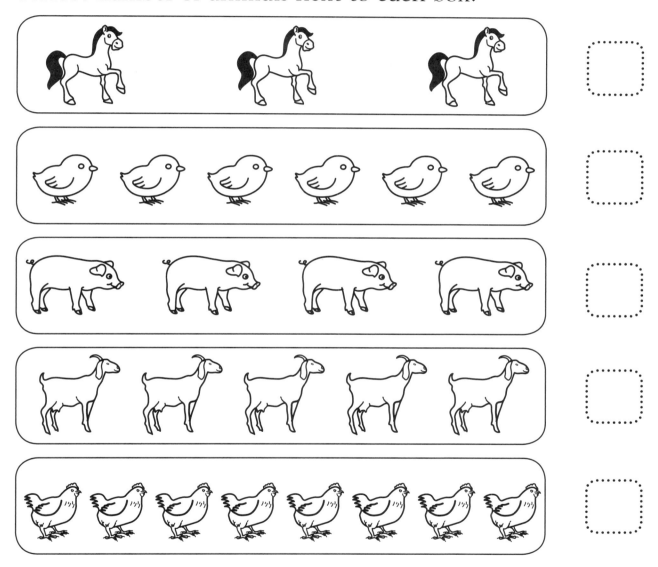

Count the chickens and the chicks. How many are there altogether? Circle the correct number.

7   14   16

1234567891234567891 2

Compare the sizes of two objects to find the biggest.

Circle the biggest animal in each row below.

Draw a bigger turtle in the box.

1 2 3 4 5 6 7 8 9 1 2 3 4 5 6 7 8 9 1 2

Learn to draw objects that are bigger or smaller.

Look at each picture, and follow the directions.

Draw a bigger sun.

Draw a bigger flower.

Draw a smaller star.

Compare the lengths of two objects to find which is shorter and which is longer.

Look at each row carefully. Follow the directions.

Circle the longer snake.

Circle the shorter penguin.

Circle the horse with the shorter tail.

Circle the animal with the longer legs.

Circle the girl whose hair is longer.

1 2 3 4 5 6 7 8 9 1 2 3 4 5 6 7 8 9 1 2

Learn to draw objects that are longer or shorter.

Look at each picture. Follow the directions for each.

Longer

Draw a fish that is longer.

Shorter

Draw a bird with a shorter beak.

Look at the snake. How many dots long is this snake?
Count the dots, and circle the correct number.

● ● ● ● ● ● ● ● ● ● ● ● ● ● ● ● ● ● ● ●

12   18   20

Compare the weights of objects to find the heaviest.

Which weighs more? Circle the heavier object in each box.

Meg's cat weighs 9 pounds.
Her dog weighs 15 pounds.
Which weighs more?

....

1 2 3 4 5 6 7 8 9 1 2 3 4 5 6 7 8 9 1 2

Learn to draw things that are heavier or lighter.

Look at the mouse below. In the empty box, draw an animal that is heavier than a mouse.

Look at the elephant below. In the empty box, draw an animal that is lighter than an elephant.

Look at the three animals. Circle the animal that is the heaviest.

Learn position words, which tell us where an object is placed.

Look at the picture below. Circle the words to answer each question.

Where is the squirrel?	next to the tree	up in the tree
Where is the bird's nest?	below the tree branch	on the tree branch
Where are the children?	up in the tree	in front of the tree

Look at the insects below. Which one is in the middle? Circle the insect in the middle.

Review position words:

inside   outside   above

     below   on   under

Look at the picture below. Circle the answer to each question.

Where is the cat?	inside the basket	outside the basket
Where is the dog?	above the table	below the table
Where is the bird?	inside the cage	outside the cage
Where is the cake?	under the table	on the table

Learn to tell the time. A clock has two hands. The hour hand is short. The minute hand is long. The hour hand on this clock points to 3. The minute hand points to 12. That means the time is 3 o'clock.

3 o'clock

What time is shown on the clocks below?

o'clock

o'clock

o'clock

o'clock

Draw the hour hand on the clock to show two o'clock.

Remember: The hour hand is shorter than the minute hand.

123456789123456789 12

Practice using clocks. When you write the word *o'clock*, that means the minute hand on the clock is pointing to 12. The hour hand points to the hour number.

Draw the hour hand on the clocks below to show the time that is under the clock.

Remember: The hour hand is shorter than the minute hand.

5 o'clock

2 o'clock

9 o'clock

6 o'clock

This clock is missing four numbers. Write the missing numbers in their correct places on the clock.

Learn the concept of using money to buy items.

Draw a line from each toy to the dollars that match the price of the toy.

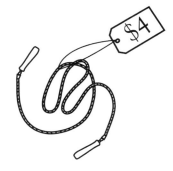

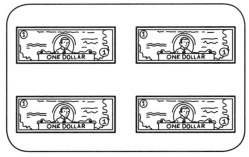

The price for a small jar of marbles is 3 dollars. The price for a large jar of marbles is 4 dollars. How many more dollars is the large jar?

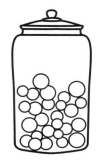

1 2 3 4 5 6 7 8 9 1 2 3 4 5 6 7 8 9 1 2

Count coins and bills to find the total amount of money.

Count the money in each pocket. Draw a line from each pocket to the correct amount written in the middle column.

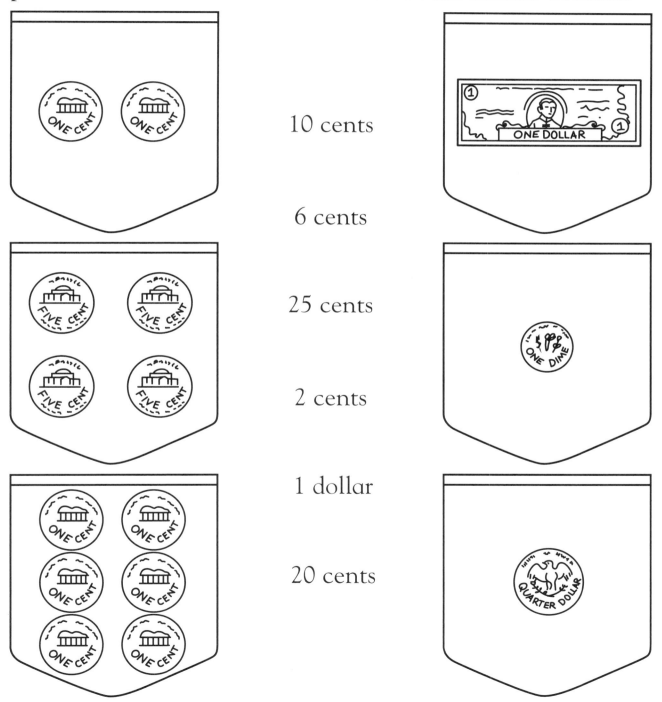

10 cents

6 cents

25 cents

2 cents

1 dollar

20 cents

Parents' Notes

The math in this book is designed for children who have the ability to count from zero to 20, with a good understanding of the order and value of numbers.

Contents

By working through the math activities in this book, your child will practice:
- reading, writing, and counting numbers to 20;
- the concept of same and different;
- the concept of more than and less than;
- the language and symbols of addition;
- the language and symbols of subtraction;
- the concept of simple number bonds;
- continuing simple sequences and patterns;
- recognizing simple 2-D shapes;
- measuring and comparing quantity, size, length, and width of objects;
- sorting objects into sets, adding sets, and finding totals;
- using positional words, such as *top*, *bottom*, *above*, *below*, and *others*;
- telling and writing the time;
- recognizing money and counting coins.

How to Help Your Child

It is very likely that children will not be able to read the instructions in this book. Therefore, parents, guardians, or helpers should work closely with children as they progress through this book, whether the child can read well or not. Both parents/helpers and children can gain a great deal from working together. Most children can understand math very well even if they are not yet able to read the language, so language should not be a reason to hold them back.

Wherever possible and necessary, try to give your children practical bits of equipment to help them, especially with the concept of adding and taking away. A collection of coins, buttons, or similar small objects will be invaluable. As they become confident with the activities, the drawn objects may be sufficient.

Build your child's confidence with praise and encouragement. Celebrate their success.

Science

Author Hugh Westrup
Educational Consultant Kara Pranikoff

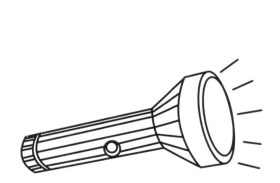

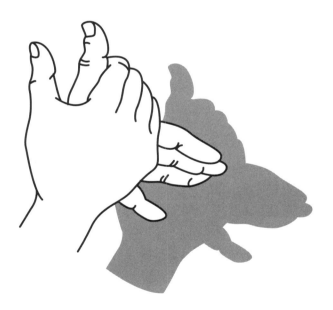

Contents

This chart lists all the topics in the Science section.

A garden is a small piece of land where flowers, fruits, and vegetables are grown. Some animals live in a garden, too.

Can you find the animals living in the garden? Point to each animal and name it.

A plant has many parts to help it grow.

Find each part of the plant and say its name.

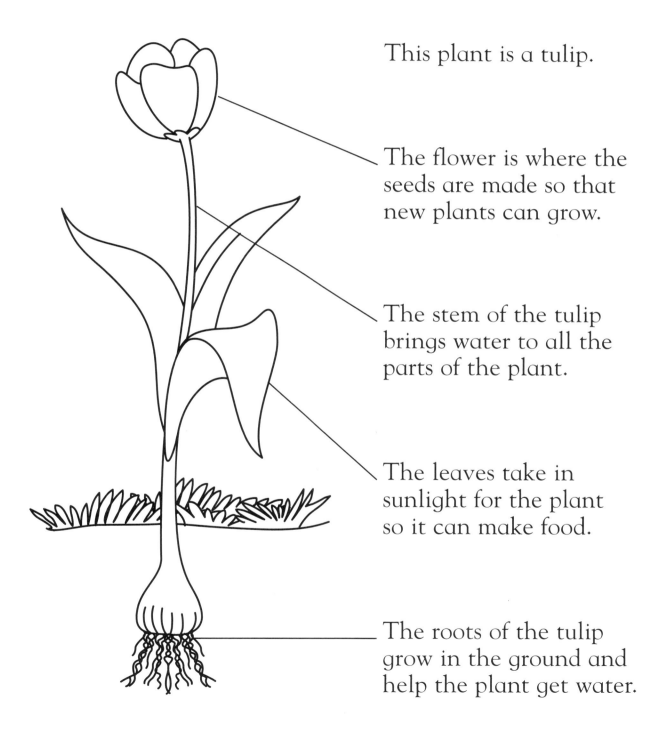

This plant is a tulip.

The flower is where the seeds are made so that new plants can grow.

The stem of the tulip brings water to all the parts of the plant.

The leaves take in sunlight for the plant so it can make food.

The roots of the tulip grow in the ground and help the plant get water.

A tree is a large plant. The stem of a tree is made out of wood.

Touch each part of the tree and say its name.

This tree has many of the same parts as the tulip plant you saw on page 103.

The leaves take in sunlight for the plant so it can make food.

The branches of the tree stretch up to the sky so that the leaves can get lots of sunlight.

The stem of the tree is made of wood. It is called the trunk. The trunk brings water to all the parts of the plant.

The roots of the tree grow in the ground and help the tree get water.

Some trees lose their leaves in the fall and grow new leaves in the spring. Trees that lose their leaves are called deciduous trees.

During the summer, deciduous trees have all their leaves. During the fall, the leaves of deciduous trees fall to the ground. During the winter, you only see the branches of a deciduous tree. During the spring, the leaves grow back. Point to each tree and name the season it is in.

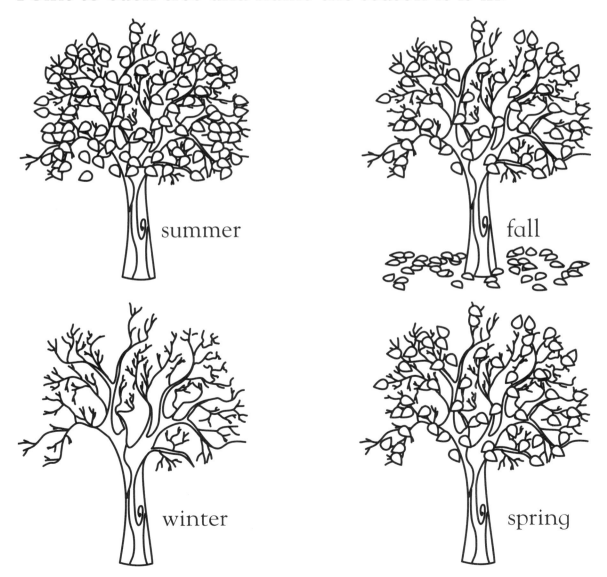

summer

fall

winter

spring

Many foods that we eat are plants.

Point to the two plants that we eat, and name them.

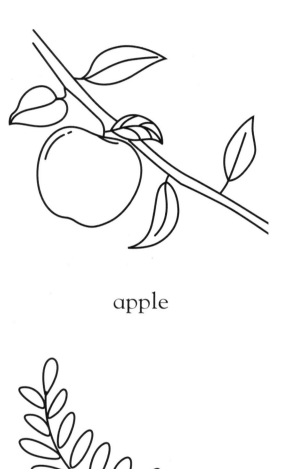

apple

tulip

fern

tomato

Vegetables come from different parts of plants.

The roots of a plant grow in the ground and help the plant get water. Carrots and potatoes are root vegetables. The stem of the plant brings water to all the parts of the plant. Asparagus and celery are stems. The leaves take in sunlight for the plant so it can make food. Spinach and lettuce are leaf vegetables.

Point to each vegetable below, and say its name. Is it a root, stem, or leaf vegetable?

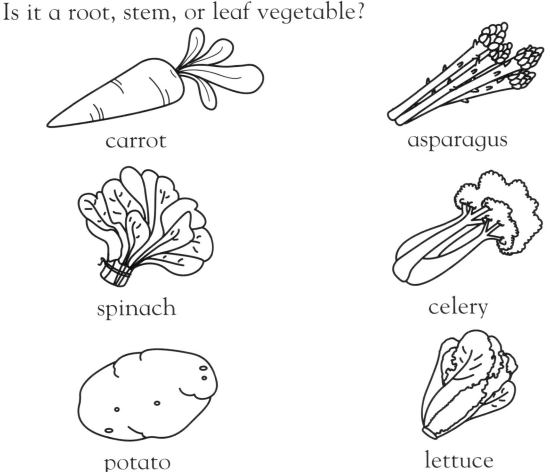

carrot

asparagus

spinach

celery

potato

lettuce

A fruit is the part of a plant that contains seeds.

Circle the fruit in each picture.

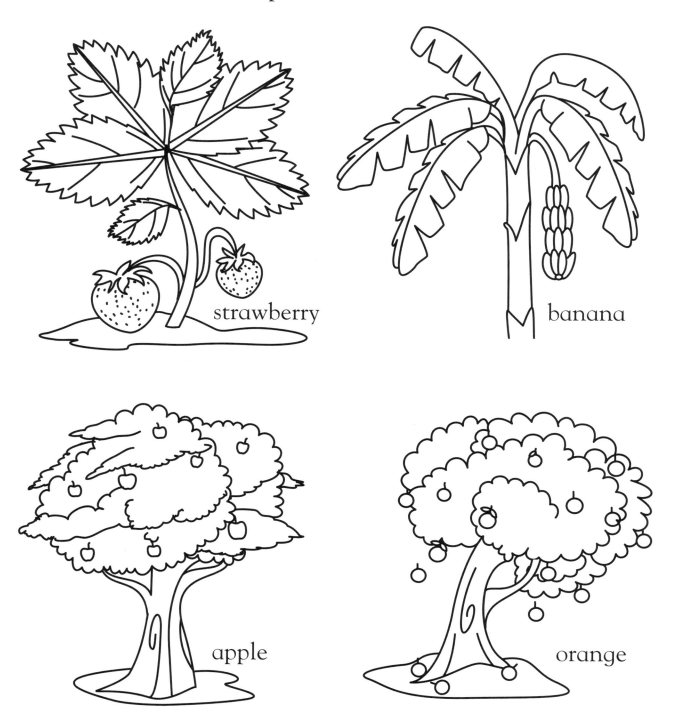

strawberry

banana

apple

orange

Many things we use are made from plants and trees.

Connect each plant with the things that are made from it.

This is a cotton plant. Many things that you wear are made from cotton. Socks and T-shirts are often made from cotton.

This is a tree. Many things you use every day are made from the wood of trees. Baseball bats and books are made from trees.

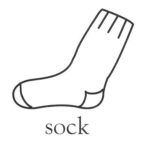

sock

book

t-shirt

baseball bat

Plants need water to grow.

TEST

What You Need:

paper towel · 2 plastic bags · water · seeds

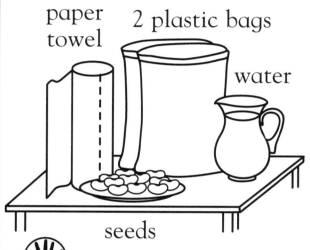

What To Do:

1. Place some bean seeds on a wet paper towel and fold it over. Place the paper towel in bag 1 and seal it.

2. Place some bean seeds on a dry paper towel and fold it over. Place the paper towel in bag 2 and seal it.

3. Put both bags in a warm, light place.

RESULT

After a week, open the bags. Describe what has happened to the seeds. Circle the picture that looks like the bag with water. Put an **X** on the picture that looks like the bag without water.

bag with wet seeds

bag with dry seeds

Plants need light to grow.

TEST

What You Need:

two seedlings of the same type of plant of equal size

two pots with soil

What To Do:

1. Plant each seedling in a pot of soil.
2. Put one pot in a dark place.
3. Put the other pot in a sunny place.
4. Check the plants every day for one week and water them if necessary.

RESULT

Watch the growth of the plants for a week. Describe what has happened to the plants. Circle the picture that looks like the plant that got sun. Put an **X** on the picture of the plant that was in the dark.

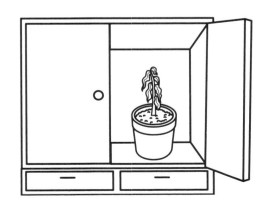

Seeds need to travel to different places to grow new plants. They travel to find a place that has light and water.

Seeds travel in many ways. Match the seeds to the way they travel.

strawberry

acorn

dandelion

burr

These seeds have a parachute of fine hairs. They are carried by the wind.

The hooks of this seed stick to the fur of animals passing by.

These seeds are eaten with fruit, pass through the animal, and grow in a new place.

Squirrels bury these seeds to eat in the winter.

A mountain is land that rises high above the ground around it. Mountains are made of soil and rocks. Trees grow on some mountains. Very high mountains can be covered in snow.

The animals in the picture live in the mountains. Can you name them all? Color the picture.

An ocean is a large body of water. Ocean water is salty. Many animals live in the ocean.

Draw a picture of an animal that lives in the ocean. Then color the picture.

A rain forest is a forest where it rains almost every day. Many plants and animals live in the rain forest.

Color the animals and plants in this picture of a rain forest. Can you name all the animals?

Some animals eat only plants. They are called herbivores. Some animals eat only other animals. They are called carnivores.

Circle all of the animals that are herbivores. Point to the animals that are carnivores and say their names out loud.

cow

tiger

crocodile

beaver

horse

deer

Some animals eat both plants and animals.
These animals are called omnivores.

Human beings are omnivores. What do you like to eat?
Draw your favorite food that comes from a plant in the
Plants box. Draw your favorite food that comes from an
animal in the **Animals** box.

What I Like to Eat

Plants

Animals

We see with our eyes.

Color the eyes the same as yours. Then write your name beside the picture.

....

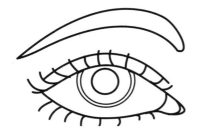 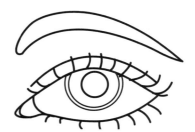

Draw the missing eyes on these animals.

Hot and cold describe the temperature of something. Something that is hot has a high temperature. Something that is cold has a low temperature. A thermometer is used to measure how hot or cold something is.

Point to the pictures of the things that are hot.
Circle the pictures of the things that are cold.

snowman   soup   ice cream

candle flame   ice water   fire

We hear with our ears.

Circle the things you can hear with your ears.

car

book

log

bell

cell phone

lamp

A noise can be loud or quiet. If you are close to a noise, it sounds loud. If you are far away from a noise, it sounds quiet.

The dog is barking. Which child hears the dog's bark the loudest? Color that child's shirt red. Which child hears the dog's bark the quietest? Color that child's shirt blue. Then color the whole picture.

We use our fingers to feel things. Our fingers tell us if things are hard, soft, rough, smooth, hot, or cold.

TEST **What You Need:**

Gather up a variety of objects from around your house. The objects shown below will work well for this activity, but you can choose others if you like.

tennis ball

orange

wooden spoon

metal spoon

bagel

plastic bottle

 What To Do:

1. Ask an adult to help you choose items from around the house.

2. Close your eyes and ask the adult to pass you something.

RESULT

Can you tell what you are holding?
Feel the object and describe it.

We use our nose to smell things.

Circle the things you can smell with your nose.

lemon

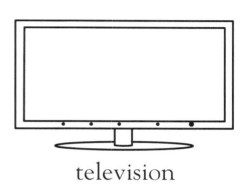

television

garbage

flower

spoon

skunk

The nose can detect many different smells.

TEST

What You Need:

1 cup of lemon juice

1 cup of peanut butter

1 cup of vinegar

1 cup of chopped banana

 What To Do:

Close your eyes and ask an adult to pass you a cup to smell. What do you smell? Name the food you are smelling.

RESULT

Put an **X** next to the foods you identified correctly.

Peanut butter	
Banana	
Vinegar	
Lemon juice	

We taste food with our tongues.

Foods can taste sweet, salty, or sour. What do these foods taste like? Connect each food to its taste.

lemon

sweet

salty

candy

sour

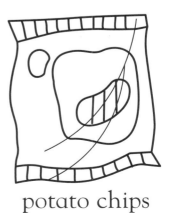

potato chips

Animals come in many shapes and sizes.

Animals move in different ways. Some animals walk and run. Some animals swim. Some animals fly. Animals that fly have wings. Circle each animal that has wings.

fly

cat

turtle

bat

bird

fish

Some animals are wild. Other animals can be kept in a house. These animals are tame.

Circle the animals that are wild. Point to the animals that are tame and can be kept in a house.

dog

gorilla

fox

goldfish

hamster

lion

Tame animals can live in your home and be kept as pets.

Do you have a pet?

If you have a pet, what kind of animal is your pet?

What is your pet's name?

Do you have a friend who has a pet?

If you have a friend who has a pet, what kind of animal is that pet?

What is the name of your friend's pet?

Draw your favorite pet.

Pets need special care to keep them happy and healthy.

The pictures below show some of the things pets need to be happy and healthy. Point to the pictures of the things pets need and name them all. Can you think of anything else pets need?

food and water   exercise

home   medical care

home

food and water

exercise

medical care

Motion is how things move.

The words in the box describe some of the ways things move. Say the words aloud and point to the picture of the motion each word describes.

| spin | slide | fall | fly | bounce | roll |

bounce

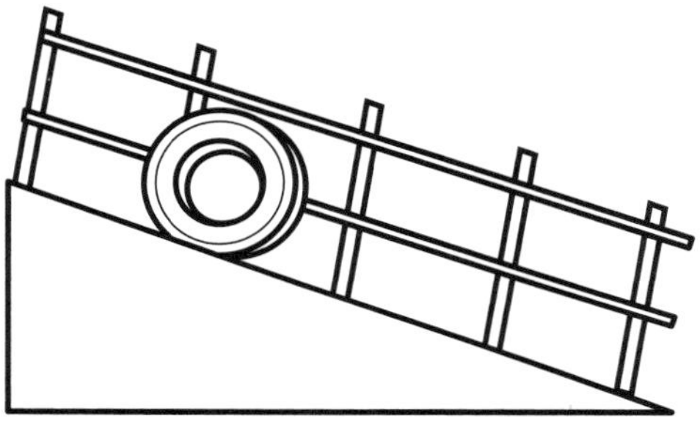

roll

spin

slide

fly

fall

When you move something away from you, you push it.
When you move something closer to you, you pull it.

Look at each picture. Put an **X** in the box to say if the movement shows pushing or pulling.

pull ☐ push ☐

pull ☐ push ☐

pull ☐ push ☐

pull ☐ push ☐

Light helps us to see.

Circle the things that generate light.

tree

campfire

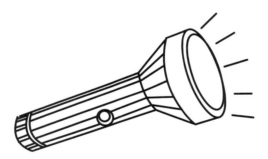

flashlight

sun

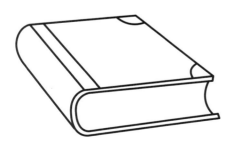

book

lamp

A shadow is a dark patch that forms where an object blocks out light.

TEST

What You Need:

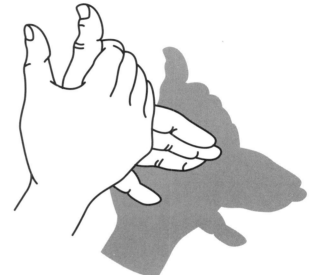

flashlight

What To Do:

1. In a dark room, turn on the flashlight and lay it on a table, pointing toward a wall.

2. Stand between the flashlight and the wall. Put your hands together, as shown above, to make the shadow of the dog.

3. What other shadows can you make on the wall?

RESULT

Can you explain what makes the shadow?

A rainbow is an arch of colors that appears when the sun shines through rain.

Color the rainbow.

You can make a rainbow by shining a light through water.

TEST **What You Need:**

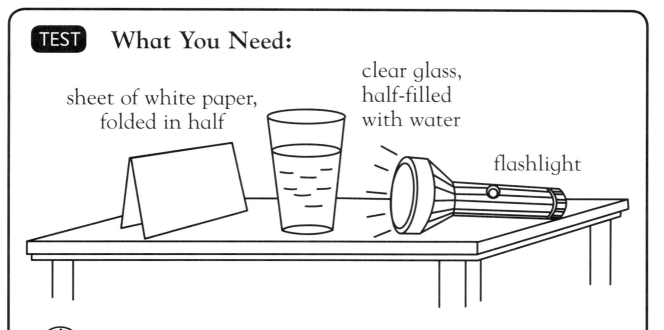

clear glass,
half-filled
with water

sheet of white paper,
folded in half

flashlight

What To Do:

1. In a dark room, stand the paper a few inches behind the glass.

2. Turn on the flashlight and shine it through the water onto the paper.

RESULT

What happens?
Draw what you
see on the paper.

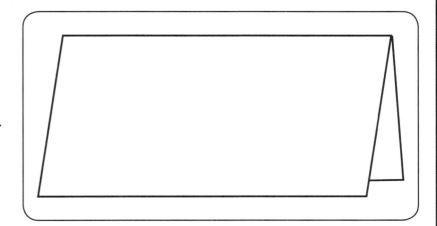

The things around you are solids, liquids, or gases.

Solid things keep their shape. Liquid things take the shape of the container they are in. Gases get bigger to fill the space they are in. Circle all the liquids. Point to the solids.

books

candy

juice

balloons

milk

water

Air is a gas. Air is invisible but you can feel it and see that it is there by blowing bubbles.

TEST

What You Need:

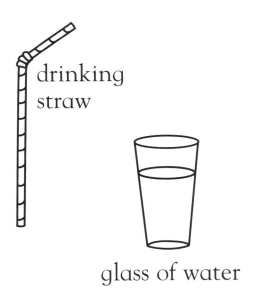

drinking straw

glass of water

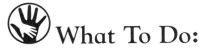 **What To Do:**

1. Blow through the straw. Feel the air coming out of the other end with your hand.

2. Put the straw in the glass of water and blow.

RESULT

Draw what you see happening when you blow through the straw in the water. Why does this happen?

You can fill a balloon with air.

TEST

What You Need:

balloon

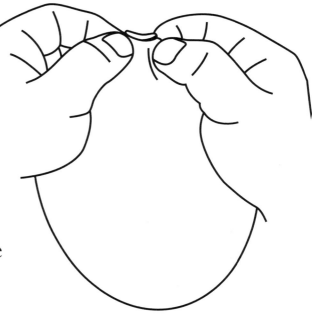

What To Do:

1. Ask an adult to blow into a balloon and fill it with air.

2. Take the balloon in your fingers and hold the mouth firmly to keep the air in.

3. Stretch the mouth of the balloon. Can you hear the air make a squeaky noise as it escapes?

4. Now let go of the balloon.

RESULT

Describe what happened to the balloon. Why do you think this happened?

Wind is moving air.

Draw a circle around the things that use the wind.
Color the picture.

Liquid takes the shape of the container it is in.

TEST

What You Need:

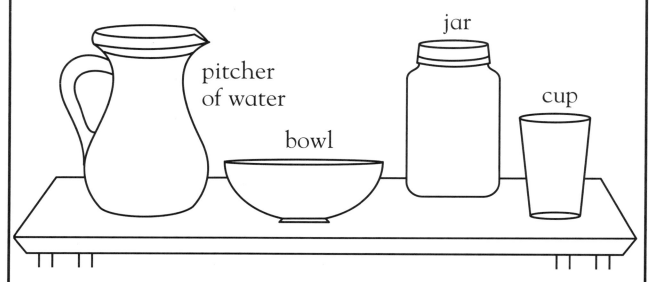

jar

pitcher
of water

cup

bowl

 What To Do:

1. Pour the water from the pitcher into a cup. See how the water fills the cup and becomes the same shape as the cup. Next, pour the water into a jar.

2. Now pour the water into a bowl. See how the water fills the bowl and becomes the same shape as the bowl.

RESULT

Describe what happens to the water when you pour it into different containers.

Bubbles are liquid filled with air.

TEST

What You Need:

2 tablespoons of
dish soap

water

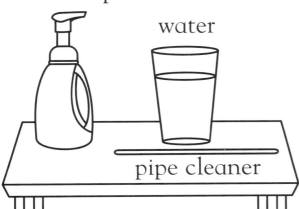

pipe cleaner

 What To Do:

1. In a cup, mix together
   the dish soap and
   the water.

2. Bend the top of the pipe
   cleaner into a loop.

3. Dip the pipe cleaner into
   the bubble mixture and
   then blow into the loop
   to make bubbles.

RESULT

Draw what happens.

What is inside the bubbles?

Solids keep their shape.

Draw a line between each object and the shape it matches.

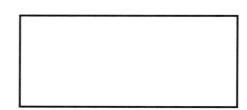

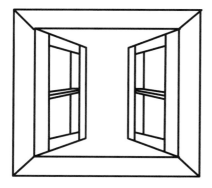

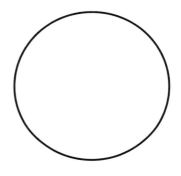

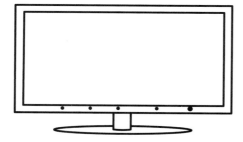

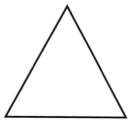

Water can be liquid or solid.

TEST

What You Need:

bowl   water pitcher   ice-cube tray

 What To Do:

1. Pour water into a pitcher. Is this water solid or liquid?

2. Pour the water from the pitcher into an ice-cube tray.

3. Put the ice-cube tray in the freezer for 5 hours.

4. Take the ice-cube tray out of the freezer and put the ice cubes in a bowl. Is the ice solid or liquid?

5. Keep the bowl of ice on a counter overnight. Look at the bowl in the morning.

RESULT

What happened to the water in the freezer?
What happened to the ice in the bowl?

What makes the water change between a solid and a liquid?

Freezing is when a liquid changes into a solid.
Freezing happens when it is very cold.

Look at the pictures. Circle the thing that will freeze
in the cold.

juice

book

rain

puddle

car tire

ball

milk

baseball bat

soup

Melting is when a solid turns into a liquid.
Melting happens when it is very warm.

Draw a circle around the objects that melt when it is hot.

apple

book

chocolate

ball

ice cream

sneakers

snowman

hat

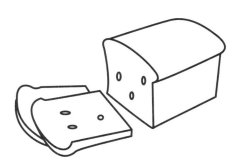

bread

Parents' Notes

The science covered in this book is similar to the work your child will do in kindergarten. The topics covered are intended to introduce children to simple scientific ideas and ways of thinking about the world.

Contents

By working through the science activities in this book, your child will practice:
- reading and writing;
- associating pictures and words;
- making observations about the world around him or her;
- categorizing animals and plants by type;
- recognizing habitats;
- finding the differences between types of plants and types of animals;
- performing experiments;
- describing the difference between liquid, solid, and gas;
- using positional words;
- noticing the weather;
- asking questions about what they see.

How to Help Your Child

Kindergarteners will not be able to read most of the instructions. Therefore, parents, guardians, or helpers should work closely with children as they progress through the activities. Both parents/helpers and children can gain a great deal from working together.

Perhaps the most important thing you can do—both as you go through the activities and in many everyday situations—is encourage children to be curious about the world around them. Whenever possible, ask them questions about what they see and hear. Ask them questions such as "Why?," "What if?," and "What do you think?" Do not be negative about their answers, however silly they may be. There is almost certainly a logic to their response, even if it is not correct. Explore and discuss their ideas with them.

Build your child's confidence with praise and encouragement. Celebrate their success.

Geography

Author Mark Shulman
Educational Consultant Kara Pranikoff

Contents

This chart lists all the topics in the Geography section.

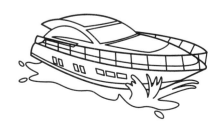

Geography is about the world around you. The people who study geography are called geographers. Geographers study nature. They study things such as the mountains, rivers, and forests. Geographers also study the way humans use and change nature when they make things like cities, parks, and bridges.

Circle the things that a geographer might study.

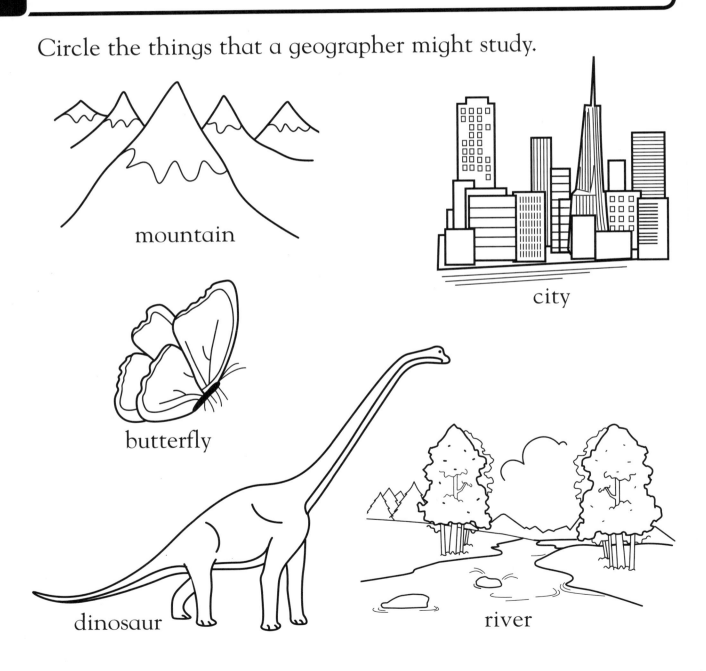

mountain

city

butterfly

dinosaur

river

You live on a planet called Earth. Earth is one of eight planets in our solar system. All the planets in a solar system share the same sun. Earth travels around the sun once every year. When your part of Earth is tilted toward the sun, it is summer. When your part of Earth is tilted away from the sun, it is winter.

Here is a picture of our solar system.
Earth is the third planet from the sun.
Circle the planet Earth.

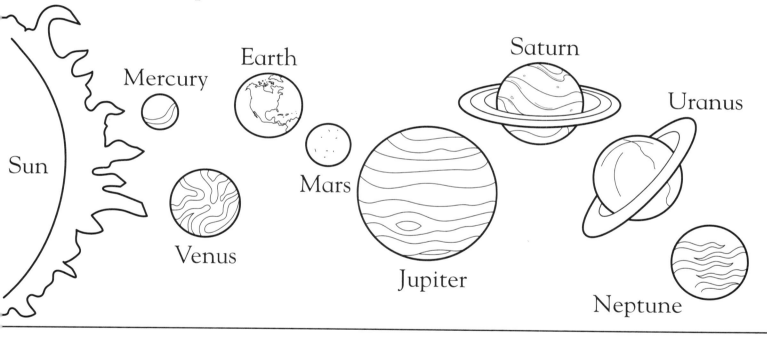

Put a check (✓) for the correct answer.

When is Earth tilted toward the sun?   winter [ ]   summer [ ]

What does Earth travel around once every year?   sun [ ]   moon [ ]

A globe is a map of planet Earth. It is shaped like a ball, just like planet Earth. A globe shows all the land and water on Earth. Most globes are small enough for a person to hold.

Look at the globe below, and then read the list at the side of it. Circle the things in the list that you can find on the globe.

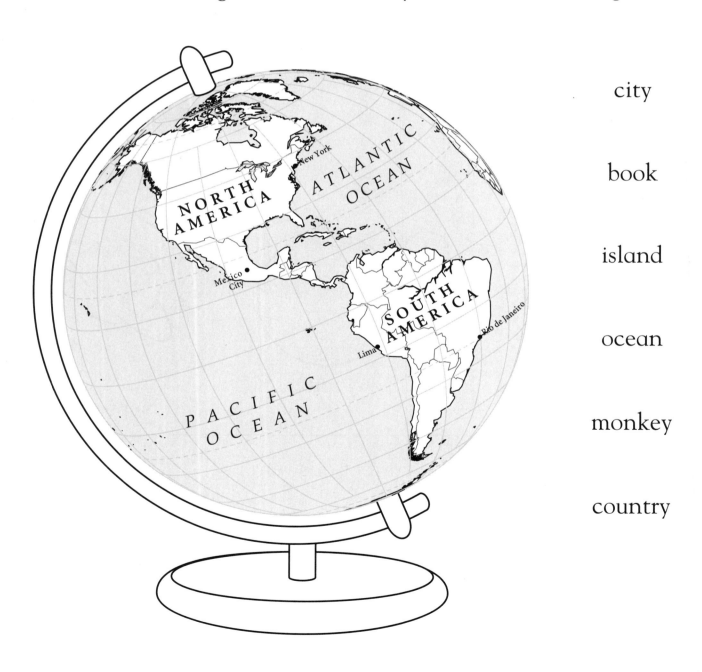

city

book

island

ocean

monkey

country

There are many different kinds of maps. A globe is shaped like a ball. Other maps are flat. They may be printed on paper, as charts, or in books. You can also see maps on the screens of computers, tablets, or phones. Flat maps can show the whole Earth or a part of it in a lot of detail.

Look at the different kinds of maps below. Write a **P** in the box under a map if the map is on paper. Write an **S** if the map is on a screen. Write a **G** if the map is a globe.

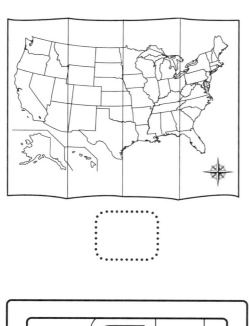

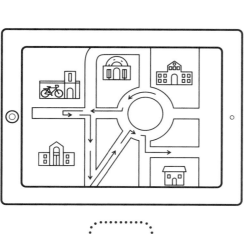

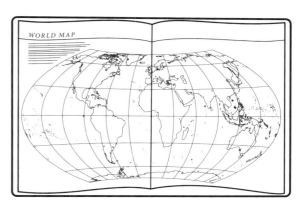

Different maps are used to show and explain different kinds of places. A park map shows you what is in a park. A street map shows you the streets you can travel along. A map of a room shows you the things in that room.

Below are pictures of three different places: a city, a park, and a bedroom. Draw a line to connect each place with its map.

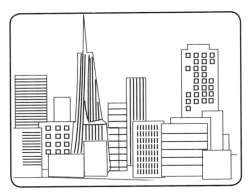
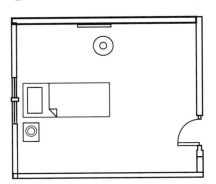

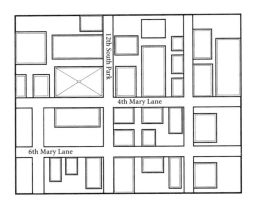

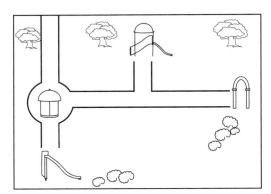

People use different maps for different reasons. A person driving a car may use a street map. Hikers may need a park map. Students and teachers may need a map of their school. There are many other kinds of maps as well.

Look at the different types of maps below. Who would use each kind of map? Draw a line to connect each map with the people who may need it.

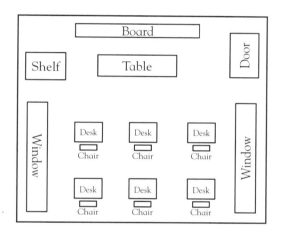

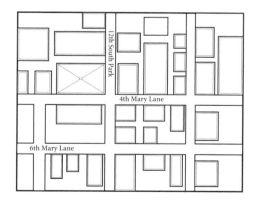

There are four directions that you need to know about to be able to read a map. Those directions are "north," "south," "east," and "west." No matter where you are, these directions can help you reach the place that you want to go to.

Look at the globe of Earth below.
Then place your finger in the middle of Earth.
Move your finger north, up to the **N**.
Now, move your finger south, down to the **S**.

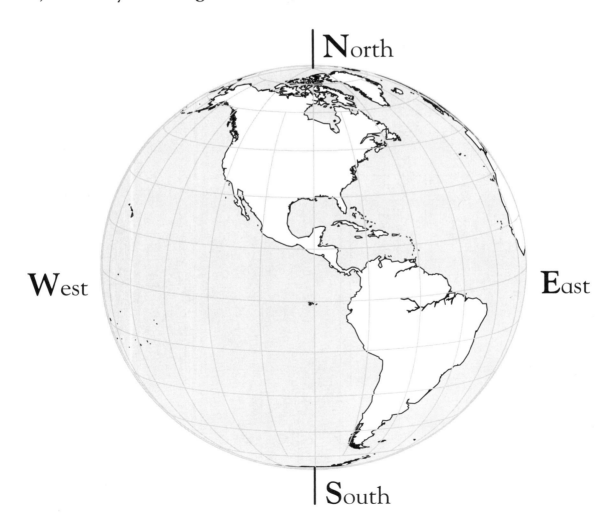

North

West

East

South

Most maps have a tool called a compass rose. It lets you know which direction the top of the map is pointing toward. Most maps have north at the top and south at the bottom. On such maps, west is on the left and east is on the right.

This is the compass rose you will see on a map.
Color the compass rose. Trace in the letters **N**, **S**, **E**, and **W**.

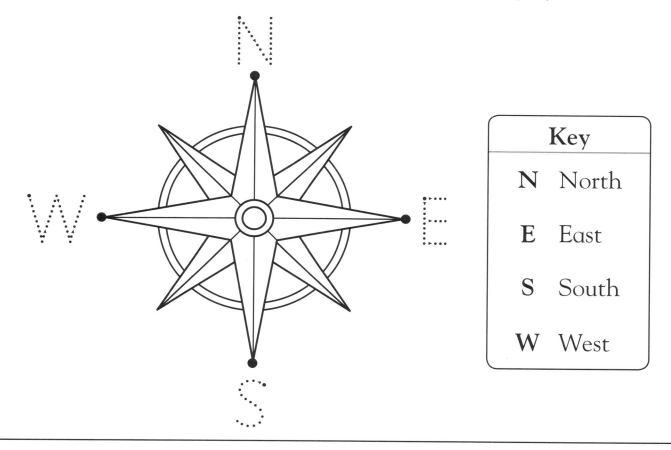

Key	
N	North
E	East
S	South
W	West

Complete the four sentences below.

N is for ....   **E** is for ....

S is for ....   **W** is for ....

The direction "north" is usually found at the top of a map. When you are going north, you are moving toward the top of Earth. You may know about the frozen North Pole. That is where you will end up if you keep going north!

Find the word "north" on the compass rose, and then circle it.

Now, look at the map of an amusement park below. Imagine you are standing at the **X** (**✗**). Which two rides are to the north of you? Circle them on the map.

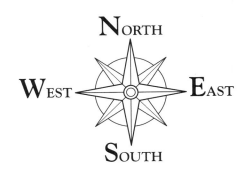

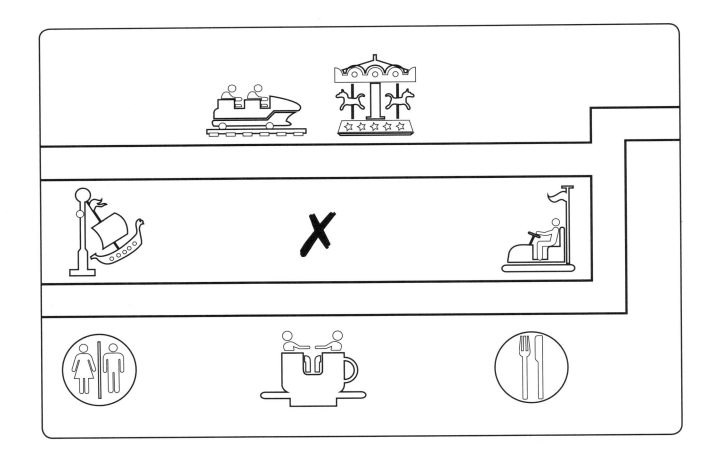

The direction "south" is usually found at the bottom of a map. When you are going south, you are moving toward the bottom of Earth. Have you heard about the freezing South Pole? That is where you will find yourself if you keep going south!

Find the word "south" on the compass rose, and then circle it. Now look at the map of North America. Find the country of Canada. Then color the country directly south of Canada.

The direction "east" is usually found at the right side of a map. When you are going east, you are moving sideways across Earth from left to right. Did you know that the sun rises in the east?

Look at the town map below. Imagine you are standing at the **X** (✗). Which two buildings are to the east of you? Circle them on the map.

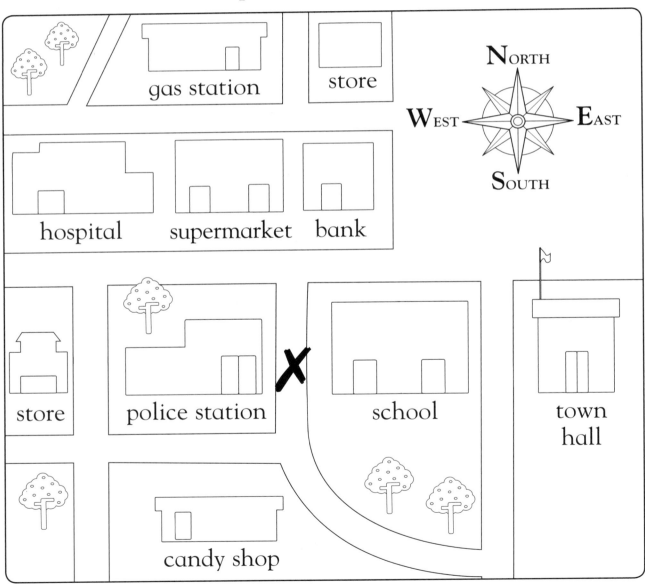

The direction "west" is usually at the left side of a map. When you are going west, you are moving across Earth from right to left. The sun sets in the west. If you can see the sun setting, you are facing west, and it is time for bed!

Look at the map of Australia below. It shows where some animals are found. Imagine you are standing at the X (✗). Circle the animal that can be found to the west of you.

kangaroo

koala

AUSTRALIA

wombat

squirrel glider

In geography, you study both the natural world and the human world. Think about a road on a mountain. The mountain is part of the natural world. It was part of our world long before there was a road. The road is part of the human world. People built the road. Geography is about understanding both the natural and the human world, and how they work together.

Use the words "natural" and "human" to complete the sentences below.

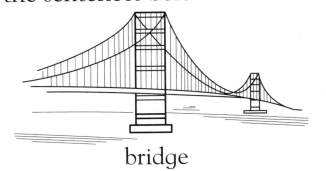

bridge

river

A river is part of the .... world.

A bridge is part of the .... world.

Circle the picture that shows the natural world.
Put an **X** on the picture that shows the human world.

airport

mountain

Your world has things from the natural world and things from the human world. The flowers and trees in a park are part of the natural world. The house you live in and your school are part of the human world.

Look around you. Draw something that is part of the natural world. Then draw something that is part of the human world.

Natural World

Human World

Maps of the natural world can help people understand it better. These maps can show mountains, rivers, lakes, types of trees, and even the weather. This information can help people plan a trip as well as pack the right clothes and equipment for it.

Draw lines connecting each natural place with its map.

island

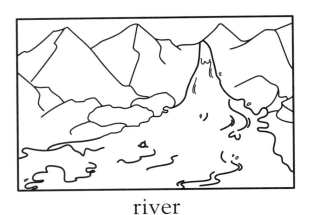

river

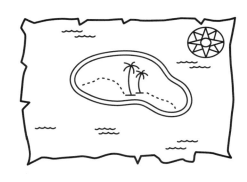

Earth

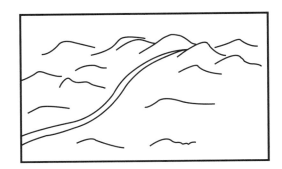

There are seven very large areas of land on Earth. These huge areas are called continents. When you look at a globe or a flat map of Earth, you will see the seven continents. The largest continent is Asia. The smallest continent is Australia.

Look at this map of the world. It shows all seven continents. Then follow the instructions below the map.

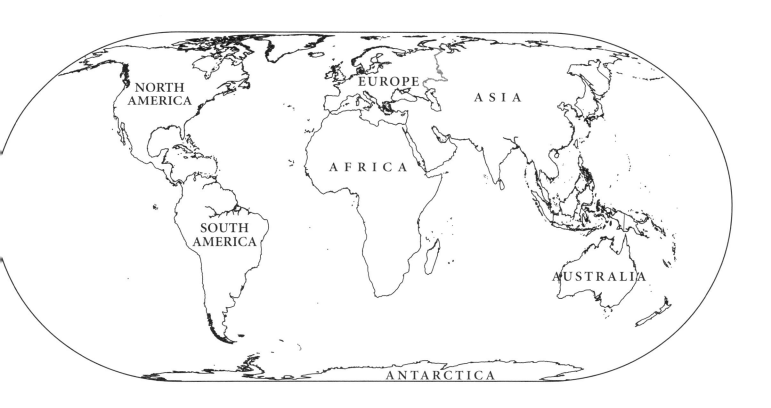

Color all the continents green.
Hint: Everything you do not color in this map is water.

Circle the name of the largest continent.
Put an **X** on the name of the smallest continent.

Mountains and hills are high areas of land. Hills are not as high as mountains. Some mountains are so tall that their tops reach the clouds. The tallest mountains have snow on top, even in summer.

Look at the two pictures below. Color the mountains brown. Color the hills green. Then answer the questions.

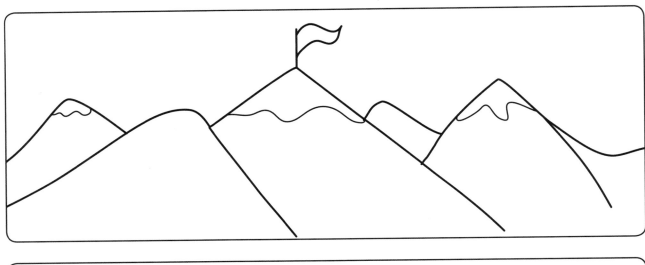

What is on top of the tallest mountain?   ....

What is on top of the tallest hill?   ....

Forests are large areas of land that are covered with trees. There are many forests on Earth. Many different kinds of animals live inside a forest. Some are large and others are small.

Look at the picture of a forest below. There are many different kinds of animals living in this forest. Circle the animals that you can find.

The driest places on Earth are called deserts. Many are very hot in the daytime and cold at night, but some are always cold. Deserts get very little rain. Most people do not like to live in such dry places. However, a number of plants and animals have learned to live in the desert.

Look at the picture of a desert below. Circle the different kinds of animals and plants that you can find in the picture.

An island is a piece of land that is completely surrounded by water. Islands can be very large, or they can be very small.

Look at the islands of Hawaii below. Then complete the activities.

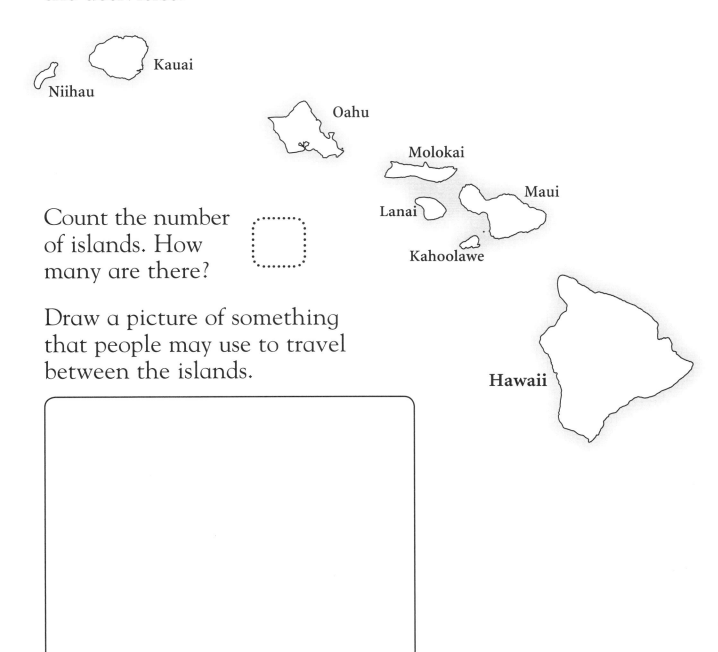

Count the number of islands. How many are there?

Draw a picture of something that people may use to travel between the islands.

An ocean is a very, very large body of water. There are five oceans on Earth, and they cover most of the planet. They are home to many different kinds of animals, such as whales, sea turtles, and fish. In fact, there are more animals in the oceans than there are on land.

Look at the map of the world below. It shows the continents surrounded by oceans. Color the oceans.

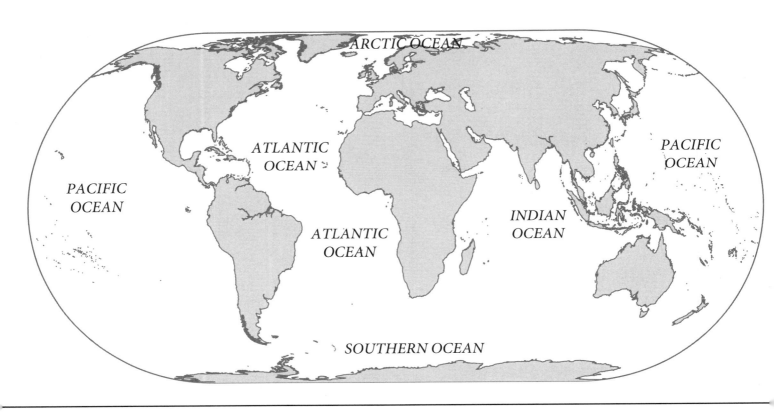

ARCTIC OCEAN

ATLANTIC OCEAN

PACIFIC OCEAN

PACIFIC OCEAN

INDIAN OCEAN

ATLANTIC OCEAN

SOUTHERN OCEAN

Circle the animals that live in the ocean.

whale

rabbit

seal

A lake is a large body of water surrounded by land. Some lakes are very big. People would need a large boat to go across a big lake. Other lakes are much smaller. People can cross them in a small boat.

Circle the things made by humans that you might see at a lake. Color the animals that you might also see there.

dinosaur

sailboat

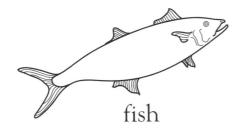

fish

baseball

life jacket

duck

Water flows from high places to low places. A small amount of flowing water is called a stream. A large amount of flowing water is called a river. Many towns and cities are built along rivers. Rivers can be long and wide and may move very quickly. You might need a bridge or a boat to get across a river.

Circle the three things you can use to get across a river.

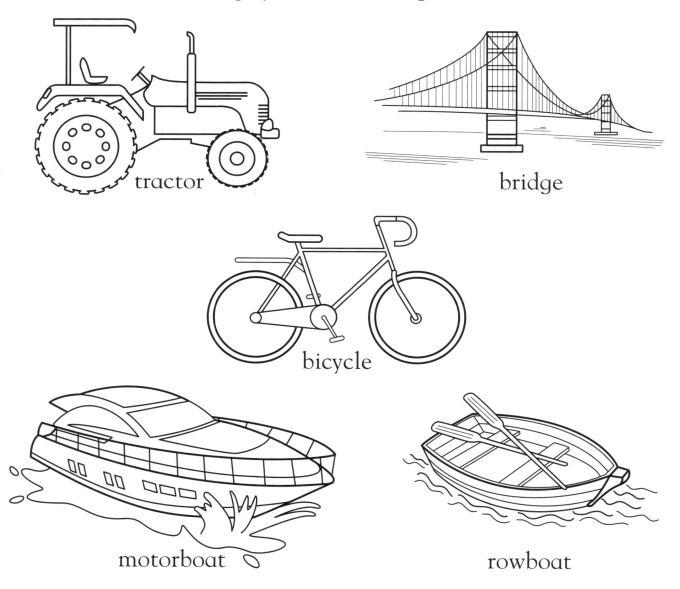

tractor

bridge

bicycle

motorboat

rowboat

The places humans make are part of the human world. We build roads, bridges, and tunnels to help us go places. We make cities, towns, and villages to live in. We create parks and playgrounds so we can enjoy them. All of these things can be found on a map.

Circle the pictures of things that belong to the human world.

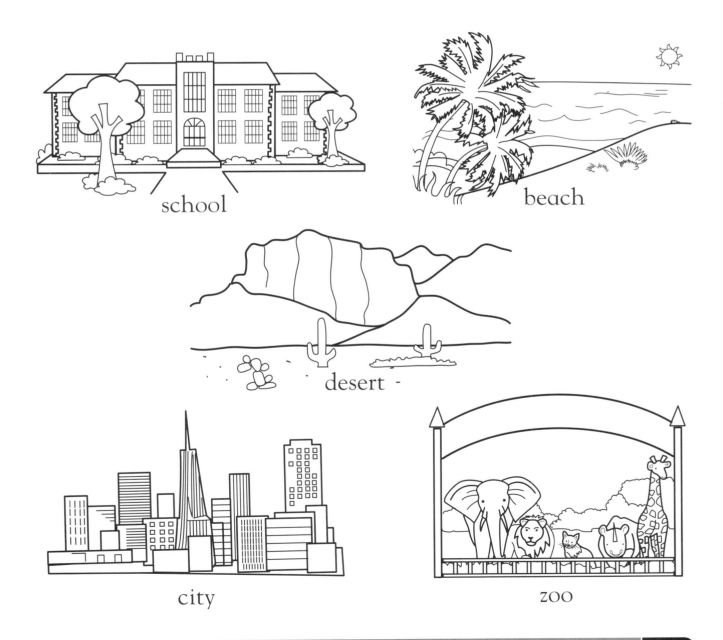

school

beach

desert

city

zoo

A country is an area of Earth that people identify as one place.

Look at the map of the world. Then follow the instructions below. You can ask an adult for help.

Circle the country you live in.

Write the name of your country.

....

Write the name of the leader of your country.

....

What language do most people speak in your country?

....

All the people in a country share the same leader, such as a president or a queen. They usually speak the same language. Every country has its own flag, too.

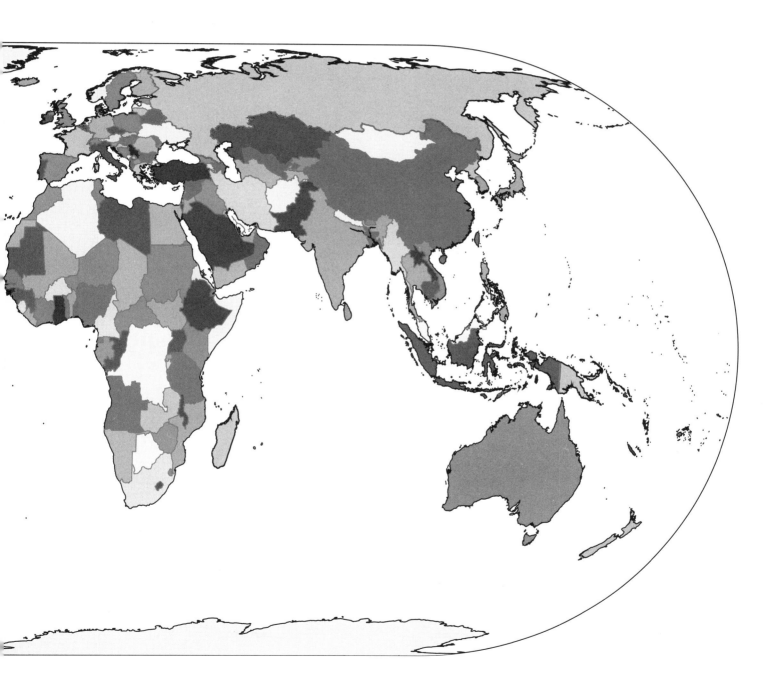

Many countries are divided into smaller regions. In some countries, like the United States (US), these smaller regions are called states.

Here is a map of the United States, which is one large country.

If you live in the US, color in your state. If you don't live in the US, color in a state you would like to visit.

What is the name of the state you colored?

....

Name a state that is next to the state you colored.

....

Name a state that is far away from the state you colored.

....

The United States is divided into 50 states. A few of these states are small, but some are very large and are filled with many towns and cities.

Some countries are divided into smaller regions known as provinces, rather than states. Canada has ten provinces (and three other regions called territories).

ARCTIC OCEAN

PACIFIC OCEAN

YUKON TERRITORY

NORTHWEST TERRITORIES

NUNAVUT

C A N A D A

NEWFOUNDLAND AND LABRADOR

BRITISH COLUMBIA

ALBERTA

SASKATCHEWAN

MANITOBA

QUÉBEC

ONTARIO

PRINCE EDWARD ISLAND

NEW BRUNSWICK

NOVA SCOTIA

Look at the map of Canada above.

The name of one of the provinces begins with the letter **O**. Find this province and color it blue.

The name of one of the provinces begins with the letter **Q**. Find this province and color it green.

A city is a busy place filled with people. There are many roads, houses, and buildings close together in a city. A big city may also have museums, parks, theaters, sports stadiums, and airports.

Look at this map showing a part of a city. Then follow the instructions given below.

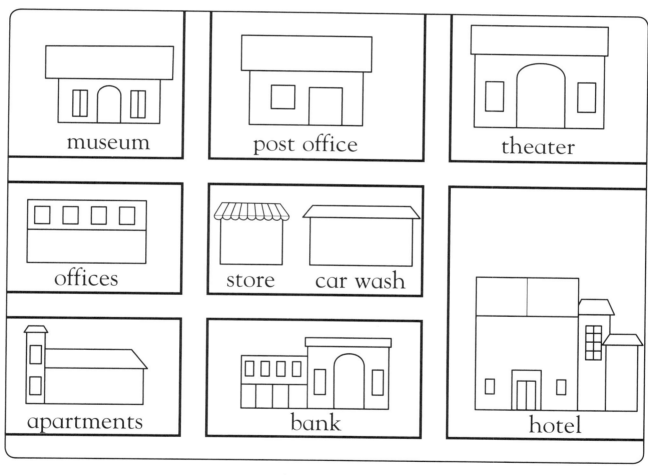

museum

post office

theater

offices

store   car wash

apartments

bank

hotel

Name three things in this city.

....

....

....

Our Earth is a very big planet. The land on Earth is divided into seven large continents. These continents are further divided into countries.

Look at the shaded areas in each pair of globes below. Which is bigger? Circle the correct globe.

planet Earth

continent of North America

continent of Australia

continent of Asia

continent of Africa

country of Nigeria

Some countries are divided into states, as we learned on pages 176 and 177. Some states are very big, while others are very small. States have cities, which can be big or small.

Look at the shaded areas in each pair of maps below. Which is bigger? Circle the correct map.

United States of America

state of California

state of Texas

state of Ohio

city of Portland

state of Oregon

Maps tell us about a place using symbols, sometimes shown as pictures. The symbols are explained in what is known as a key. A map's key is a list of the different symbols that the map uses. It helps you read the map.

Match each map symbol to the thing you think it stands for. Ask a grown up for help.

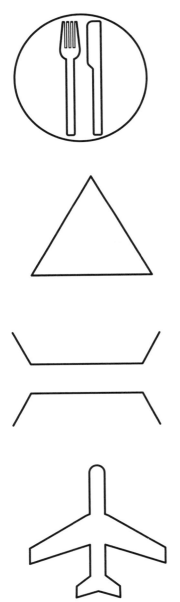

It can be hard for people to find their way around the natural world without a map. Nature maps tell you what you will find in an area of the natural world. Each symbol in the key stands for a different part of the natural world.

Look at this nature map. Then follow the instructions given below.

Draw lines to connect each symbol to the name of the place it stands for.

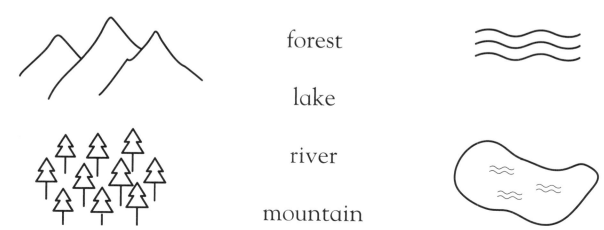

forest

lake

river

mountain

A city is a big place. Maps can help you find your way around a city. They show you which roads you can take. A city map also shows you where to find the places you want to visit. Without a map, it is easy to get lost.

Look at this map of a part of a city. Draw a line to connect each symbol on the map to the name of the place you think it stands for.

bike store

candy store

gift shop

hotel

fire department

library

A map of a park can show you the activities you can do there. It can also show you how to get to the places you want to visit. The map also shows you where to get help.

Look at the map of a park below. Then, read the list of activities you can do in the park. Draw a line to connect each activity to the symbol on the map that it stands for.

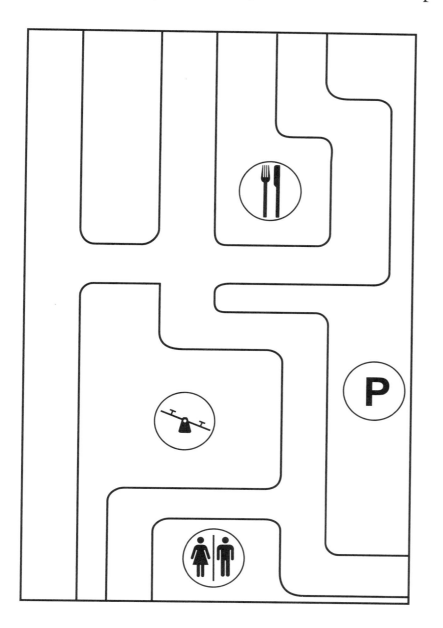

play on the see-saw

eat a picnic

use the restroom

park your car

Some map keys use symbols that are not pictures. Instead, they use letters as symbols to tell you what to find there.

Look at this map of a school and its key. The key uses letters to represent different places in the school.

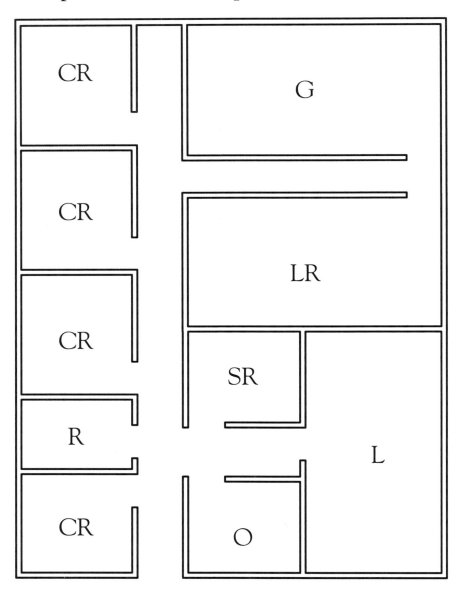

Key

LR	lunch room
O	office
SR	science room
L	library
G	gym
R	restroom
CR	classroom

Imagine you are at the gym and you need to reach the restroom. Draw a path on the map to find your way.

Some map keys do not use words at all. They have symbols that are small pictures of the places or things that are shown on the map.

Look at this map of a zoo. It has small pictures of animals as symbols to show where each can be found in the zoo.

Key

Imagine you are standing in front of the lions. You want to go see the alligators. Draw a path on the map to find your way.

Road maps are some of the most commonly used maps. They can show you the roads in a town or a city, or roads that cross much larger areas, such as the highways running from state to state across the whole country.

Here is a map of three states in the US. The states are Washington, Oregon, and California. Use the compass rose to help you answer the questions below.

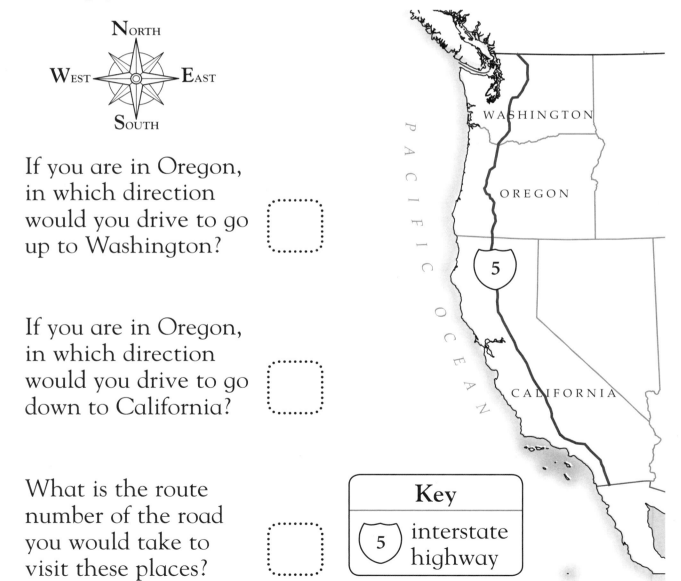

If you are in Oregon, in which direction would you drive to go up to Washington?

If you are in Oregon, in which direction would you drive to go down to California?

What is the route number of the road you would take to visit these places?

Key

5 interstate highway

A map of your neighborhood can help you find your way around the area close to your home. It can also show you the different kinds of places you will find there.

Imagine the map below is of your neighborhood. Answer the questions that follow, using the map, its key, and the compass rose.

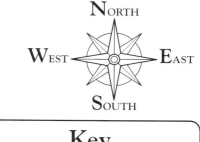

Which is closer to the park, the school or the supermarket?

....

What is to the east of your home?

....

If you are at the school, in which direction will you go to reach the library?

....

Some maps tell you the choices you have when you visit a place. A park map, for example, helps you plan what you might do when you visit that park.

Look at this park map. Use direction words such as "left," "right," "next to," "in front of," and similar words to describe the path you would take to enjoy the activities given below. Trace your path on the map using your finger.

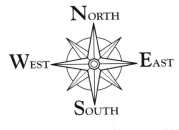

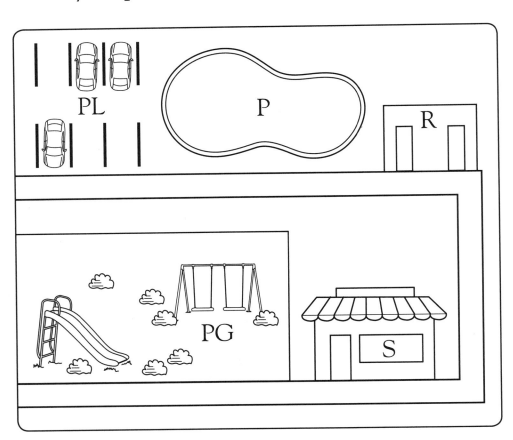

Key

PG	playground
PL	parking lot
R	restroom
S	snack bar
P	pool

Start at the parking lot. Then go to the pool. After swimming, wash your hands in the restroom. Then go down to the snack bar. After eating in the snack bar, play at the playground. That's a busy day at the park.

Where is the restroom? It is .... the pool.

A map can also help you to find your way when you are inside a building. You can still use a compass rose with this type of map.

Look at this map of a school. Answer the questions below, using only the map and the compass rose to help you.

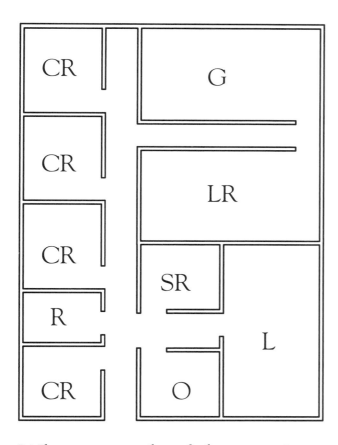

NORTH

WEST **E**AST

SOUTH

Key	
LR	lunch room
O	office
SR	science room
L	library
G	gym
R	restroom
CR	classroom

What is south of the gym? ....

What is north of the lunch room? ....

What is to the east of the office? ....

Which rooms are on either side
of the restroom? ....

Where do you want to go? What do you want to do?
When you want to answer these questions, you use a map.

Jess and Miguel need different kinds of maps. Read about their trips below. Then put a check (✓) next to the map that each child needs.

Jess and her mother are driving across the United States to see Grandma and Grandpa.

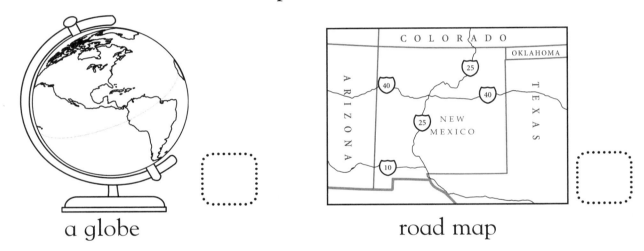

a globe   road map

Miguel and his brother are going to the video-game store in their town.

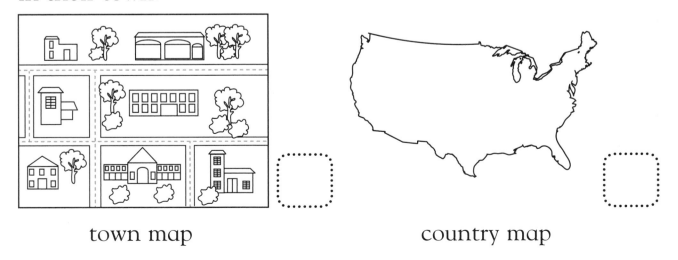

town map   country map

There are different kinds of maps. Each map is useful at a different time. Which map do you need?

Tanya and Leon also need maps. Below, read about what they need them for. Then put a check (✔) next to the map that each child needs.

Tanya and her parents are planning to buy furniture for their house.

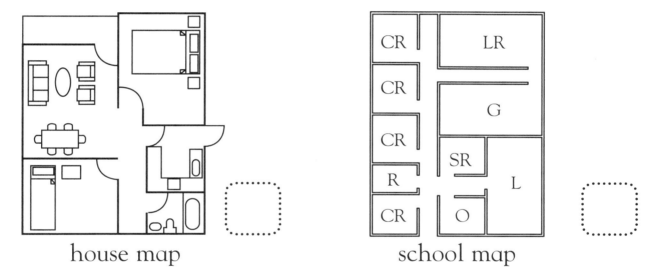

house map   school map

Leon and his babysitter want to go for a picnic in a park.

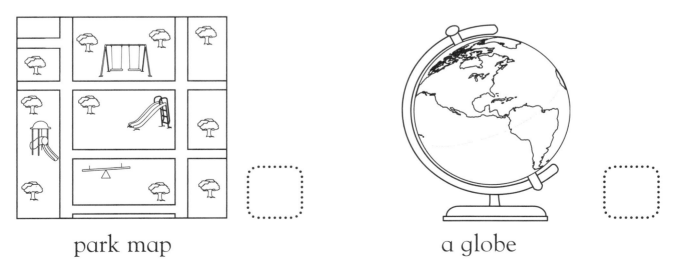

park map   a globe

Parents' Notes

The geography section of this book is intended to support the concepts that are taught to your child in kindergarten. The topics covered will test your child's knowledge of the world around him or her. By working through the activities, your child will learn basic geography concepts in a fun and informative way.

Contents

The geography activities are intended to be completed by a child with adult support. The topics covered are as follows:

- planet Earth and globes;
- the natural and the human (man-made) world;
- bodies of water such as oceans, rivers, and lakes;
- landforms such as mountains, hills, islands, and deserts;
- types of maps and their keys;
- compass directions;
- continents, countries, provinces, and territories;
- cities and states.

How to Help Your Child

As you work through the pages with your child, make sure he or she understands what each activity requires. Read the facts and instructions aloud. Encourage questions and reinforce observations that will build confidence and increase active participation in classes at school.

By working with your child, you will understand how he or she thinks and learns. When appropriate, use props and objects from daily life to help your child make connections with the world outside.

If an activity seems too challenging for your child, encourage him or her to try another page. You can also give encouragement by praising progress made as a correct answer is given and a page is completed. Above all, have fun!

Language Arts

Author Anne Flounders

Contents

This chart lists all the topics
in the Language Arts section.

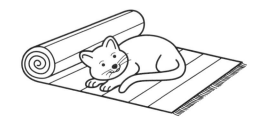

Lowercase letters are the small letters.
The first letters of the alphabet are **a** through **n**.

Trace lowercase letters **a** through **n**.
Then write these letters in lowercase on your own.

a a a a art	h h h h ham
b b b b bad	i i i i ill
c c c c cat	j j j j jet
d d d d dot	k k k k kit
e e e e egg	l l l l lot
f f f f fit	m m m m mad
g g g g get	n n n n not

The letters in most words are in lowercase.
The last letters of the alphabet are **o** through **z**.

Trace lowercase letters **o** through **z**.
Then write these letters in lowercase on your own.

o o o o · · · odd	u u u u · · · up
p p p p · · · pat	v v v v · · · vet
q q q q · · · quit	w w w w · wet
r r r r · · · rag	x x x x · x-ray
s s s s · · · sit	y y y y · · · yes
t t t t · · · tap	z z z z · · zip

Can you think of some words beginning with
the letters **a** through **z**?

Uppercase letters are used in the names of people, places, or events. These are the letters **A** through **N** in uppercase.

Practice writing the uppercase letters. First trace the letters. Then write uppercase letters **A** through **N** on your own.

A A A · · · · April

H H H · · Hannah

B B B · · · Brad

I I I I · · · Ivan

C C C · · · Cody

J J J · · · Joe

D D D · · · Dan

K K K · · · Kim

E E E · · · Easter

L L L · · Logan

F F F · · · Fred

M M M Morgan

G G G · Grace

N N N · · Nora

Uppercase letters are used at the beginning of a sentence and in titles. Here are the letters **O** through **Z** in uppercase.

Practice writing the uppercase letters. First trace the letters. Then write uppercase letters **O** through **Z** on your own.

O O O O Owen

U U U Uma

P P P Paul

V V V Vic

Q Q Q Quinn

W W W Will

R R R Randy

X X X Xavier

S S S Sam

Y Y Y Yoko

T T T Tom

Z Z Z Zach

Can you think of some names beginning with the letters **A** through **Z**?

Books have covers. Covers give information about books.

Description	Instruction
The title is the name of the book.	Look at the book's cover. Draw a box around the title.
The author is the person who wrote the book.	Draw a line under the author's name.
A book title uses uppercase letters. People's names also start with uppercase letters.	Circle all the uppercase letters.
The title and picture on a book's cover can give you a clue as to what the book will be about.	What do you think you would read in this book? Finally, color the book cover.

Silly Skunk
Stories

Rosy **S**niffin

Stories have a beginning, a middle, and an end.

Look at the pictures below. Then tell the story they show aloud. What happens first? What happens next? What happens last? When you have told the story, color the pictures.

1.

2.

3.

4.

The letter **a** can sound like the **a** in "apple" (short "a") or the **a** in "ape" (long "a").

Each word is missing its short "a." Write the letter to complete the word. Then read each word aloud.

w_g

b_t

s_d

c_p

f_n

g_s

Two words that end in the same sound are called rhyming words. Rhyming words begin with different sounds.

Read the sentences aloud. Draw a line under the rhyming words.

My dad was mad.

A mat is flat.

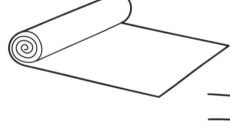

Put the rag in the bag.

The rat sat on the cap.

Rhyming words often have similar spellings. Sometimes rhyming words can have completely different spellings.

Read each word aloud. Find the pairs of rhyming words in the balloons. Color each pair the same color.

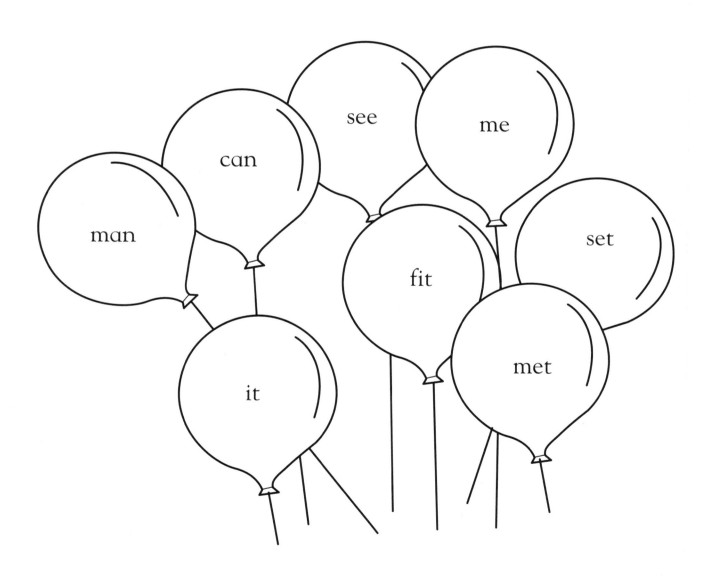

A nursery rhyme is a poem or song for children.
Nursery rhymes are passed down through the years.

Read the nursery rhyme aloud. Underline the rhyming words.
Draw a picture that illustrates the nursery rhyme.

Hey, diddle, diddle,
The cat and the fiddle,
The cow jumped over the Moon.
The little dog laughed
To see such sport,
And the dish ran away with the spoon.

Saying words aloud can make it easier to figure out if they rhyme. Here are some more rhyming words to practice.

Find the rhyming words to practice. Draw a line between each pair.

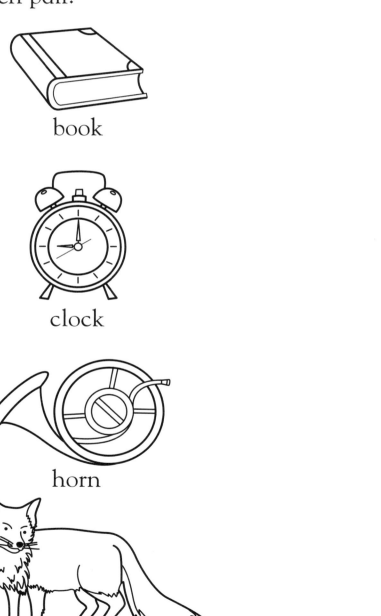

book

clock

horn

fox

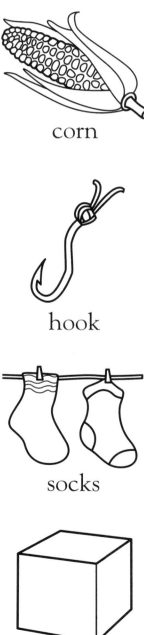

corn

hook

socks

block

Some words are used often in reading and writing.
You can learn to recognize these words.

Read the words aloud. Use them to complete sentences.

| off | out | from | in | to | for |

I gave the bag .... Bob.

The gift is .... you.

Jane took the book .... me.

The dog is .... the house.

We are .... of the car.

The lid is .... the pot.

A character is a person or animal in a story.

Read the story aloud.

> A wolf liked to look at the stars. One night,
> he walked along looking up at the stars.
> He didn't see a hole in the ground and fell into it.
> Another wolf passing by said, "You see the stars far
> away. Why don't you see the ground under your feet?"

Below, circle the character that this story is about.

A setting is where and when a story takes place.

Read the story aloud.

Jenny and Jack climbed on a sled. They zoomed down a hill. The winter air turned their cheeks cold. The sled stopped at the bottom of the hill.
Jack said, "Let's ride again!"

Circle the picture that shows the setting of the story.

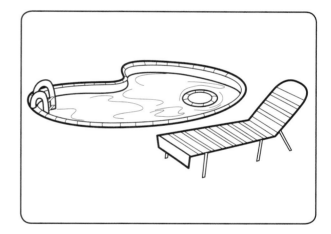

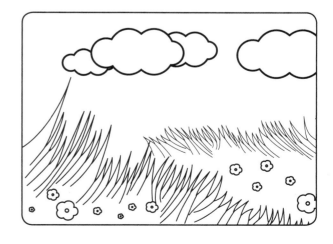

The letter **e** can sound like the **e** in "egg"
(short "e") or the **e** in "eel" (long "e").

Each word is missing its short "e." Write the letter
to complete the word. Then read each word aloud.

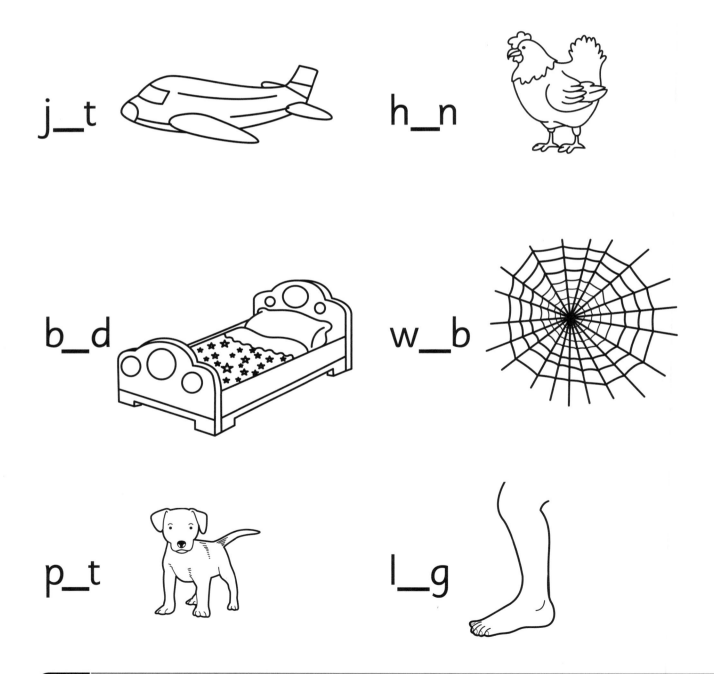

j_t

h_n

b_d

w_b

p_t

l_g

Rhyming words in a sentence make it more fun to read. Here are some more rhyming words.

Read the sentences aloud. Draw lines under the rhyming words.

I led the red hen.

She fed the wet pet.

A bird can rest in a nest.

Ten men saw the pen.

People read for different reasons.
Sometimes they read to learn.

Read the text below.

A map helps you find your way. A map can show your home. It can show your school. A map can show you how to go from your home to your school.

Circle the picture that shows what the text is about.

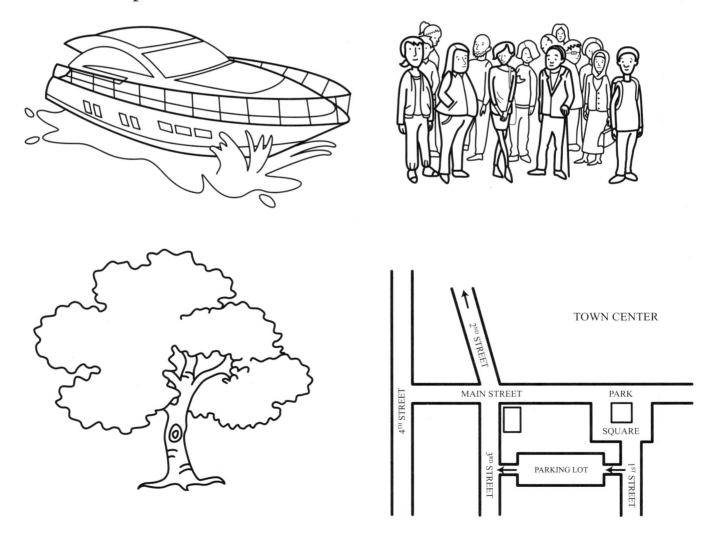

 Labels are a text feature.
They give information about a picture.

Write labels naming the parts of the tiger.
Use the words from the word bank.

| back | ear | eye | leg | nose | tail |

A noun names a person, a place, or a thing.

Circle the words that are nouns.

bird

run

train

man

pull

leaf

car

book

A verb is an action word. It names anything one can do or be.

Circle the words that are verbs.

sun

kick

jump

door

hide

sing

frog

hold

The letter **i** can sound like the **i** in "big" (short "i") or the **i** in "ripe" (long "i").

Each word is missing its short "i." Write the letter to complete the word. Then read each word aloud.

d_g

k_d

s_t

r_p

b_b

p_n

One way to create a word that rhymes with another word is to change the first letter of the word.

Make rhyming words using letters from the letter bank.

r	d	w	p	f	t

_in   _in

_id   _id

_ig   _ig

Adjectives are words that describe people, places, or things.

Draw a line between the picture and
the word that describes it.

funny

red

soft

loud

Telling or writing information in order helps it make sense.

This story is out of order. What happens first, next, and last? Write 1, 2, and 3 by the pictures to put them in the correct order.

Make sense of information by telling
or writing it in order.

Read the text below. Then look at the pictures.
Number the pictures 1, 2, 3, and 4 to show
the order in which the story happened.

Meg wanted to sell lemonade. First, she made the lemonade.
Next, she set up her stand. Then, she hung up a sign.
Finally, Meg sold lots of lemonade to her friends!

The letter **o** can sound like the **o** in "dog" (short "o") or the **o** in "rope" (long "o").

Each word is missing its short "o." Write the letter to complete the word. Then read each word aloud.

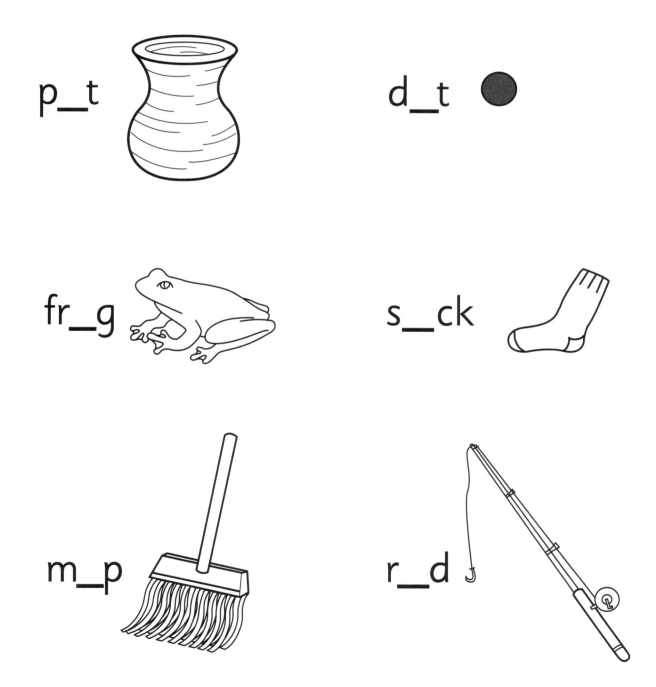

p_t

d_t

fr_g

s__ck

m_p

r_d

If words end with the same sound, they are rhyming words.

Read the sentences aloud. Circle the rhyming words.

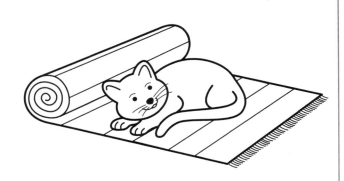

The cat sits on the mat.

Bob likes corn on the cob.

Lots of dogs sit on logs.

The pot is not too hot.

Words can name a general idea or topic, such as "place" or "job." Other words are more specific, such as "city" or "teacher."

Find the words that name foods in the spaces. Color those spaces red. Find the words that name animals in the spaces. Color those spaces green.

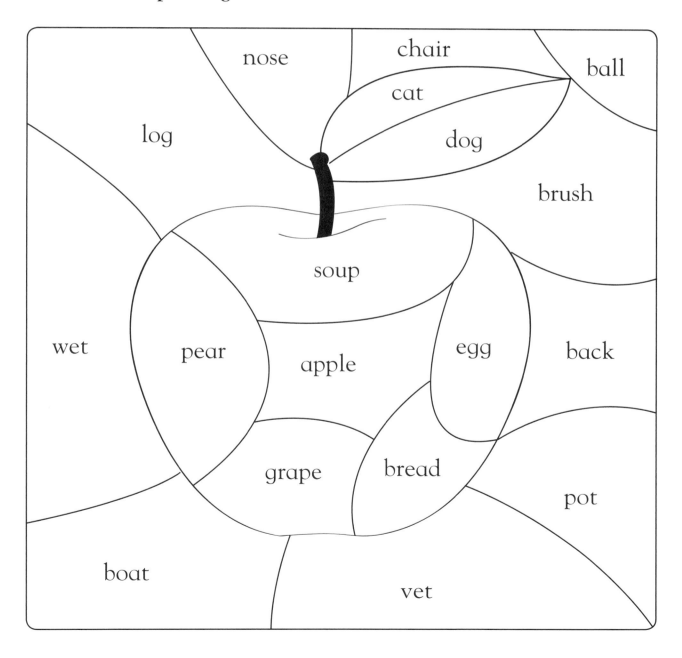

Singular means one. Plural means more than one. To make some words plural, add an **s** at the end of the word.

Make these words plural.

bat_

pig_

cane_

pan_

Add **es** to make a plural of words that end
in **ch**, **sh**, **s**, or **x**.

Make these words plural.

fox__

dish__

match__

dress__

A story has a title, or name. Stories are made up by authors. Stories also have characters and a setting.

Write down the title, author, characters, and setting of your favorite storybook. Write down why you like it.

My Favorite Storybook

Title: ....

Author: ....

Characters: ....

Setting: ....

Why I like this book: ....

....

Draw a picture of something that happens in your favorite storybook.

Books about true events are called nonfiction books. Nonfiction books can inform us about a subject.

Write down the title, author, and subject of your favorite true book. Write down why you like it.

My Favorite True Book

Title: ....

Author: ....

Subject: ....

Why I like this book: ....

....

....

Draw a picture of what your favorite true book is about.

The letter **u** can sound like the **u** in "up"
(short "u") or the **u** in "use" (long "u").

Each word is missing its short "u." Write the letter
to complete the word. Then read each word aloud.

r_g

b_d

h_t

c_b

b_s

p_p

Using a rhyme in a sentence can make it easier to remember.

Read the sentences aloud. Draw lines under the rhyming words.

It is fun to run.

Can you cut a nut?

A bug is on the mug.

The fox is in the box.

Some words sound alike but are spelled differently.
These are called homophones.

Read each pair of words aloud. They sound alike!
Trace the letters that change the spelling of the words.

te a   te e   s o n   s u n

to e   to w   ta i l   ta l e

ha i r   ha r e   bl ew   bl ue

This popular song names different parts of the body.

Sing or say the song. As you sing, point to the parts named.
Then use words from the song to label the parts of the body.

Head, shoulders, knees and toes, knees and toes.
Head, shoulders, knees and toes, knees and toes.
And eyes, and ears and mouth and nose.
Head, shoulders, knees and toes, knees and toes.

Question words help people think about and understand what they read, do, or see.

The animals are running a race in the park. Look at the picture. Then answer the questions.

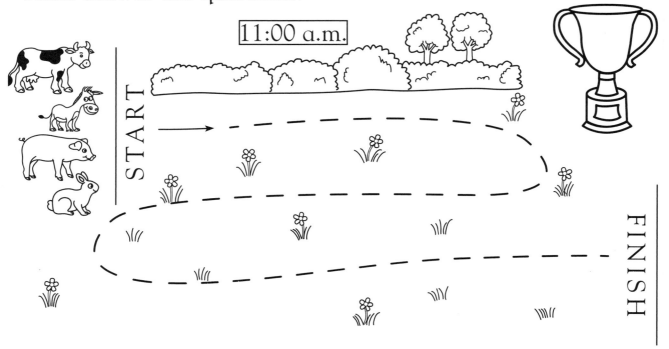

11:00 a.m.

START

FINISH

Who is running the race? Circle the answer in the picture.

What will the winner of the race get? Draw a box around it.

Where will the runners go? Trace the answer with your pencil.

When is the race? Circle the answer.

Why do you think the race is in a park? Talk about your ideas.

How will the runners know where to go? Draw a box around the answer.

Question Words

> Question words are words that help people ask for information.

Select question words from the word bank to best complete each question.

Who	What	Where	When	Why	How

.... do you tie a shoe?

.... is at the door?

.... are there clouds in the sky?

.... is my dog?

.... will we eat dinner?

.... time is it?

Consonant Blends

FACTS

Letters are used together to make new sounds.
These letters are called blends.

Use the letters from the letter bank to
complete each word. Say the words aloud.

bl	br	cl	cr	gl	gr

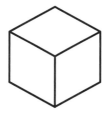

__ock

__ue

__ips

__apes

__ush

__ab

Certain letters make special sounds when they are used together.

C + H makes the sound that starts the word "chip."
S + H makes the sound that starts the word "sheep."
T + H makes the sound that starts the word "thin."
Draw a line to connect each word to its sound.

shoes

TH

chair

cheese

SH

think

three

CH

ship

Sometimes one word has more than one meaning.
Some words are both nouns and verbs.

Use the words in the word bank to write
the names of the pictures.

| box | duck | fall | train |

....

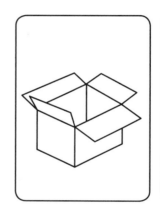 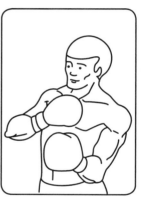

....

....

....

Every letter has an uppercase and a lowercase form.

For each letter, fill in the missing uppercase
or lowercase letter.

_____ a   B _____   C _____   _____ d

_____ e   _____ f   _____ g   H _____

I _____   _____ j   K _____   L _____

_____ m   _____ n   _____ o   P _____

_____ q   _____ r   _____ s   T _____

_____ u   V _____   _____ w   X _____

y _____   Z _____

Some words are easy to recognize.
Others need to be sounded out.

Say the words describing these pictures aloud.
Then write the words.

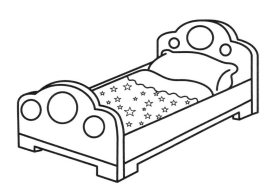

....

....

....

....

....

....

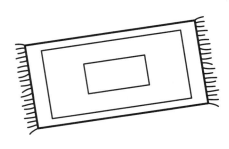
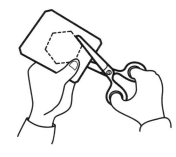

....

....

....

People can share ideas and give information through writing.

Complete the sentences to describe your day.

My Day

My name is ....

Here is what happened to me today/yesterday. (Circle one.)

First, ...

....

Then, ...

....

Finally, ...

....

I felt ....

.... !

Parents' Notes

The language arts section of this book provides a fun way to help your child build kindergarten literacy skills. All of the activities support the language arts work that your child will encounter in kindergarten.

Contents

The language arts activities in this book are intended for a child to complete with adult support. These topics will help children understand the world of words around them:

- writing the letters of the alphabet;
- uppercase and lowercase letters;
- short vowel sounds;
- consonant blends;
- sight words;
- rhyming words;
- sound-alike words;
- ordering events using temporal words;
- forming plurals with -s and -es;
- nouns, verbs, and adjectives;
- question words;
- story characters;
- story settings;
- text features;
- reading for personal enjoyment.

How to Help Your Child

On each page, read the facts and instructions aloud. Provide support while your child completes the activity. Encourage questions and reinforce observations to build confidence and increase participation at school.

Throughout, children will learn how to decode short CVC (consonant-vowel-consonant) words. This will help them recognize these words as they read and later on help them with longer words, too.

As you work through the pages, help your child connect the content to specific personal experiences. For example, as you read a book together, explore the book cover. Ask your child to retell a story you have read, using temporal words such as "first," "next," "then," and "finally." Encourage your child to practice writing skills by helping him or her write short letters to family and friends or label pictures he or she has drawn.

Be sure to praise your child as he or she completes a page, gives a correct answer, or makes progress. This will help build the child's confidence and enjoyment in learning. Above all, have fun!

Spelling

Author Linda Ruggieri

Contents

This chart lists all the topics in the Spelling section.

We spell words with letters. A set of these letters is called the alphabet. Each letter has a different shape and sound.

Read the letters of the alphabet aloud or sing them.

A a

apple

B b

ball

C c
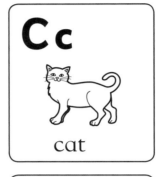
cat

D d

door

E e
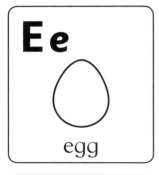
egg

F f
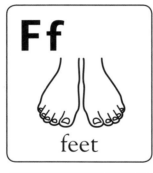
feet

G g
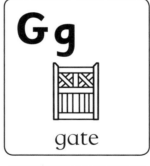
gate

H h

hen

I i

ice

J j

jar

K k

kite

L l

lamp

M m

mop

N n

nest

O o

octopus

P p

pencil

The alphabet has 26 letters. Each letter has an uppercase and a lowercase form.

Q q
queen

R r
rabbit

S s
sun

T t
turtle

U u
umbrella

V v
violin

W w
watch

X x
x-ray

Y y
yak

Z z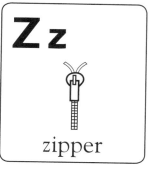
zipper

Write the letter that begins the name of each picture below.

_pple

_en

_est

Activities using the alphabet help children identify, read, and write uppercase and lowercase letters.

Trace the uppercase and lowercase letters of the alphabet wherever they are missing.

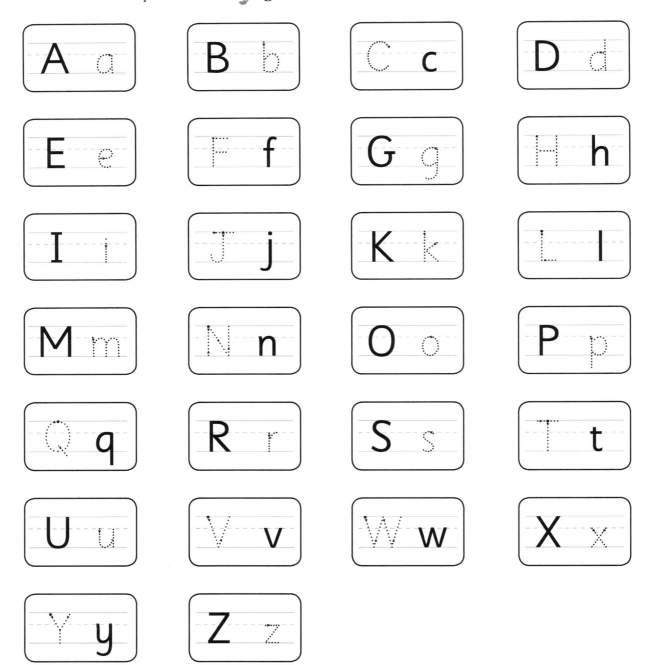

Matching the uppercase and lowercase letters of the alphabet helps children with reading and writing.

Draw a line from each sock on the top clothesline to the sock with the matching lowercase letter on the bottom clothesline.

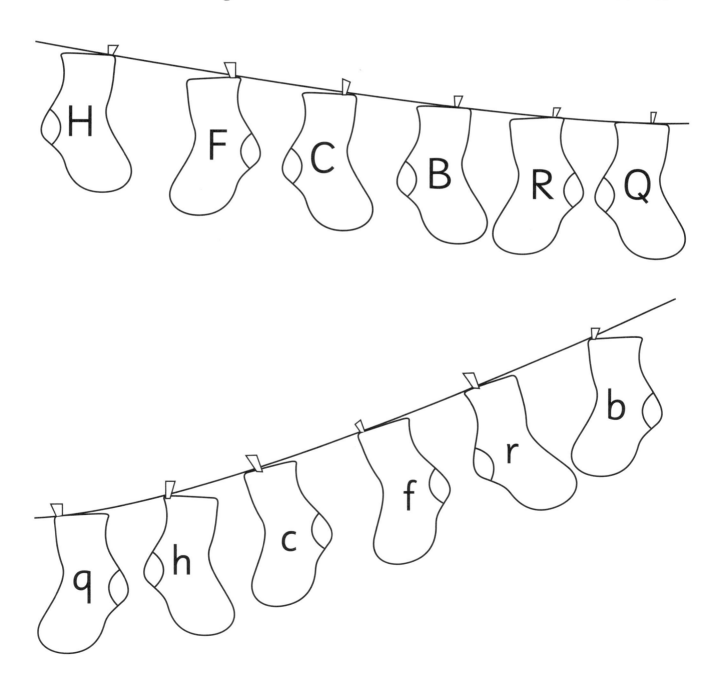

Words are spelled with letters. Some letters are consonants and some are vowels. The letters **a, e, i, o,** and **u** are vowels. The letter **y** is sometimes a vowel and sometimes a consonant. The other letters of the alphabet are consonants.

Read each picture's name aloud. Circle the vowel you hear in the middle of each word.

sun   bed   hen   log

cat   pin   pup   wig

Look at each picture and write the consonant that begins the name of each picture.

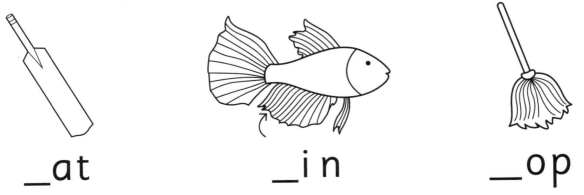

_at   _in   _op

Each letter has a different sound. For example, the letters **b-a-t** spell "bat." The letters **b-u-g** spell "bug."

Look at each picture and say its name aloud. Then write the letters of its name in the boxes in the correct order.

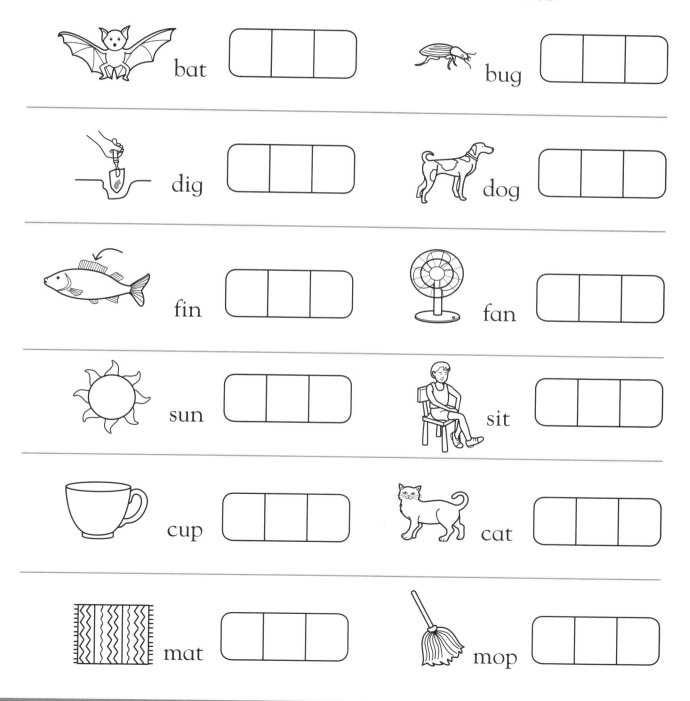

bat

bug

dig

dog

fin

fan

sun

sit

cup

cat

mat

mop

The letter **b** begins the word "book." The letter **c** begins the word "cat." The letter **d** begins the word "duck." The letter **f** begins the word "fun."

Trace the uppercase and lowercase letters in each row. Circle the picture in each row whose name begins with the same letter.

Bb Bb Bb   leaf   bell

Cc Cc Cc   cup   pot

Dd Dd Dd   hen   dog

Ff Ff Ff   fan   net

The letter **g** begins the word "gift." The letter **h** begins the word "hut." The letter **j** begins the word "jump." The letter **k** begins the word "kite."

Trace the uppercase and lowercase letters in each row. Circle the picture in each row whose name begins with the same letter.

Gg Gg Gg   gate   boat

Hh Hh Hh   house   mouse

Jj Jj Jj   duck   jam

Kk Kk Kk   kite   bed

★ Consonants l, m, n, and p

FACTS

The letter **l** begins the word "lamp." The letter **m** begins the word "mop." The letter **n** begins the word "net." The letter **p** begins the word "pan."

Trace the uppercase and lowercase letters at the beginning of each row. Circle the two words in each row that begin with the same letter.

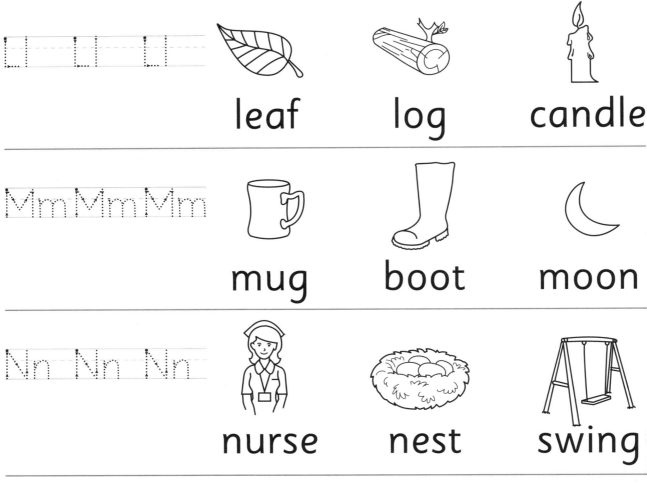

leaf   log   candle

mug   boot   moon

nurse   nest   swing

puppy   bat   pencil

The letter **q** begins the word "quilt." The letter **r** begins the word "rabbit." The letter **s** begins the word "sock." The letter **t** begins the word "top."

Trace the uppercase and lowercase letters at the beginning of each row. Circle the two words in each row that begin with the same letter.

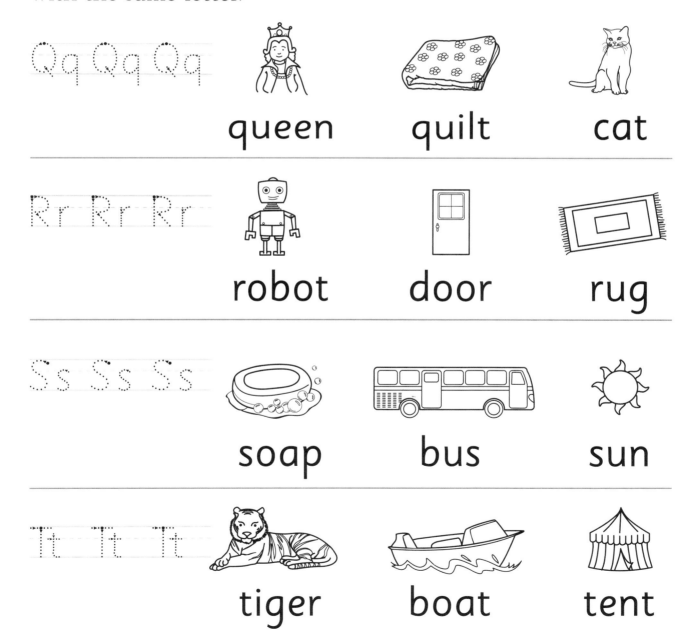

Qq Qq Qq

queen   quilt   cat

Rr Rr Rr

robot   door   rug

Ss Ss Ss

soap   bus   sun

Tt Tt Tt

tiger   boat   tent

The letter **v** begins the word "van." The letter **w** begins the word "window." The letter **x** begins the word "x-ray." The letter **y** begins the word "yard." The letter **z** begins the word "zebra."

Trace the uppercase and lowercase letters at the beginning of each row. Circle the word or words in each row that begin with the same letter.

Vv Vv Vv   van   pin   vase

WwWwWw   worm   fan   window

Xx Xx Xx   x-ray   book   chick

Yy Yy Yy   yak   yogurt   shoe

Zz Zz Zz   zebra   zipper   sun

Words have different sounds based on the order of the letters they contain. If the beginning, middle, or final letters of a word change, a new word with a different sound is made.

Read each pair of words below. Then underline the letters that are different in each pair.

box   fox

pen   pan

coat   boat

rug   run

hen   ten

nail   pail

Each letter in a word has a different sound. Identifying the initial sound of a word helps you to say it.

Read each picture's name on the left. Using a letter from the box, complete the rhyming picture's name on the right.

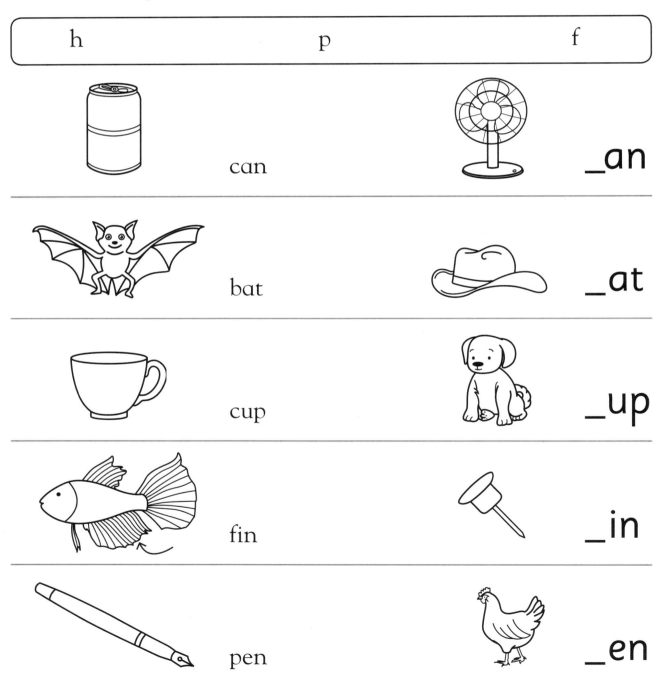

h	p	f

can   _an

bat   _at

cup   _up

fin   _in

pen   _en

Recognizing simple consonant-vowel-consonant words builds knowledge of words, their sounds, and spellings.

Read each picture's name on the left. Using a vowel from the box, complete the picture's name on the right.

o	a	u

leg 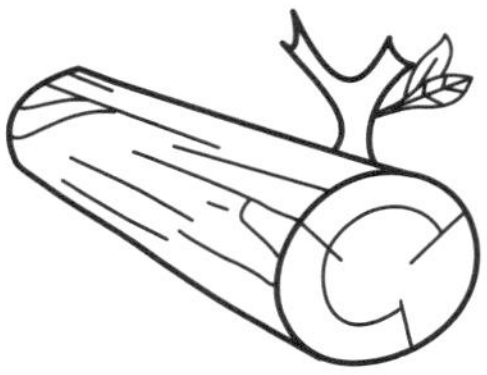   l_g

hut    h_t

pin    p_n

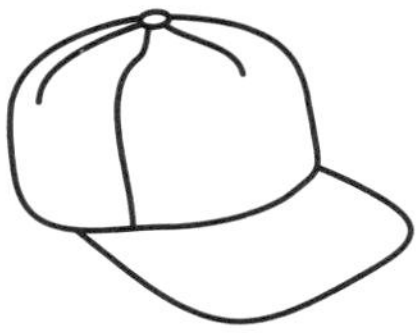

cap    c_p

map    m_p

The ending sounds of words can be short or extended. Some letters produce short, or stop, sounds, such as the **t** in "bat." Other words end with extended, or continuous, letter sounds. For example, the letter **r** can be extended in "far."

Look at the first picture in each row. Read its name aloud. Look at the other two pictures in the row. Find the picture's name that ends in the same sound as the first picture's name. Circle that picture and its name.

man   web   run

bat   cat   dog

star   bell   car

Words can be broken up into letters and the sounds of the letters.

Read the words aloud and write each letter in a separate box.

bug

pin

hen

net

web

fan

bus

pup

The long sound of the vowel **a** says its name. You hear the long "a" sound in the word "snake."

Read each picture's name aloud. Circle the names of the six pictures that have the long "a" sound. Make an **X** on the names of the two pictures that have the short "a" sound, as heard in "cat."

gate   whale   face   apple

cake   grapes   bat   train

Read the sentence below. Circle the two words that have the long "a" sound.

Owen and I like to play in the rain.

The long sound of the vowel **e** says its name. You hear the long "e" sound in the word "cheese."

Read each picture's name aloud. Circle the names of the six pictures that have the long "e" sound. Make an **X** on the names of the two pictures that have the short "e" sound, as heard in "pen."

key   bee   read   eagle

egg   feet   bed   leaf

Fill in the letter **e** to complete the long "e" names of the bunny's body parts.

t__th   f__t

The long sound of the vowel **i** says its name. You hear the long "i" sound in the word "lion."

Read each picture's name aloud. Circle the names of the six pictures that have the long "i" sound. Make an **X** on the names of the two pictures that have the short "i" sound, as heard in "tin."

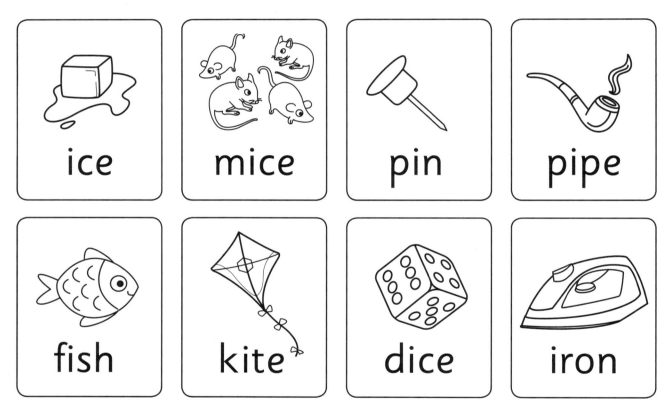

ice   mice   pin   pipe

fish   kite   dice   iron

Read the sentence below. Circle the two words that have the long "i" sound.

The tiger is a big
cat that has stripes.

The long sound of the vowel **o** says its name. You hear the long "o" sound in the word "boat."

Read each picture's name aloud. Circle the names of the six pictures that have the long "o" sound. Make an **X** on the names of the two pictures that have the short "o" sound, as heard in "pot."

oval   open   goat   mop

yogurt   log   toast   soap

Read the sentence below. Circle the two words that have the long "o" sound.

Jenny likes to eat yogurt and toast.

The long sound of the vowel **u** says its name. You hear the long "u" sound in the word "cube."

Read the words on the balloons aloud. Color the five balloons that have words with the long "u" sound. Make an **X** on the two balloons that have words with the short "u" sound, as heard in "fun."

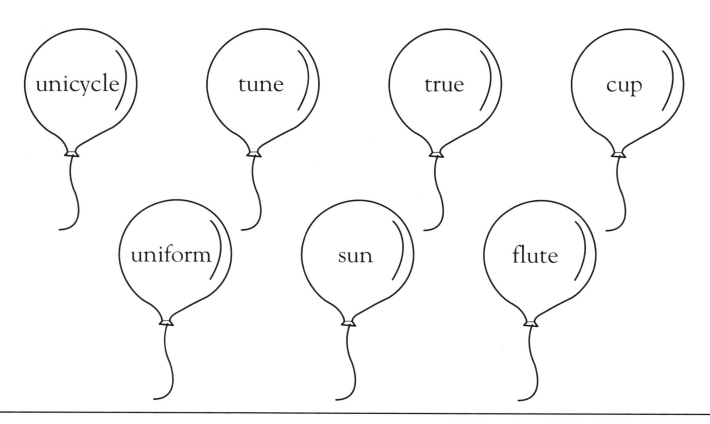

Read the sentence below. Circle the three words that have the long "u" sound.

Brandon is using a tube of glue.

The letter **y** can be tricky. Sometimes, it makes the long "e" vowel sound, as in the word "funny." Sometimes, it makes the long "i" vowel sound, as in the word "sky."

Circle the letter **y** in each word below. Read the word aloud. Listen to the "e" sound **y** makes in each word.

 puppy

 bunny

 lady

 happy

 candy

 baby

Write the letter **y** to complete each word below. Read the word aloud. Listen to the "i" sound **y** makes in each word.

 sk_

 fl_

 cr_

 fr_

 b_e

 sp_

The word "apple" begins with the short sound of the vowel **a**. Some other words with the short "a" sound are "ax," "bag," and "rat."

Circle the names of the four pictures that have the short "a" sound. Make an **X** on the names of the two pictures that have the long "a" sound.

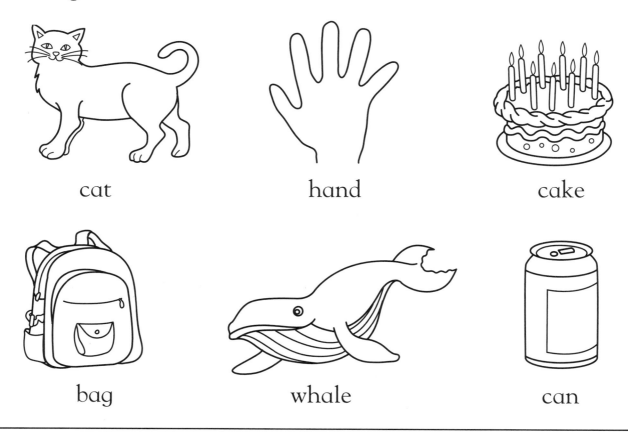

cat   hand   cake

bag   whale   can

For each word below, fill in the letter **a** to complete the word.

h_t   f_n   c_ndy

The word "egg" begins with the short sound of the vowel **e**. You also hear the short "**e**" sound in the words "elbow," "desk," and "hen."

Read each picture's name in the word wheel aloud. Color each section of the wheel in which the picture's name has the short "e" sound.

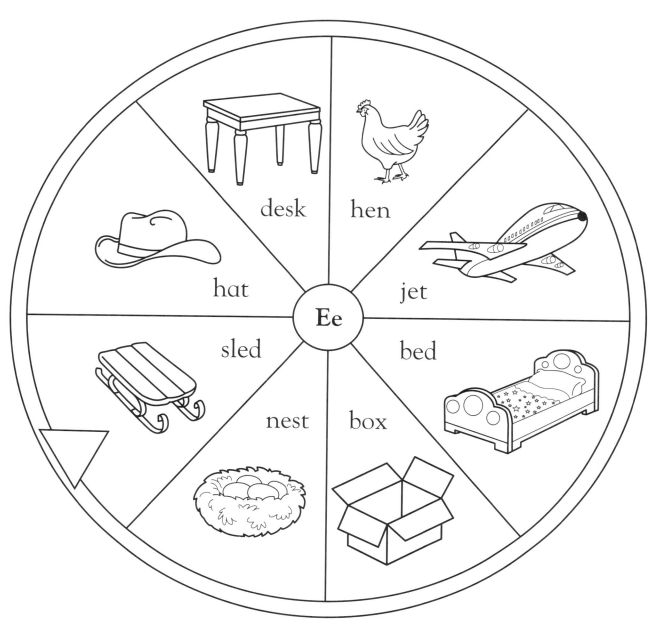

desk

hen

hat

jet

Ee

sled

bed

nest

box

The word "pin" has the short sound of the vowel **i**. You also hear the short "i" sound in the words "pig," "fin," and "fish."

Read each picture's name in the word wheel aloud.
If the word has the short "i" sound, underline the letter **i**.
Make an **X** on the words that have the long "i" sound.

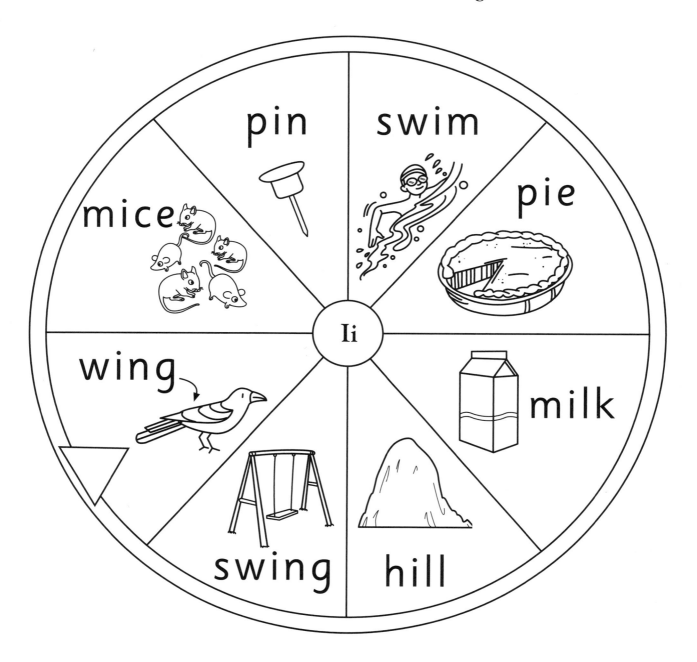

The word "dog" has the short sound of the vowel **o**. You also hear the short "o" sound in the words "top" and "mop."

Read each picture's name aloud. Circle the six names that have the short "o" sound. Make an **X** on the two names that have the long "o" sound.

dog

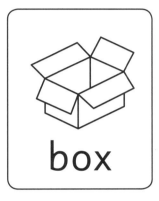
box

soap

mop

log

boat

fox

sock

Read the sentence below. Circle the three words that have the short "o" sound.

The dog jumped over a log to run after the frog.

FACTS

The word "umbrella" has the short sound of the vowel **u**. You also hear the short "u" sound in the words "drum," "pup," and "sun."

Read each picture's name aloud. Circle the six names that have the short "u" sound. Make an **X** on the two names that have the long "u" sound.

drum

cup

unicorn

duck

sun

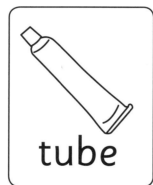
tube

jump

under

Read the sentence below. Circle the three words that have the short "u" sound.

The bug is snug in the rug.

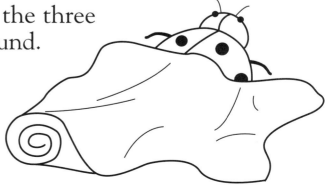

The individual letter sounds in simple words can be changed to make new words.

Read each picture's name on the left. Fill in the letter to complete the picture's name on the right.

 box    _ox

 jet   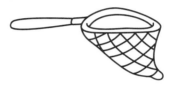 _et

 bug   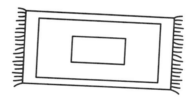 _ug

 hen    _en

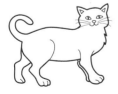 cat    _at

 fan   _an

To identify spoken words, let your child listen to the beginning sounds of the words.

Look at the picture of each animal. Say the letter on the animal aloud. Then draw a line to match each animal to its name.

   monkey

   lion

   fish

   zebra

> Rhyming words have the same ending sound. For example, "cap" and "nap" end with the same letter sound.

FACTS

Read the pictures' names in each box aloud. Circle "yes" if the words rhyme and "no" if the words do not rhyme.

cat — mat   yes   no

pan — can   yes   no

sun — box   yes   no

mop — top   yes   no

hat — bat   yes   no

jet — net   yes   no

pig — wig   yes   no

dig — pin   yes   no

Every word has one or more syllables, or beats. For example, the word "boat" has one syllable, the word "butter" has two syllables, and the word "dinosaur" has three syllables.

Read each animal's name aloud. As you say the word, count the number of its syllables. Circle the correct number.

lion
1 2 3

fish
1 2 3

horse
1 2 3

elephant
1 2 3

pig
1 2 3

raccoon
1 2 3

Every syllable has one vowel sound. For example, the word "tomato" has three vowel sounds and three syllables.

Read each sentence aloud. Circle the number of syllables in each underlined word.

My snack today is a <u>banana</u>.

1   2   3

Do you have any <u>crayons</u>?

1   2   3

Turn off the <u>radio</u>.

1   2   3

Let's bake a <u>cake</u>.

1   2   3

Let's sit at the <u>table</u>.

1   2   3

I see an orange <u>butterfly</u>.

1   2   3

Sight words, or high-frequency words, are words commonly used in speaking and writing. The spelling of some of these words does not follow the usual letter-sound pattern.

Practice reading and using the sight words listed below.

all	four	on	too
am	get	please	under
are	good	ran	was
at	have	say	what
be	he	she	who
but	into	so	will
came	like	that	with
did	no	there	yes
do	now	they	you
eat	of	this	your

Learning to spell and use sight words improves fluency in reading.

Read each sentence below. Circle the correct sight word to complete the sentence.

I know the days of has the week.

Do you your have a red crayon?

Does she her have a brother?

That girl be is my friend.

Kate went to am the zoo.

A cat is in so the tree.

Words are made with letters that are placed in order from left to right.

Find the words from the word box in the rectangles below.
Each rectangle has three words hidden in it.
Circle the words and read them aloud.

bat	cat	milk	rat	horse
drum	doll	kiwi	pear	

Food Words

p e a r g o j k i w i q v m i l k

Toy Words

d o l l r j h i b a t x d r u m x

Animal Words

c a t j z p r a t g u l h o r s e

Print, or written text, is made up of letters and words that are read from left to right.

Read the words in each sentence aloud. Circle the word at the end of each line.

I see a bed.

I see a tree.

I see a horse.

I see a jar.

I see a kite.

Words in a sentence are read from left to right. At the end of a line, you return to the left side of the next line to continue reading.

Draw a line from the word in the box to the same word on the right.

 James has a ball.

ball

The dog is on the chair.

chair

 Sara has a flower.

flower

The bird is in a nest.

nest

 Clarissa has a book.

book

Words are combined to form sentences. The words in a sentence are separated by a single space between each word.

The sentences below tell a story. Count the words in each sentence. Circle the number of words each sentence contains.

I have a bear.

| 1 | 2 | 3 | 4 | 5 | 6 | 7 |

It is a brown bear.

| 1 | 2 | 3 | 4 | 5 | 6 | 7 |

It is not a big bear.

| 1 | 2 | 3 | 4 | 5 | 6 | 7 |

The little bear sits in a chair.

| 1 | 2 | 3 | 4 | 5 | 6 | 7 |

My little bear is a teddy bear.

| 1 | 2 | 3 | 4 | 5 | 6 | 7 |

Each sentence ends with a punctuation mark, such as a period (.).

Look at each sentence below. The spaces between words are missing. Draw a line between the letters where each space should be. Add a period at the end of each sentence.

Icanjump

Ilikeswings

Mycatisasleep

Icanflyakite

A sentence is a group of words that expresses a complete thought. Sentences can be long or short.

Read each sentence aloud. Count the words in each sentence and circle the correct number.

I like ice cream.

1   2   3   4   5   6

I like vanilla ice cream.

1   2   3   4   5   6

I like vanilla ice-cream cones.

1   2   3   4   5   6

I like rainbow sprinkles, too.

1   2   3   4   5   6

Complete the sentence below.

My favorite ice-cream flavor is ....

Count the words above. Write the number.

Sentences that end with rhyming words are called rhyming sentences. Some poems have rhyming sentences.

Read each sentence aloud. Look at each picture and pick the correct word to complete the rhyme.

The dog has a toy mouse.

The dog is in a ....

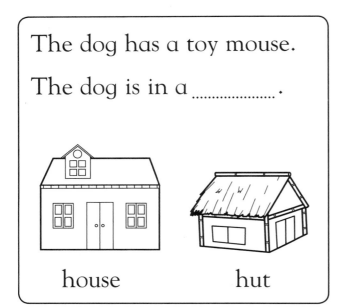

house   hut

The boy has a pet duck.

The duck sat in the ....

wagon   truck

The pig lives in a pen.

The pig is named ....

Bob   Ben

Kate saw a ladybug.

The ladybug was on a ....

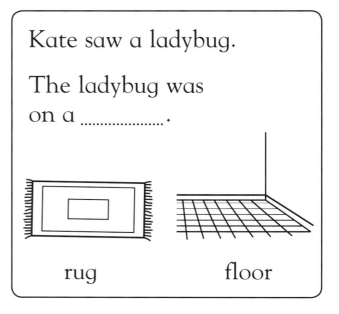

rug   floor

You read words from left to right, top to bottom, and then page by page.

The pictures in the boxes below tell a story. Follow the numbers to read the story and answer the questions.

The puppy barks.

The puppy is given food.

The puppy eats her food.

Finally, the puppy sleeps.

In which picture does the puppy bark?

In which picture does the puppy eat?

In which picture does the puppy sleep?

In which picture is the puppy given food?

FACTS

Knowing the sounds that letters make helps children recognize words and builds reading skills.

Read the story aloud. Circle the correct word to answer each question.

A Puppy Named Pooky

Joey has a little puppy.
She is a funny puppy.
The puppy is named Pooky.
One day, Pooky went to hide.
Where are you, Pooky?
Pooky was under the table.

What is the story about?

a cat   a puppy

Is the puppy big or little?

big   little

What is the name of the puppy?

Joey   Pooky

Where was Pooky hiding?

under the table   under the bed

Children should be able to read with purpose and understanding. Regular reading reinforces fluency so that children read accurately, quickly, and with expression.

Read all about the life of a frog in the four boxes.
Pick the correct word to complete each sentence below.

The Life of a Frog

1. "Ribbit!" That may be a frog calling. Let's visit the pond. Frogs live on land and in water.

2. Many frogs eat insects. They use their long tongues to catch them.

3. Frogs have long, strong back legs. They are good jumpers and swimmers.

4. Frogs lay eggs. The eggs hatch into tadpoles. The tadpoles grow up to be frogs.

Frogs live on land and in _____.

| water | caves |

Many frogs eat _____.

| insects | fish |

Frogs have long back _____.

| tails | legs |

Frogs are good _____.

| jumpers | crawlers |

Parents' Notes

The work covered by the spelling section of this book is similar to that taught to children in kindergarten. Working through the activities will help your child to develop strong spelling skills, which are vital to his or her understanding of letters, words, and sentences.

Contents

The spelling activities in this book are intended to be completed by a child with adult support. The topics covered are:

- letters of the alphabet;
- uppercase and lowercase letters;
- vowels and consonants;
- long and short vowel sounds;
- consonant sounds;
- understanding the sequence of letters to learn words;
- initial, middle, and final sounds in CVC (consonant-vowel-consonant) words;
- syllables;
- common sight words, such as "the," "of," "to," "you," "she," "my," "is," and "are";
- understanding print and learning to read sentences;
- reading kindergarten-level text with fluency, purpose, and understanding.

How to Help Your Child

As you work through the pages with your child, make sure he or she understands what each activity requires. Read the facts and instructions aloud. Encourage questions and reinforce observations that will build confidence and increase active participation in classes at school.

By working with your child, you will understand how he or she thinks and learns. This workbook is designed to help your child understand the concept of letters and words. When appropriate, use props such as pictures or flash cards to help your child visualize letters and words.

If an activity seems too challenging, encourage your child to try another page. Always remember to make learning fun!

Certificate

Congratulations to

....

for successfully finishing this book.

GOOD JOB!

You're a star.

★ ★ ★ ★ ★

Date

....

Answer Section

Kindergarten

JUMBO

Workbook

⭐ Read and Write 1, 2, and 3

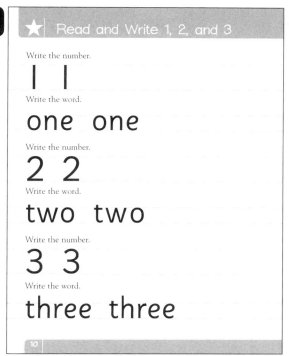

Write the number.

| |

Write the word.

one one

Write the number.

2 2

Write the word.

two two

Write the number.

3 3

Write the word.

three three

Very young children need lots of practice at forming the correct shapes for the numbers. Whether they can form the number shapes well or not, they should recognize the numbers and have an understanding of the amount they represent.

11

Read and Write 4 and 5 ⭐

Write the number.

4 4

Write the word.

four four

Write the number.

5 5

Write the word.

five five

How many?

Recognizing and being able to read the word that corresponds to each number may be difficult for very young children, but should be expected of many five year olds.

⭐ Circles and Ovals

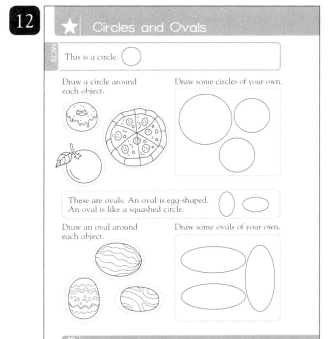

FACTS This is a circle.

Draw a circle around each object.

Draw some circles of your own.

These are ovals. An oval is egg-shaped. An oval is like a squashed circle.

Draw an oval around each object.

Draw some ovals of your own.

Children should be able to draw a circle fairly well. They could use coins to draw around. The oval is often described as being similar to an egg shape or a "squashed circle," which is fine as an introduction at this age.

The Same ⭐

Circle the animal that is the same.

The phrase "the same as" is used to represent an equivalence of some sort. In these questions, children need to recognize an animal in the right column which "is the same as" the animals shown in the left column.

★ Counting 1 to 5

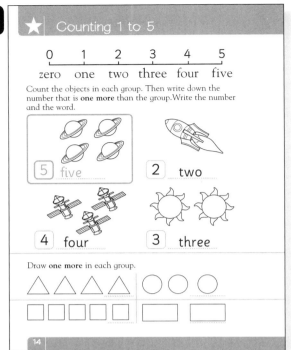

0   1   2   3   4   5
zero one two three four five

Count the objects in each group. Then write down the number that is **one more** than the group. Write the number and the word.

5 five

2 two

4 four

3 three

Draw **one more** in each group.

Number lines are commonly used with young children who should be encouraged to point to the numbers, and move along to find out what is "one more than." Basic shapes are also reinforced throughout the book.

15

Counting Things ★

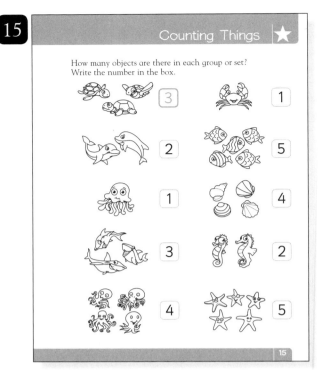

How many objects are there in each group or set? Write the number in the box.

3   1

2   5

1   4

3   2

4   5

Children should be able to count up to five objects with confidence. To begin they might need to use a finger to actually touch each object as they count but they should be encouraged to recognize the number of objects just by looking, at least up to 10 or 12.

16

★ Triangles

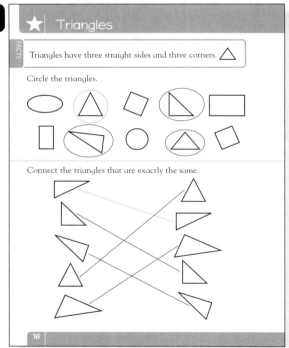

Triangles have three straight sides and three corners.

Circle the triangles.

Connect the triangles that are exactly the same.

The main point of this page is for children to recognize the general name for a three-sided shape and examples of different types. It is not required for them to know the specific names and definitions at this stage.

Not the Same, Different ★

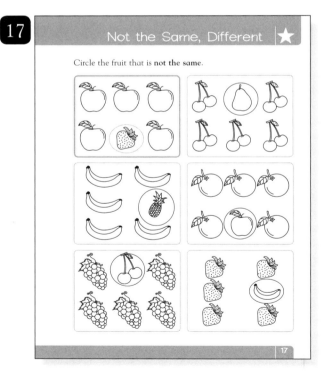

Circle the fruit that is **not the same**.

Children should be able to recognize that one of the fruits in each group is not the same as the rest. The phrases "is not the same" and "different" can be used interchangeably at this age.

★ Color and Pattern

Color the ovals green. Color the triangles blue.

Draw the next shape.

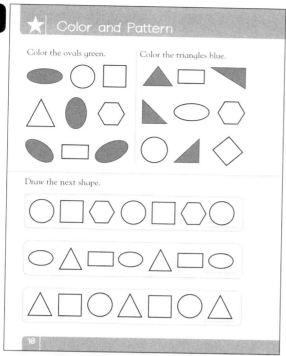

This page helps children in two ways. First, children should recognize the simple patterns and be able to continue them. Secondly, the same shapes are used throughout and parents/helpers can reinforce previous learning by asking them to name the shapes in the patterns.

19

Matching ★

Connect the matching numbers, pictures, and words.

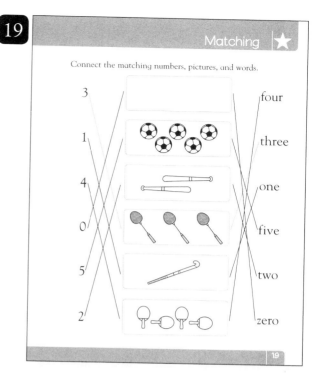

The work on this page will help children to match a number with its corresponding word as well as the number of objects.

★ Which Has More?

In each row, cross out (X) the group that has more.

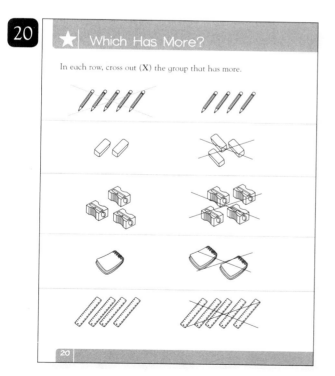

On this page, your child will need to count carefully. Ask your child to tell you which group has more objects. If the child is ready, you can also ask "How many more?"

21

More Than ★

Draw the flowers and write the numbers to complete each sentence.

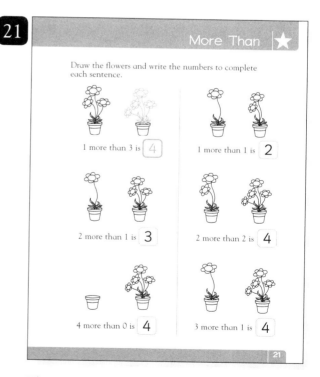

1 more than 3 is [4]   1 more than 1 is [2]

2 more than 1 is [3]   2 more than 2 is [4]

4 more than 0 is [4]   3 more than 1 is [4]

The words "1 more than" can be considered the beginnings of addition with the symbols "+" and "=" being introduced fairly soon. Draw a simple number line from 0 to 5 if it helps your child.

★ Keeping Skills Sharp

Cross out (X) all the triangles below.

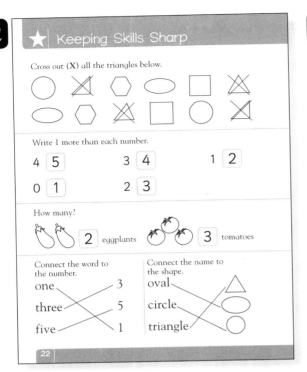

Write 1 more than each number.

4 **5**   3 **4**   1 **2**

0 **1**   2 **3**

How many?

2 eggplants   **3** tomatoes

Connect the word to the number.

one ⟍ 3
three ⟋ 5
five ⟍ 1

Connect the name to the shape.

oval
circle
triangle

These pages review the work covered so far and should act as a reminder and a test of what has been learned. As ever, no pressure should be applied to children nor should a time limit be set.

Keeping Skills Sharp ★

Circle the vegetables that are **not the same** as the carrot.

Draw a smiley face ☺ next to the group that has more.

What is 1 more than each number?

3   **4**

5   **2**

Write the answer.

1 more than 3 is   **4**

2 is one more than   **1**

Children should be encouraged to read the words, although they may need help in doing so.

★ Read and Write 6

Write the number.

6 6

Write the word.

six six

Draw 6 circles. ◯

Draw six ovals. ⬭

Draw 6 squares. ▢

Draw six triangles. △

It is very likely young children will recognize the shapes of the numbers 6 and 7 but will still need practice in their formation.

Read and Write 7 ★

Write the number.

7 7

Write the word.

seven seven

Cross out (X) the groups with 7 animals.

As with all the other numbers, the sooner children recognize the number and associate it with the corresponding word the better.

26

★ Squares

This is a square. A square has four sides of the same length and four corners.

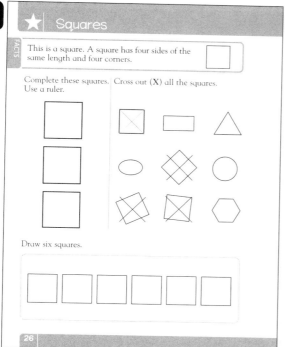

Complete these squares. Use a ruler.

Cross out (X) all the squares.

Draw six squares.

The square is one in a series of special shapes children need to learn. The definition of a square can include the term "four right angles" also. Although a knowledge of right angles would not normally have been taught by this age, it would be helpful if the parent/helper explains the term.

Mirror Image ★

Draw the other half of each object.

Children are likely to be familiar with words such as "reflection" and should find this page straightforward and enjoyable. Have a small mirror at hand so children can check their drawing by placing it along the dotted line of symmetry.

★ Read, Write, and Draw 8

Write the number.

8 8

Write the word.

eight eight

Count the objects and write the answers in numbers and words.

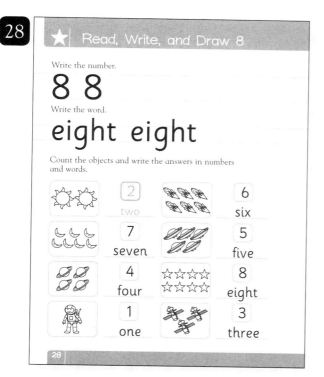

If children need extra practice writing any of the numbers from 0 to 9, allow them time to do this on a lined piece of paper.

29

Read, Write, and Draw 9 ★

Write the number.

9 9

Write the word.

nine nine

Circle the groups with 9 items.

Emphasis is given to recognizing number shapes and the corresponding number words to improve childen's math vocabulary.

★ Read, Write, and Draw 10

Write the number.

10 10

Write the word.

ten ten

Draw 10 circles.

Draw 10 triangles.

How many toes are on two feet?

10

Draw two hands.

The drawing exercises on this page are only intended to help children count to ten and keep a mental note as they draw. It is not meant for them to spend ages carefully drawing each shape.

Adding ★

This is a special sign +. It means **add**. We can also say **plus**.

What is the answer?

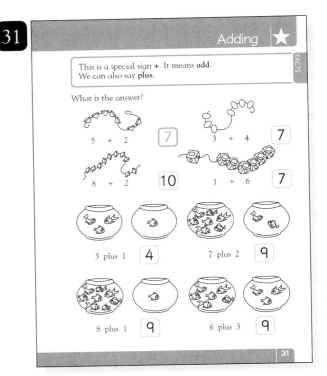

5 + 2   7

3 + 4   7

8 + 2   10

1 + 6   7

3 plus 1   4

7 plus 2   9

8 plus 1   9

6 plus 3   9

This page introduces the plus "+" sign. Children will need to be able to read it, write it, and understand its implications. It is important they learn that the operation of adding can be shown through different phrases such as "add," "plus," "increase" or "increase by," or "more than."

★ Taking Away

This is a special sign –. It means **minus**, **subtract**, and **take away**.

Draw the apples and write the numbers that make each sentence true.

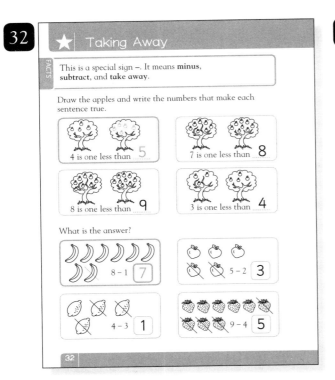

4 is one less than 5

7 is one less than 8

8 is one less than 9

3 is one less than 4

What is the answer?

8 – 1   7

5 – 2   3

4 – 3   1

9 – 4   5

This page introduces the minus "–" sign. Children should know various ways of saying the operation of subtraction such as "reduce" or "reduce by," "take away," "less than" etc.

Counting Up and Down ★

Count up.

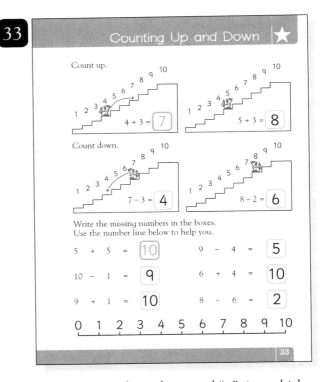

4 + 3 = 7

5 + 3 = 8

Count down.

7 – 3 = 4

8 – 2 = 6

Write the missing numbers in the boxes.
Use the number line below to help you.

5 + 5 = 10

9 – 4 = 5

10 – 1 = 9

6 + 4 = 10

9 + 1 = 10

8 – 6 = 2

0 1 2 3 4 5 6 7 8 9 10

This page introduces the special "=" sign, which will become more important as children move through school. Encourage them to look carefully at each question before answering it, as they may add instead of subtract or vice versa.

34

★ 4-sided Shapes

Here are some 4-sided shapes.

Square   Rectangle   Kite

Cross out (X) the squares.

Cross out (X) the rectangles.

Cross out (X) the kites.

Cross out (X) the rectangle shapes.

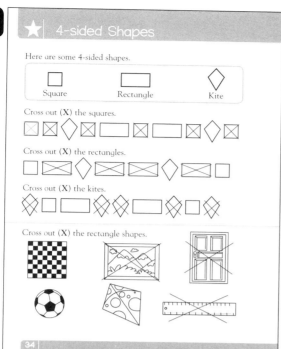

Children should notice similarities between these shapes like having four straight sides. More importantly, children should notice the differences, like having equal sides or right angles.

Dot-to-dot ★

Connect the dots to make a number or shape.

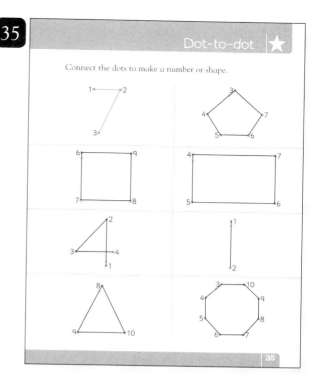

This page reviews number order.

★ Keeping Skills Sharp

Connect the word to the number.

seven   6
nine   10
eight   9
six   7
ten   8

Draw the other half.

Write the answers.

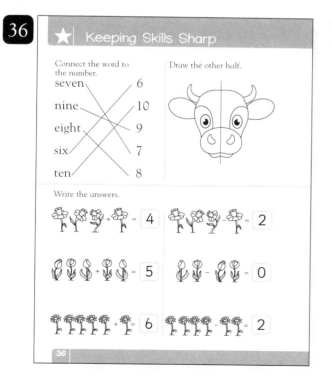

🌸🌸🌸 + 🌸 = 4   🌸🌸🌸 - 🌸 = 2

🌷🌷🌷 + 🌷🌷 = 5   🌷🌷 - 🌷🌷 = 0

🌼🌼🌼🌼🌼 + = 6   🌼🌼🌼🌼 - 🌼🌼 = 2

This test will check how well previous pages have been learned.

37

Keeping Skills Sharp ★

How many candies? Draw the candies in the jar.

6 + 3 = 9

7 + 1 = 8

Write the answers. Use the number line below to help you.

plus   is   7

plus   is   10

Write the answers. Use the number line below to help you.

Four add four is   8   Nine plus one is   10

Eight plus one is   9   Two add three is   5

0 1 2 3 4 5 6 7 8 9 10

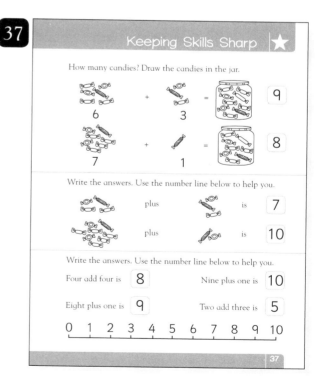

Very young children may need help with the words in the last problem.

Write the number.

l l l l

Write the word.

eleven   eleven

Write the number.

l2 l2

Write the word.

twelve   twelve

Write the number.

l3 l3

Write the word.

thirteen   thirteen

As children develop their mathematical understanding of numbers they will learn about larger numbers.

Write the number.

l4 l4

Write the word.

fourteen fourteen

Write the number.

l5 l5

Write the word.

fifteen   fifteen

How many?

12   11   15   13   14

This page provides extra practice with larger numbers.

Connect all the animals that are the same.

Connect all the shapes that are the same.

Connect all the fruits that are the same.

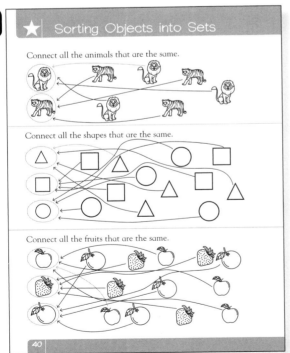

Sorting objects into sets helps to develop logical thinking. Parents/helpers can ask children why they have made a particular selection and encourage them to talk about the attributes of the objects in the sets.

Continue each pattern.

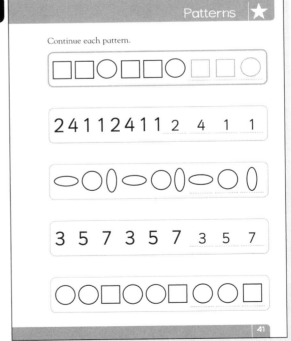

2 4 1 1 2 4 1 1 2   4   1   1

3 5 7 3 5 7 3   5   7

As with sorting objects, children should be recognizing attributes of groups and objects, and using this knowledge to continue the patterns.

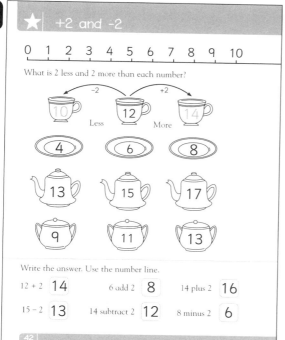

42

0 1 2 3 4 5 6 7 8 9 10

What is 2 less and 2 more than each number?

-2   +2
10   12   14
Less   More

4   6   8

13   15   17

9   11   13

Write the answer. Use the number line.

12 + 2 **14**   6 add 2 **8**   14 plus 2 **16**

15 – 2 **13**   14 subtract 2 **12**   8 minus 2 **6**

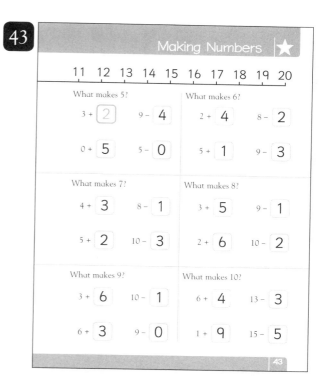

11 12 13 14 15 16 17 18 19 20

What makes 5?
3 + 2   9 – 4
0 + 5   5 – 0

What makes 6?
2 + 4   8 – 2
5 + 1   9 – 3

What makes 7?
4 + 3   8 – 1
5 + 2   10 – 3

What makes 8?
3 + 5   9 – 1
2 + 6   10 – 2

What makes 9?
3 + 6   10 – 1
6 + 3   9 – 0

What makes 10?
6 + 4   13 – 3
1 + 9   15 – 5

These pages contain addition and subtraction
questions. The number line should be useful
but encourage children to work without it
(by covering it) if they seem confident.

44

Write the number.
16 16
Write the word.
sixteen sixteen

Write the number.
17 17
Write the word.
seventeen seventeen

Write the number.
18 18
Write the word.
eighteen eighteen

Children may need help to spell out big words
on this page.

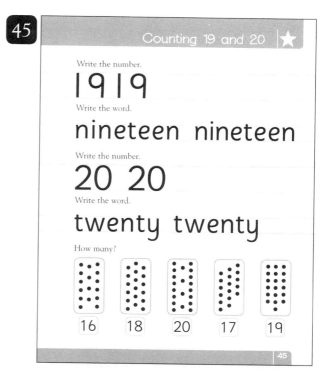

Write the number.
19 19
Write the word.
nineteen nineteen

Write the number.
20 20
Write the word.
twenty twenty

How many?

16   18   20   17   19

Children can mark each dot with a line
or number as it is counted. This is time
consuming, but can be helpful when
counting higher than 10.

★ Practice the Numbers

Connect the matching numbers, picture sets, and words.

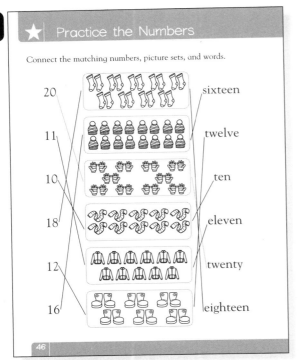

20   sixteen

11   twelve

10   ten

18   eleven

12   twenty

16   eighteen

This page reviews numbers from 10 to 20.
The numbers are shown as figures, in sets,
and as words.

47

Comparing Sizes ★

Draw a taller giraffe.   Draw a larger elephant.

Draw a longer snake.

Draw a thinner cat.

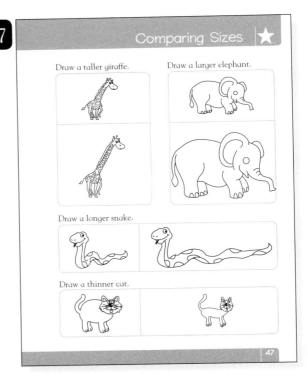

Children need to know words that relate to size
and position, such as "behind" and "larger."

★ Comparing Length

Circle the longest vine.

Circle the skinniest bench.

Circle the longest bush.

Circle the skinniest fence.

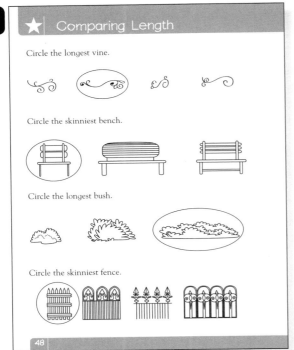

This page practices words to do with length.

49

Position ★

Draw a circle...
next to the cat.   above the dog.

below the owl.   beneath the monkey.

beside the donkey.   on top of the cow.

Ask children to point out the position words
on this page as well. Ask them if they know
the opposite position or can identify them on
this page.

★ More Positions

What is in the middle of the park?
A signpost

What is beneath the tree?
A bench

What is on the tree?
A bird

What is beside the pond?
A bush

What is in the pond?
A duck

Draw a dog next to the tree.

Take opportunities to use position words in real-life situations with children.

Days of the Week ★

Write the days of the week in the right order.

| Sunday | Monday | Thursday | Friday |
| Tuesday | Saturday | Wednesday |

Sunday   Monday   Tuesday   Wednesday

Thursday   Friday   Saturday

What day comes before Tuesday?
Monday

What is two days after Monday?
Wednesday

How many days are there in a week?
Seven

How many days are there in two weeks?
Fourteen

Children should know the days of the week by now and this page gives them the opportunity to read the names and talk with parents/helpers about the right order of days. Encourage your child to learn how to spell the words too.

★ Keeping Skills Sharp

The numbers below go from eleven to twenty, in order. Write the missing numbers.

11   12   13   14   15
16   17   18   19   20

How many are there in each group?

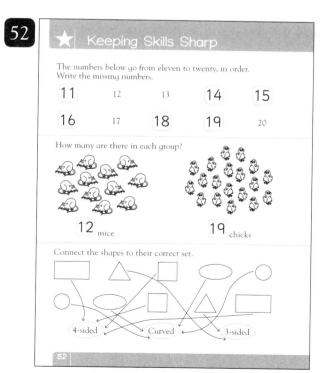

12 mice

19 chicks

Connect the shapes to their correct set.

4-sided   Curved   3-sided

These two revision pages provide a good indication of the success children have had with the math activities completed so far.

Keeping Skills Sharp ★

Write the answers.

$12 - 2 = 10$ $17 - 7 = 10$ $20 - 2 = 18$

$14 - 4 = 10$ $11 - 2 = 9$ $18 - 8 = 10$

Write 2 more than each number.

18 20   12 14   15 17   11 13

Write 2 less than each number.

19 17   14 12   20 18   17 15

Draw a snake that is shorter than the one shown.

Fill in the missing days.

Monday   Tuesday   Wednesday   Thursday

Friday   Saturday   Sunday

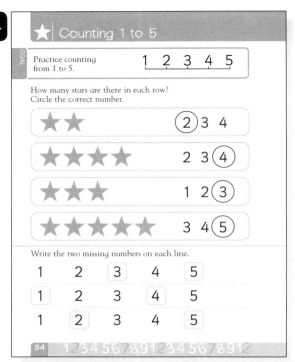

54

★ Counting 1 to 5

GOAL
Practice counting from 1 to 5.

1 2 3 4 5

How many stars are there in each row?
Circle the correct number.

★ ★   (2) 3 4

★ ★ ★ ★   2 3 (4)

★ ★ ★   1 2 (3)

★ ★ ★ ★ ★   3 4 (5)

Write the two missing numbers on each line.

1 2 3 4 5
1 2 3 4 5
1 2 3 4 5

Let children count as they place a finger on
each star. Then ask them to write the number
under or on each star as they count, which will
help reinforce their counting skills.

55

Counting 6 to 10 ★

GOAL
Practice counting from 6 to 10.

6 7 8 9 10

How many apples are there in each row?
Circle the correct number.

🍎🍎🍎🍎🍎   5 6 (7)

🍎🍎🍎🍎🍎🍎   (6) 7 8

🍎🍎🍎🍎🍎🍎   5 (8) 9

🍎🍎🍎🍎🍎🍎🍎   6 8 (10)

Circle any ten flowers below.   **Answers may vary**

Many children enjoy learning while touching
or moving objects. Extend the activity on
this page by providing cut-out paper apples
that can be counted along with each row
of apples on the page.

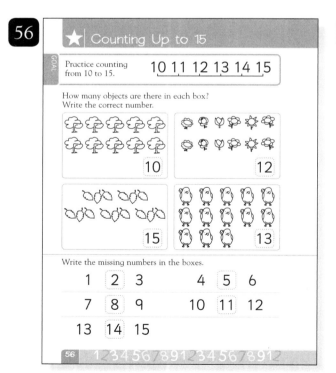

56

★ Counting Up to 15

GOAL
Practice counting from 10 to 15.

10 11 12 13 14 15

How many objects are there in each box?
Write the correct number.

10   12

15   13

Write the missing numbers in the boxes.

1 [2] 3   4 [5] 6
7 [8] 9   10 [11] 12
13 [14] 15

To reinforce counting in groups, arrange twenty
pennies into groups of two, four, six, and eight.
Let children practice counting the pennies in each
group, followed by adding up the numbers to find
the total number of pennies.

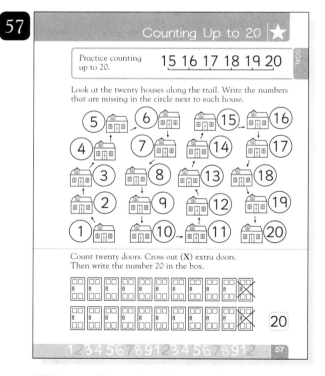

Counting Up to 20 ★

GOAL
Practice counting up to 20.

15 16 17 18 19 20

Look at the twenty houses along the trail. Write the numbers
that are missing in the circle next to each house.

(5) (6) (15) (16)
(4) (7) (14) (17)
(3) (8) (13) (18)
(2) (9) (12) (19)
(1) (10) (11) (20)

Count twenty doors. Cross out (X) extra doors.
Then write the number 20 in the box.

20

Children will have fun following the trail as
they count and write the missing numbers.
Point to the numbers and explain that numbers
increase by one on each step of the trail.

★ | **What Makes 10?**

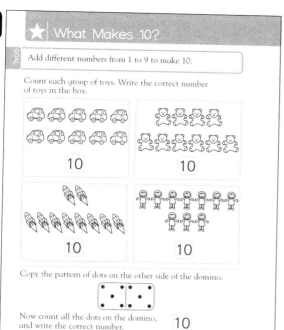

GOAL
Add different numbers from 1 to 9 to make 10.

Count each group of toys. Write the correct number of toys in the box.

10   10

10   10

Copy the pattern of dots on the other side of the domino.

Now count all the dots on the domino, and write the correct number.   10

Encourage children to look for patterns to help them determine quantities and gain confidence in their math skills. For example, three and three should become instantly recognizable as six. Let them move objects to match the patterns on the page.

59

Practice Making 10 | ★

GOAL
Review how to make 10.

Write the numbers from 1 to 10 in the circles next to each car on the path below.

1   10
2   9
3   8
4   7
5 → 6

Learning what makes ten is key to understanding our number system. Try the following exercise: cut out ten circles. Label each circle with a number and a corresponding series of dots. Have children practice selecting groups of circles that make ten.

60

★ | **What Makes 20?**

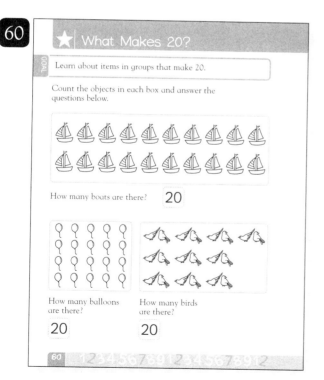

GOAL
Learn about items in groups that make 20.

Count the objects in each box and answer the questions below.

How many boats are there?   20

How many balloons are there?   How many birds are there?

20   20

Draw a row of twenty squares. Number each square from 1 to 20, and let children see and count the numbers. Then cut out twenty cardboard circles, and let children arrange them in groups to see how many ways they can make twenty—four groups of five, a group of four and two groups of eight, and so on.

61

Practice Making 20 | ★

GOAL
Review ways to make 20, such as 10 + 10.

Solve these equations.

6 + 14 = 20   9 + 11 = 20   8 + 12 = 20

5 + 15 = 20   3 + 17 = 20   16 + 4 = 20

13 + 7 = 20   18 + 2 = 20   19 + 1 = 20

Circle the equation that adds up to 20.

12 + 4 + 6   (5 + 5 + 10)   4 + 4 + 9

Follow the path to the castle and write the missing numbers on each stone.

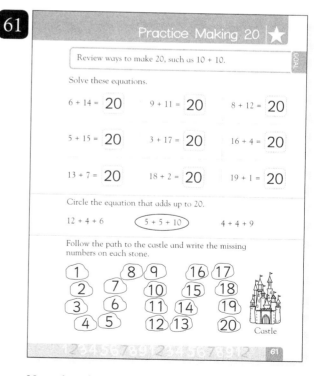

1   8 9   16 17
2   7   10   15 18
3   6   11 14   19
4 5   12 13   20
Castle

Have fun playing a game: create a set of twenty cards, and number them 1 through 20. Create another set of twenty cards, but this time use star stickers to represent the numbers. Let children match each number card with its corresponding star-sticker card.

★ Recognizing Shapes

Learn that objects have shapes, and shapes have names.

Look at the objects. Circle the correct shape of the object in each row.

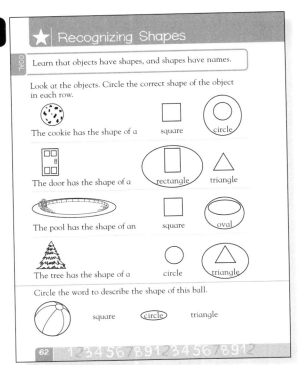

The cookie has the shape of a · square · circle

The door has the shape of a · rectangle · triangle

The pool has the shape of an · square · oval

The tree has the shape of a · circle · triangle

Circle the word to describe the shape of this ball.

square · circle · triangle

Help children identify shapes. After reading a picture book, review the pages and point out circles, squares, and triangles in the illustrations. Take turns as you look at each page to see how many shapes you can find in each scene.

Different Shapes ★

Learn to identify different shapes.

Look at the shapes in each row. Circle the shape that is different.

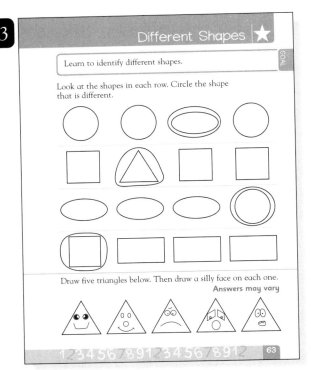

Draw five triangles below. Then draw a silly face on each one.

Answers may vary

Reinforce problem-solving skills in creative ways. After baking a pan of brownies, let children help decide how you will cut them up. Let your child estimate how many servings of brownies you can cut.

★ Describing Shapes

Describe shapes by the number of sides and corners.

Circle the word that correctly completes each sentence.

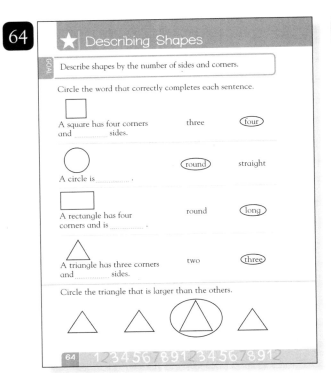

A square has four corners and .... sides. · three · four

A circle is .... · round · straight

A rectangle has four corners and is .... · round · long

A triangle has three corners and .... sides. · two · three

Circle the triangle that is larger than the others.

Make a simple jigsaw puzzle to reinforce shapes: cut up the front of an old cereal box or an old greeting card into circles, squares, triangles, and rectangles. Engage children in describing the shapes as they work to put the puzzle together.

Comparing Shapes ★

Shapes can vary in size. Learn to find the shapes that are larger.

Look at the shapes in each box. Color in the largest shape.

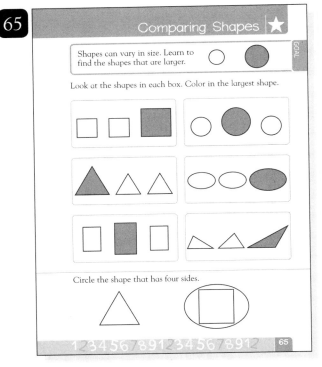

Circle the shape that has four sides.

Cut scrap paper into a variety of shapes and sizes. Guide children in sorting the paper first by shapes, and then into size order. You can provide plastic containers for easy sorting.

★ Creating Shapes

Learn to draw shapes.

Look at each shape and make it into an object.

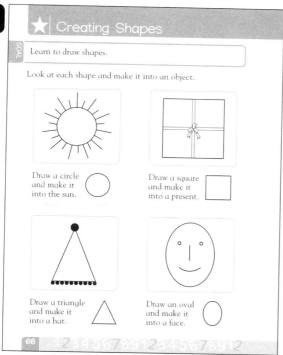

Draw a circle and make it into the sun. ◯

Draw a square and make it into a present. ▢

Draw a triangle and make it into a hat. △

Draw an oval and make it into a face. ◯

Encourage shape skills and tactile learning with colorful clay: provide children with four lumps of colored clay. Ask them to form a circle, a square, a triangle, and an oval using the clay.

More Shapes ★

Practice finding and counting shapes.

Color the circles red. ◯ Color the rectangles yellow. ▢
Color the squares blue. ▢ Color the triangles green. △

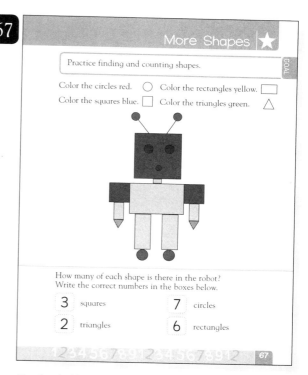

How many of each shape is there in the robot?
Write the correct numbers in the boxes below.

3 squares   7 circles

2 triangles   6 rectangles

Guide children in using the key. Color each shape in the key to illustrate how they should color the shapes on the robot. Review as they begin to color to check their understanding.

★ Shape Patterns

Learn to draw shapes and continue patterns.
Patterns are repeated sets of objects.

Draw the shape to continue the pattern in each row.

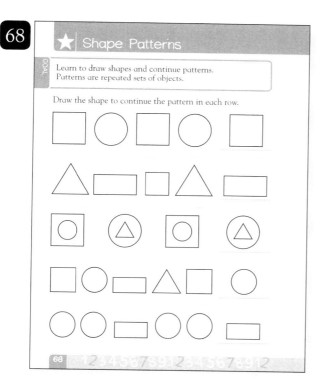

To extend their knowledge of shapes, ask children to draw a picture of their room, a toy, or the playground. Encourage them to use shapes in their drawing. Review their drawings, and ask them to point to and name the shapes.

More Patterns ★

Practice continuing patterns.

Look at the cupcakes below. In each row, follow the pattern and decorate the tops of the undecorated cupcakes with the correct design.

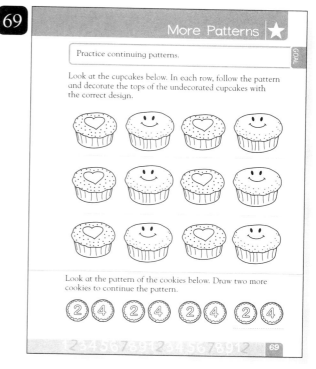

Look at the pattern of the cookies below. Draw two more cookies to continue the pattern.

Have fun and reinforce math skills by using stickers. Start a simple pattern and let them continue it. Then have them create a pattern of either the shapes or colors of the stickers.

70

★ The Same

Learn to identify objects that are the same.

Look at each row of animals. Circle the two animals that are the same.

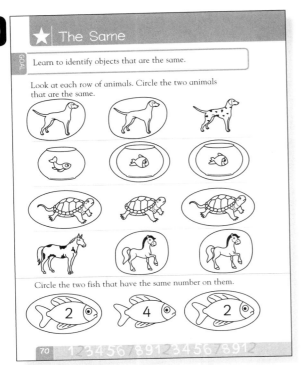

Circle the two fish that have the same number on them.

Which Has the Same? ★

Learn to compare characteristics, such as numbers and letters.

Put the balls into the correct boxes: Draw a line from each ball with a number on it to the number box. Draw a line from each ball with a letter on it to the letter box.

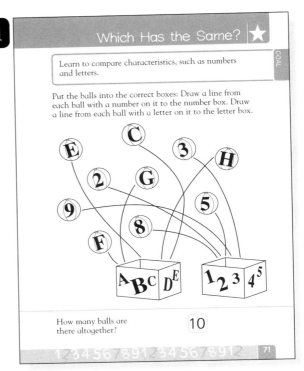

How many balls are there altogether? 10

Reinforce accuracy of numbers. Write the numbers from 1 to 20 on scraps of paper. Include four numbers that are written incorrectly, backward, or missing a part. Ask children to find the numbers that are not correct.

Many children need help determining the difference between letters and numbers, and the difference between numbers and letters that look similar—6 and 9, 1 and 7, E and F, and so on. The activity on this page will reinforce those skills.

72

★ Not the Same

Learn to find things that are not the same, or different.

Circle the leaf in each row that is different.

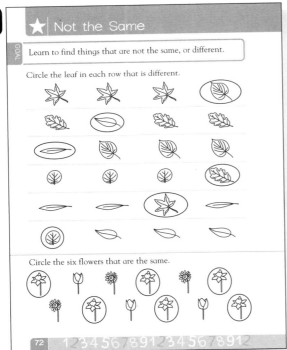

Circle the six flowers that are the same.

Which is Different? ★

Learn to identify (spot) which is different.

Circle the animal in each row that is different.

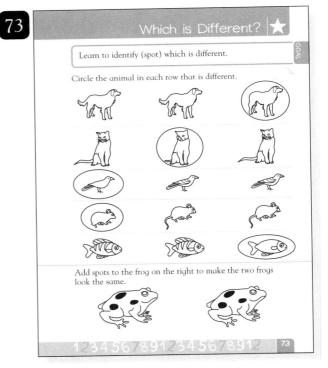

Add spots to the frog on the right to make the two frogs look the same.

Let children help with gardening or caring for houseplants. Reinforce classifying flowers and leaves that are the same and different. This helps build observation skills, which are important in learning math.

Read an illustrated book about animals with your child. Ask questions like, "What is different about those fish?" and "What is the same about these bears?" Describing what is different and what is the same helps children learn to compare things.

★ Which Has More?

GOAL
Count the objects to find out which set has more.

Write the letter **M** on the line under the box that has more objects.

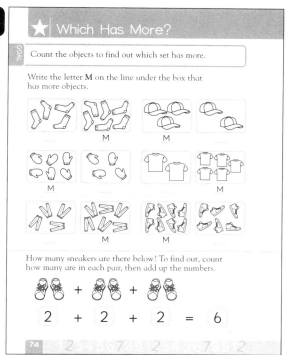

M   M

M   M

M   M

How many sneakers are there below? To find out, count how many are in each pair, then add up the numbers.

2 + 2 + 2 = 6

Encourage children to identify quantity by looking at objects without counting them. This introduces the skill of estimating. Display two jars of coins, one nearly full and one half full, and ask: "Which jar has more coins?"

75

Adding One More ★

GOAL
Learn to add one more.

Add one more to each group in the boxes. Then count the total items in the group and write the correct number.

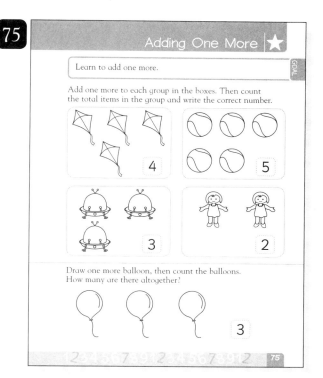

4   5

3   2

Draw one more balloon, then count the balloons. How many are there altogether?

3

Tell a simple story and draw simple pictures to reinforce adding. Here is an example: "Amy had two cookies. Adam gave her one more. How many cookies does Amy have now?"

76

★ Adding More

GOAL
Draw more shapes to add to the group. The + sign means to add.

○ + ○○ = 3

Draw two more of the same shape in each box. Then add all the shapes and write the correct number.

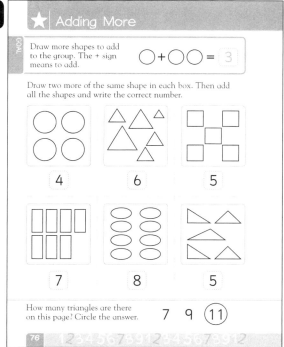

4   6   5

7   8   5

How many triangles are there on this page? Circle the answer.   7 9 (11)

Use the activities on this page to reinforce adding skills. Introduce the addition sign (+) by using it when helping children to write out the addition problems involved in adding more shapes to each box.

How Many in Total? ★

GOAL
Find the total, which is the answer you get when you add things together.   ☁ + ☁ = 6

Draw a + sign between the boxes in each row. Then count all the items in both of the boxes and write the total number.

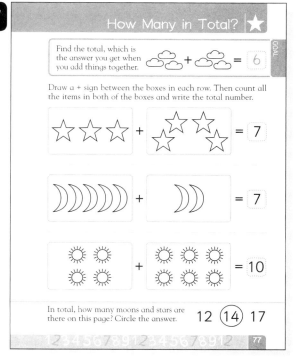

+ = 7

+ = 7

+ = 10

In total, how many moons and stars are there on this page? Circle the answer.   12 (14) 17

Combining sets can be reinforced using objects such as plastic toys or buttons. Arrange objects in small groups according to shape or color. Let children sort groups and gain an understanding of sorting and sets.

★ Which Has Fewer?

Taking Away One ★

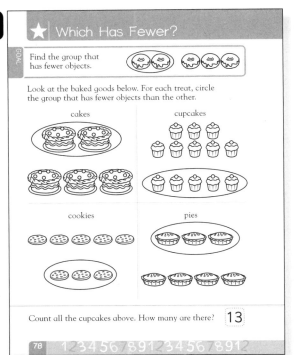

GOAL Find the group that has fewer objects.

Look at the baked goods below. For each treat, circle the group that has fewer objects than the other.

cakes   cupcakes

cookies   pies

Count all the cupcakes above. How many are there? **13**

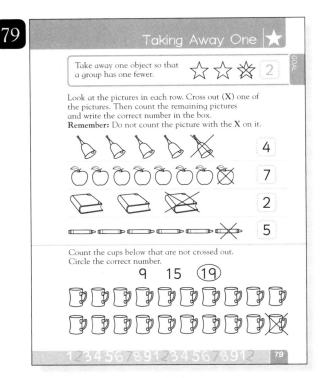

GOAL Take away one object so that a group has one fewer. **2**

Look at the pictures in each row. Cross out (**X**) one of the pictures. Then count the remaining pictures and write the correct number in the box.
Remember: Do not count the picture with the **X** on it.

4

7

2

5

Count the cups below that are not crossed out. Circle the correct number.

9   15   (**19**)

Guide children in looking for the group with fewer items. Model how to count the cakes in each group. Ask: "Which group has fewer cakes? Which group has more?"

Introduce the concept of taking away, or subtracting, with a simple story. For example, "Tim had three toy cars. Tony took one car. How many cars did Tim have left?" Use toy cars to model the story.

★ Taking Away More

Subtracting ★

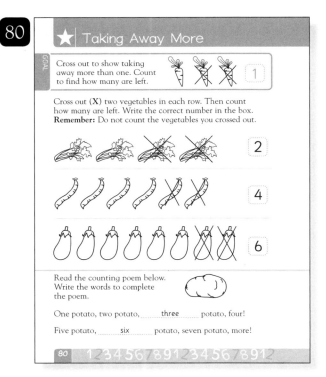

GOAL Cross out to show taking away more than one. Count to find how many are left. **1**

Cross out (**X**) two vegetables in each row. Then count how many are left. Write the correct number in the box.
Remember: Do not count the vegetables you crossed out.

2

4

6

Read the counting poem below. Write the words to complete the poem.

One potato, two potato, ___three___ potato, four!

Five potato, ___six___ potato, seven potato, more!

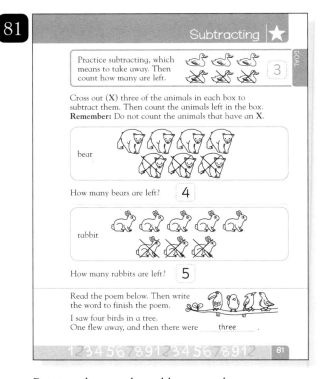

GOAL Practice subtracting, which means to take away. Then count how many are left. **3**

Cross out (**X**) three of the animals in each box to subtract them. Then count the animals left in the box.
Remember: Do not count the animals that have an **X**.

bear

How many bears are left? **4**

rabbit

How many rabbits are left? **5**

Read the poem below. Then write the word to finish the poem.
I saw four birds in a tree.
One flew away, and then there were ___three___ .

Children may need hands-on objects to be able to comprehend taking objects away and counting what's left. Use toys or plastic blocks to act out the activities on the page and to be sure children understand the basic idea of subtraction.

Point to the sample problem to make sure children know what to do. Let them count the animals that remain after making an **X** on three animals. Then ask: "How many animals will be left if you take away three?"

82

★ Sorting Objects into Sets

GOAL Add together groups to make sets of ten.

Draw a line from the group in the first column to the group in the second column that makes a set of ten.

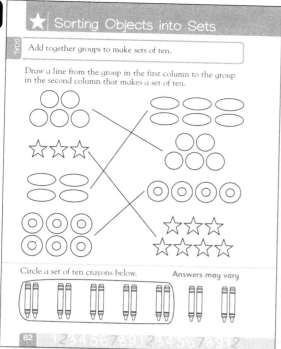

Circle a set of ten crayons below.

Answers may vary

82

Reinforce counting, sets, and shapes.
Cut cardboard into shapes, making sets
of ten of each shape. Place them in a container.
Engage children in taking them out of the
container one at a time and sorting them by
shape. Add a challenge by asking them to create
special sets, sets of five or two.

83

Which Group? ★

Learn to sort items into groups that are the same. **GOAL**

Draw a line to match the number on each child's shirt to the numbers on the flags below.

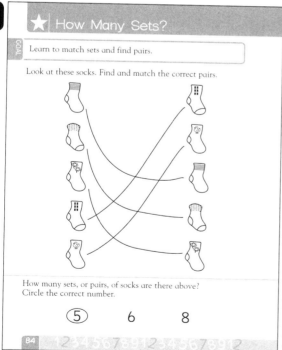

Count all of the children on this page. How many are there? **10**

83

To extend the activity on the page, make a box
under each flag. Together, count the children
matched to each flag and write the correct
number in each box.

84

★ How Many Sets?

GOAL Learn to match sets and find pairs.

Look at these socks. Find and match the correct pairs.

How many sets, or pairs, of socks are there above?
Circle the correct number.

⑤   6   8

84

Identifying sets helps children use the observation
skills they also need in reading, science, and
other areas of the curriculum. Finding and
matching sets also helps children begin to
develop problem-solving skills.

85

Counting Sets ★

Count to find the number of things in each set. **GOAL**

Count the farm animals in each box below. Then write the correct number of animals next to each box.

3

6

4

5

8

Count the chickens and the chicks. How many are there altogether? Circle the correct number.

7   ⑭   16

85

Once children understand counting, challenge
them by asking questions that require them to
add two groups of objects. Use the activity on this
page for prompts. Ask: "How many pigs and goats
are there in all?"; "How many chicks and horses
are there altogether?"

86

★ Comparing Sizes

Compare the sizes of two objects to find the biggest.

Circle the biggest animal in each row below.

Draw a bigger turtle in the box.

Reinforce size and comparison by using pictures and key vocabulary words. Ask children questions to compare size: "Which animal in this row is the smallest?"; "Which animal in this row is bigger than the smallest one, and smaller than the biggest one?"

87

Drawing Bigger or Smaller ★

Learn to draw objects that are bigger or smaller.

Look at each picture, and follow the directions.

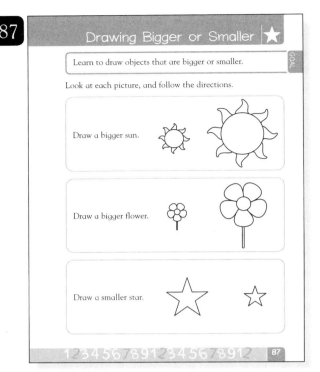

Draw a bigger sun.

Draw a bigger flower.

Draw a smaller star.

Encourage children to draw to help them learn to compare sizes. This requires little direction and lets children experiment as they develop independence in solving problems. They will also learn to use words related to size and shape.

88

★ Comparing Length

Compare the lengths of two objects to find which is shorter and which is longer.

Look at each row carefully. Follow the directions.

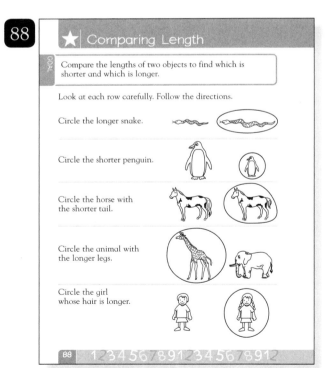

Circle the longer snake.

Circle the shorter penguin.

Circle the horse with the shorter tail.

Circle the animal with the longer legs.

Circle the girl whose hair is longer.

Ask questions about length while children are working with blocks or modeling clay. Make rows of blocks or roll out pieces of clay to different lengths. Ask: "Which is the longest?"; "Which is the shortest?"

89

Drawing Longer or Shorter ★

Learn to draw objects that are longer or shorter.

Look at each picture. Follow the directions for each.

Longer

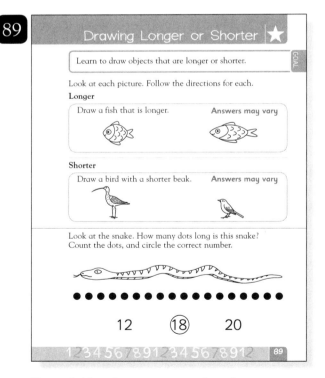

Draw a fish that is longer. Answers may vary

Shorter

Draw a bird with a shorter beak. Answers may vary

Look at the snake. How many dots long is this snake? Count the dots, and circle the correct number.

12   (18)   20

Show children how to estimate length. Display pieces of colorful yarn or strips of paper. Ask children to place them in order of length from the shortest to the longest.

★ Comparing Weight

GOAL: Compare the weights of objects to find the heaviest.

Which weighs more? Circle the heavier object in each box.

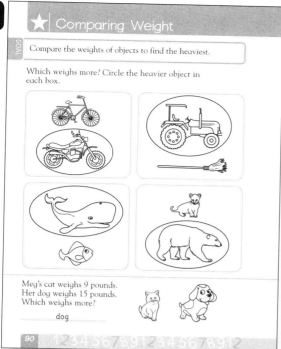

Meg's cat weighs 9 pounds.
Her dog weighs 15 pounds.
Which weighs more?

_____dog_____

Discuss with children different tools used to weigh things, such as the bathroom scale, the kitchen scale, and the scale at the supermarket. Let children use a small kitchen scale to weigh toys, dolls, or amounts of food.

Drawing Heavier or Lighter ★

GOAL: Learn to draw things that are heavier or lighter.

Look at the mouse below. In the empty box, draw an animal that is heavier than a mouse.

Answers may vary

Look at the elephant below. In the empty box, draw an animal that is lighter than an elephant.

Answers may vary

Look at the three animals. Circle the animal that is the heaviest.

Most children have prior knowledge about animals; though they may never have seen certain real animals, they have acquired knowledge from seeing animals in books and other places. Ask questions like, "How do you know that a horse is heavier than a chick?"

★ Position

GOAL: Learn position words, which tell us where an object is placed.

Look at the picture below. Circle the words to answer each question.

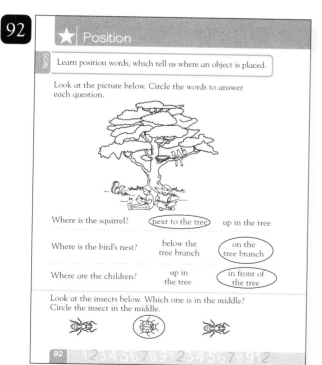

Where is the squirrel? (next to the tree) up in the tree

Where is the bird's nest? below the tree branch (on the tree branch)

Where are the children? up in the tree (in front of the tree)

Look at the insects below. Which one is in the middle? Circle the insect in the middle.

Children may need help reading the questions and answers on this page. Read them aloud if necessary. Then solicit responses. It may be helpful to ask children to point to the picture and then respond with the correct position words.

More Positions ★

GOAL

Review position words:

inside   outside   above
     below   on   under

Look at the picture below. Circle the answer to each question.

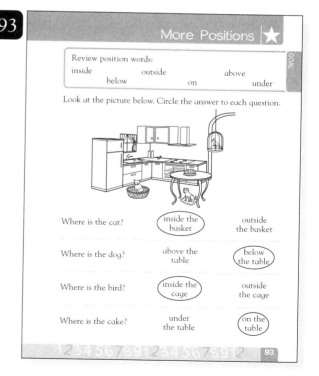

Where is the cat? (inside the basket) outside the basket

Where is the dog? above the table (below the table)

Where is the bird? (inside the cage) outside the cage

Where is the cake? under the table (on the table)

See if children can respond to the questions without reading the possible answers. Ask questions to encourage children to use the position words, and point to the correct answer, reading it aloud. This will help them make connections between pictures and words.

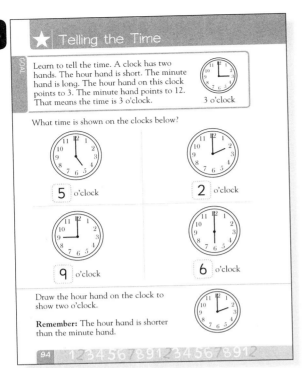

94

★ Telling the Time

Learn to tell the time. A clock has two hands. The hour hand is short. The minute hand is long. The hour hand on this clock points to 3. The minute hand points to 12. That means the time is 3 o'clock.

3 o'clock

What time is shown on the clocks below?

5 o'clock

2 o'clock

9 o'clock

6 o'clock

Draw the hour hand on the clock to show two o'clock.

Remember: The hour hand is shorter than the minute hand.

Incorporate time into daily conversations with children. Point to a clock, and say, "We have to get up at 7 o'clock tomorrow morning." Then ask, "Where will the hour hand be pointing at 7 o'clock?"

95

More Clocks ★

Practice using clocks. When you write the word *o'clock*, that means the minute hand on the clock is pointing to 12. The hour hand points to the hour number.

Draw the hour hand on the clocks below to show the time that is under the clock.
Remember: The hour hand is shorter than the minute hand.

5 o'clock

2 o'clock

9 o'clock

6 o'clock

This clock is missing four numbers. Write the missing numbers in their correct places on the clock.

Tell children that the analog clocks shown on this page, with hands that point to the time, are only one kind of clock. Explain that there are also digital clocks that are used on computers, cell phones, and alarm clocks. Digital clocks have no hands; they display numbers to tell you the time in hours and minutes.

96

★ Money

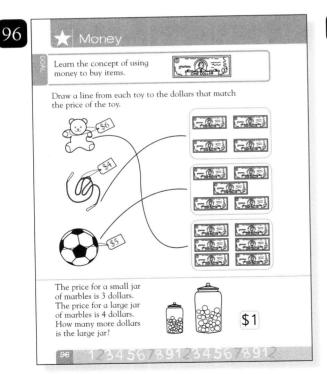

Learn the concept of using money to buy items.

ONE DOLLAR

Draw a line from each toy to the dollars that match the price of the toy.

$6

$4

$5

The price for a small jar of marbles is 3 dollars. The price for a large jar of marbles is 4 dollars. How many more dollars is the large jar?

$1

As children match written dollar amounts with the quantity of dollars shown in the right-hand column, they will become familiar with counting and recognizing amounts of money. Let children act out buying toys with fake paper dollars you create together, or fake paper dollars from a board game.

97

Counting the Money ★

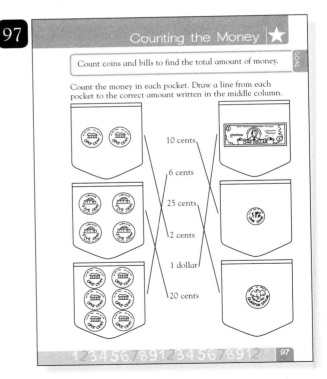

Count coins and bills to find the total amount of money.

Count the money in each pocket. Draw a line from each pocket to the correct amount written in the middle column.

10 cents

6 cents

25 cents

2 cents

1 dollar

20 cents

This activity will help reinforce children's ability to count money and recognize the value of both paper money and coins. Having coins and paper money on hand may be helpful. Let children count real coins to match the quantities listed on the page.

★ Garden

A garden is a small piece of land where flowers, fruits, and vegetables are grown. Some animals live in a garden, too.

Can you find the animals living in the garden? Point to each animal and name it.

A worm, a snail, and a bee are living in the garden.

102

What other creatures besides those pictured might live in a garden? Explore your own yard or park with your child and discover the plants and animals that live there.

Plants ★

A plant has many parts to help it grow.

Find each part of the plant and say its name.

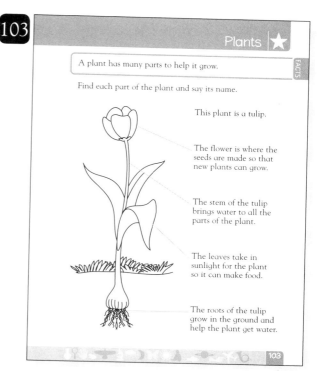

This plant is a tulip.

The flower is where the seeds are made so that new plants can grow.

The stem of the tulip brings water to all the parts of the plant.

The leaves take in sunlight for the plant so it can make food.

The roots of the tulip grow in the ground and help the plant get water.

103

Some parts of a plant have reproductive functions, others take in water, while others convert sunlight into energy or attract insects to help with pollination. Talk about the role each part plays in keeping the plant healthy.

★ Trees

A tree is a large plant. The stem of a tree is made out of wood.

Touch each part of the tree and say its name.

This tree has many of the same parts as the tulip plant you saw on page 103.

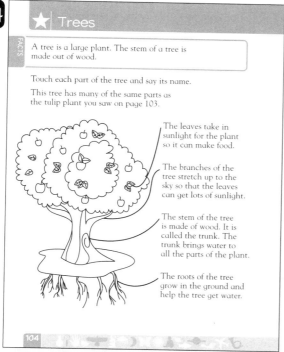

The leaves take in sunlight for the plant so it can make food.

The branches of the tree stretch up to the sky so that the leaves can get lots of sunlight.

The stem of the tree is made of wood. It is called the trunk. The trunk brings water to all the parts of the plant.

The roots of the tree grow in the ground and help the tree get water.

104

Plants may look very different, but they all have the same parts that perform the same functions. Ask your child to compare the parts of the tulip to the parts of the tree. How are they alike? How are they different?

Deciduous Trees ★

Some trees lose their leaves in the fall and grow new leaves in the spring. Trees that lose their leaves are called deciduous trees.

During the summer, deciduous trees have all their leaves. During the fall, the leaves of deciduous trees fall to the ground. During the winter, you only see the branches of a deciduous tree. During the spring, the leaves grow back. Point to each tree and name the season it is in.

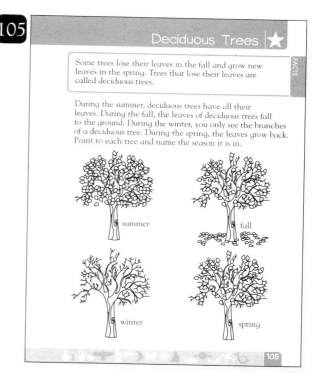

summer

fall

winter

spring

105

Children of this age will be familiar with the seasonal changes. Discuss how the leaves and trees change with each season and how these and other changes repeat themselves. These patterns of change are called cycles and are part of our environment.

★ Plants We Eat

FACTS

Many foods that we eat are plants.

Point to the two plants that we eat, and name them.

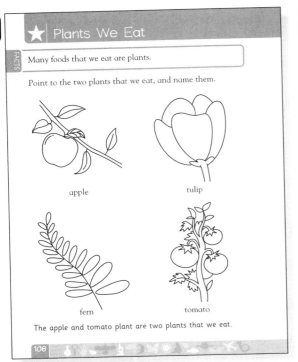

apple

tulip

fern

tomato

The apple and tomato plant are two plants that we eat.

The concept of turning plants into food (i.e., turning tomatoes into tomato sauce) is a difficult one for this age group. A hands-on activity such as cooking can make the concept easier to grasp.

Vegetables ★

FACTS

Vegetables come from different parts of plants.

The roots of a plant grow in the ground and help the plant get water. Carrots and potatoes are root vegetables. The stem of the plant brings water to all the parts of the plant. Asparagus and celery are stems. The leaves take in sunlight for the plant so it can make food. Spinach and lettuce are leaf vegetables.

Point to each vegetable below, and say its name.
Is it a root, stem, or leaf vegetable?

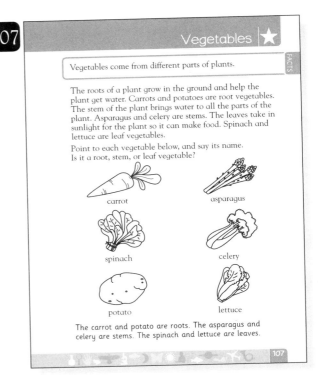

carrot

asparagus

spinach

celery

potato

lettuce

The carrot and potato are roots. The asparagus and celery are stems. The spinach and lettuce are leaves.

Your child will have learned about the different parts of plants and how we use plants for food. This exercise helps to reinforce both of these lessons.

★ Fruits

FACTS

A fruit is the part of a plant that contains seeds.

Circle the fruit in each picture.

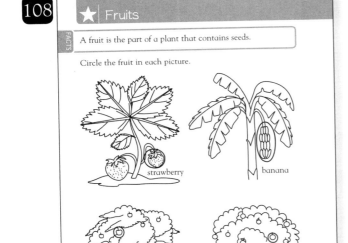

strawberry

banana

apple

orange

All fruits contain seeds, but not all fruits and seeds are easy to identify. Show your child fruits that might not be readily recognized, such as pumpkins and cucumbers, and explain that it is the seeds that make these plants fruit.

Useful Plants ★

FACTS

Many things we use are made from plants and trees.

Connect each plant with the things that are made from it.

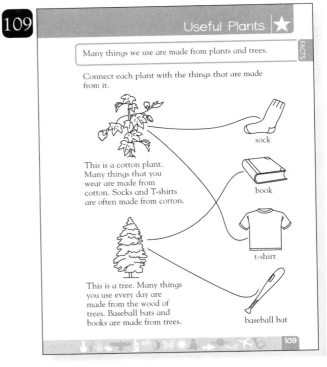

sock

This is a cotton plant. Many things that you wear are made from cotton. Socks and T-shirts are often made from cotton.

book

t-shirt

This is a tree. Many things you use every day are made from the wood of trees. Baseball bats and books are made from trees.

baseball bat

Understanding the concept that many items can be made from trees and plants can be tricky for children. Look for other things around the home that are made from plants and discuss these.

110 ★ Plants and Water

FACTS Plants need water to grow.

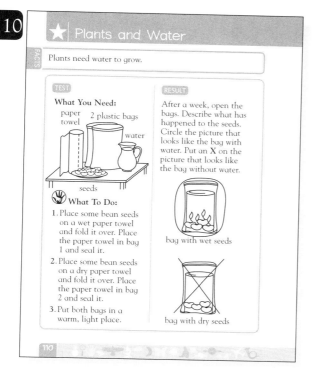

TEST

What You Need:
paper towel, 2 plastic bags, water, seeds

What To Do:
1. Place some bean seeds on a wet paper towel and fold it over. Place the paper towel in bag 1 and seal it.
2. Place some bean seeds on a dry paper towel and fold it over. Place the paper towel in bag 2 and seal it.
3. Put both bags in a warm, light place.

RESULT
After a week, open the bags. Describe what has happened to the seeds. Circle the picture that looks like the bag with water. Put an **X** on the picture that looks like the bag without water.

bag with wet seeds

bag with dry seeds

Experimentation involves observing, questioning, and sharing. The point of these activities for children is to observe what happens when a plant receives light and water and what happens when it doesn't. Ask the child to predict what

111 Plants and Light ★

FACTS Plants need light to grow.

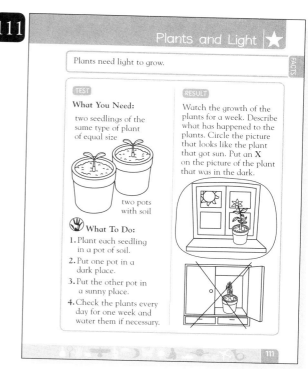

TEST

What You Need:
two seedlings of the same type of plant of equal size

two pots with soil

What To Do:
1. Plant each seedling in a pot of soil.
2. Put one pot in a dark place.
3. Put the other pot in a sunny place.
4. Check the plants every day for one week and water them if necessary.

RESULT
Watch the growth of the plants for a week. Describe what has happened to the plants. Circle the picture that looks like the plant that got sun. Put an **X** on the picture of the plant that was in the dark.

will happen to each plant. Making predictions is an important part of experimentation. Comparing results to predictions and discussing the experiment's outcome are also key activities.

112 ★ Seeds

FACTS Seeds need to travel to different places to grow new plants. They travel to find a place that has light and water.

Seeds travel in many ways. Match the seeds to the way they travel.

strawberry

acorn

dandelion

burr

These seeds have a parachute of fine hairs. They are carried by the wind.

The hooks of this seed stick to the fur of animals passing by.

These seeds are eaten with fruit, pass through the animal, and grow in a new place.

Squirrels bury these seeds to eat in the winter.

Naming and recognizing the different ways that seeds travel is an excellent way to explain how seeds move to different locations. See if your child can name other seeds that travel in the same way as those listed.

113 Mountains ★

FACTS A mountain is land that rises high above the ground around it. Mountains are made of soil and rocks. Trees grow on some mountains. Very high mountains can be covered in snow.

The animals in the picture live in the mountains. Can you name them all? Color the picture. **Colors may vary**

The animals in the picture are a bear, an eagle, a wolf, and a deer.

Where an animal lives is called a habitat. Children, at this age, are learning about Earth's many habitats. Encourage your child to discuss the wildlife that lives in mountain habitats. Take the opportunity, too, to talk about how mountains are formed.

★ Ocean

An ocean is a large body of water. Ocean water is salty. Many animals live in the ocean.

Draw a picture of an animal that lives in the ocean. Then color the picture.
Answers may vary

About 97 percent of the world's water is contained in the oceans, which have diverse habitats. Discuss the different zones of the oceans (sunlit, twilight, and dark) and explain that different animals live in different zones.

Rain Forest ★

A rain forest is a forest where it rains almost every day. Many plants and animals live in the rain forest.

Color the animals and plants in this picture of a rain forest. Can you name all the animals?
Colors may vary

The animals in the picture are a frog, a monkey, a jaguar, a toucan, and a parrot.

Most rain forests are located near the equator. Animals and plants that live in them like the hot, rainy climate. When discussing habitats with your child, you can talk to them about their own home and habitat.

★ Herbivores and Carnivores

Some animals eat only plants. They are called herbivores. Some animals eat only other animals. They are called carnivores.

Circle all of the animals that are herbivores. Point to the animals that are carnivores and say their names out loud.

cow

tiger

crocodile

beaver

horse

deer

Continue to discuss the different animals that are herbivores and those that are carnivores. Encourage your child to come up with answers by prompting them with questions such as: What do sharks eat? What do birds eat? What do spiders eat?

Omnivores ★

Some animals eat both plants and animals. These animals are called omnivores.

Human beings are omnivores. What do you like to eat? Draw your favorite food that comes from a plant in the **Plants** box. Draw your favorite food that comes from an animal in the **Animals** box.
Answers may vary

What I Like to Eat

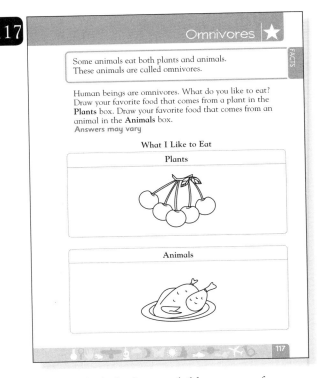

Plants

Animals

Discuss which foods your child eats come from plants and which foods come from animals. Some foods, such as cheese and milk, may be harder for children to identify, so you may need to prompt them.

★ Sight

FACTS

We see with our eyes.

Color the eyes the same as yours. Then write your name beside the picture.

Answers may vary

Draw the missing eyes on these animals.

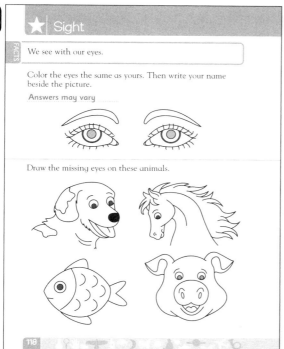

We use our sense of sight to observe our surroundings. Playing a game such as "I Spy" helps children understand how they can see, observe, and describe the world around them.

Hot and Cold ★

FACTS

Hot and cold describe the temperature of something. Something that is hot has a high temperature. Something that is cold has a low temperature. A thermometer is used to measure how hot or cold something is.

Point to the pictures of the things that are hot. Circle the pictures of the things that are cold.

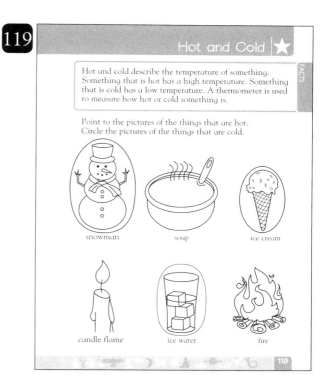

snowman   soup   ice cream

candle flame   ice water   fire

Hot and cold can be difficult concepts to describe to children of this age. Using a thermometer to test the temperature of different items to show how hot or cold something is can make this concept easier for children to grasp.

★ Hearing

FACTS

We hear with our ears.

Circle the things you can hear with your ears.

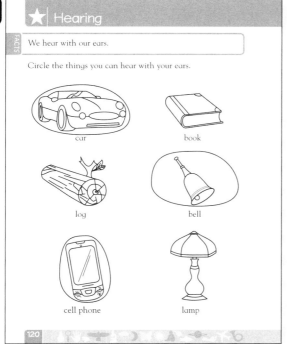

car   book

log   bell

cell phone   lamp

In this activity your child identified the sounds of objects that make noise. Have them name animals that make sounds and imitate the sound each animal makes.

Volume ★

FACTS

A noise can be loud or quiet. If you are close to a noise, it sounds loud. If you are far away from a noise, it sounds quiet.

The dog is barking. Which child hears the dog's bark the loudest? Color that child's shirt red. Which child hears the dog's bark the quietest? Color that child's shirt blue. Then color the whole picture.

Some sounds are loud and some are quiet. Play a game with your child in which you each name things that make a loud noise and things that make a quiet noise.

122

★ Touching

FACTS We use our fingers to feel things. Our fingers tell us if things are hard, soft, rough, smooth, hot, or cold.

TEST What You Need:
Gather up a variety of objects from around your house. The objects shown below will work well for this activity, but you can choose others if you like.

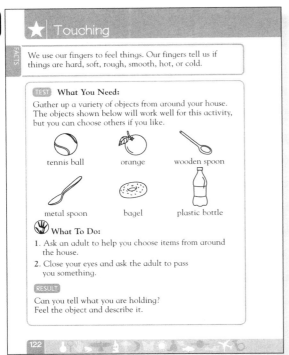

tennis ball · orange · wooden spoon
metal spoon · bagel · plastic bottle

What To Do:
1. Ask an adult to help you choose items from around the house.
2. Close your eyes and ask the adult to pass you something.

RESULT
Can you tell what you are holding? Feel the object and describe it.

Continue to support your child in this activity by having them not only identify items, but also describe how each object feels. Is it heavy? Smooth? Squishy? Encourage them to use their adjectives.

123

Smelling ★

FACTS We use our nose to smell things.

Circle the things you can smell with your nose.

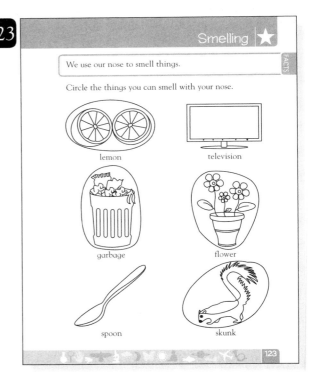

lemon · television · garbage · flower · spoon · skunk

Continue to support your child with this activity by coming up with other things that have a strong smell. What things smell sweet? What things are stinky? Think of different descriptive adjectives.

124

★ Smelling Test

FACTS The nose can detect many different smells.

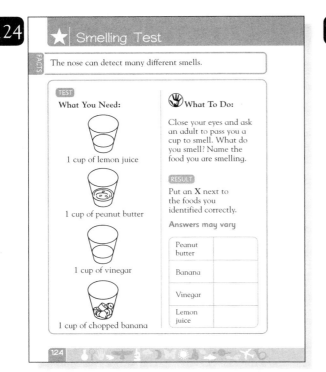

TEST
What You Need:
1 cup of lemon juice
1 cup of peanut butter
1 cup of vinegar
1 cup of chopped banana

What To Do:
Close your eyes and ask an adult to pass you a cup to smell. What do you smell? Name the food you are smelling.

RESULT
Put an **X** next to the foods you identified correctly.

Answers may vary

Peanut butter	
Banana	
Vinegar	
Lemon juice	

This science activity is a great way for children to experience how their sense of smell helps them collect information and make scientific observations.

Tasting ★

FACTS We taste food with our tongues.

Foods can taste sweet, salty, or sour. What do these foods taste like? Connect each food to its taste.

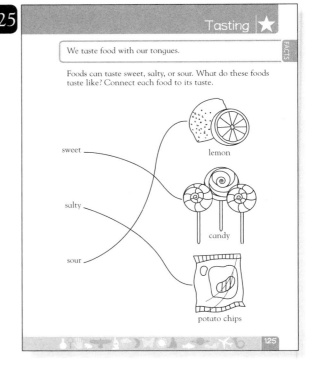

sweet · salty · sour · lemon · candy · potato chips

Encourage your child to name other foods that are sweet, salty, and sour. Which taste do they like the best? Which taste do they like the least?

★ Animals

Animals come in many shapes and sizes.

Animals move in different ways. Some animals walk and run. Some animals swim. Some animals fly. Animals that fly have wings. Circle each animal that has wings.

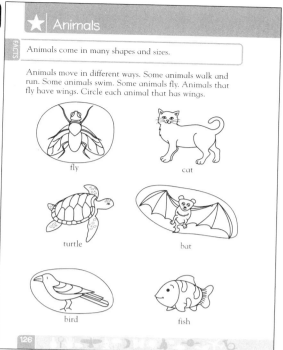

fly

cat

turtle

bat

bird

fish

Continue learning about how animals get around and move. Name animals that swim. Name animals that walk and run. How do humans move around?

127

Tame and Wild Animals ★

Some animals are wild. Other animals can be kept in a house. These animals are tame.

Circle the animals that are wild. Point to the animals that are tame and can be kept in a house.

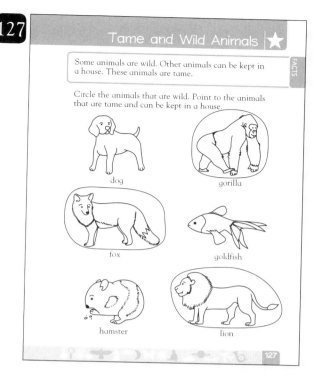

dog

gorilla

fox

goldfish

hamster

lion

Children often know the difference between tame and wild animals at this point. Encourage them to name more wild animals and where these animals live. Also, talk about how wild animals behave differently than tame animals.

128

★ Pets

Tame animals can live in your home and be kept as pets.

Do you have a pet?

If you have a pet, what kind of animal is your pet?

What is your pet's name?

Do you have a friend who has a pet?

If you have a friend who has a pet, what kind of animal is that pet?

What is the name of your friend's pet?

Draw your favorite pet.   **Answers may vary**

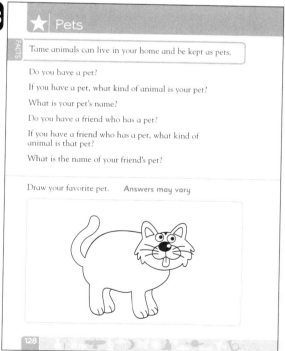

Tame animals live in captivity. Discuss with your child the different homes where tame animals might live: for instance, in a home, in a cage, in a corral.

Pet Care ★

Pets need special care to keep them happy and healthy.

The pictures below show some of the things pets need to be happy and healthy. Point to the pictures of the things pets need and name them all. Can you think of anything else pets need?

| food and water | exercise |
| home | medical care |

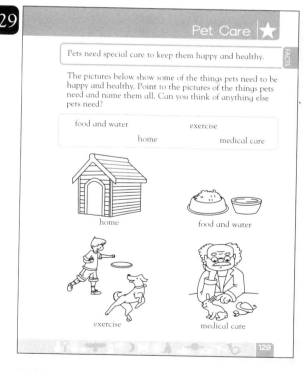

home

food and water

exercise

medical care

Unlike wild animals, which provide their own food and shelter, tame animals rely on humans to take care of them. What other needs do tame animals have? For example, they need to be bathed. Many of their needs are the same as humans'. Feel free to talk about farm animals as well as pets.

★ Motion

Motion is how things move.

The words in the box describe some of the ways things move. Say the words aloud and point to the picture of the motion each word describes.

| spin | slide | fall | fly | bounce | roll |

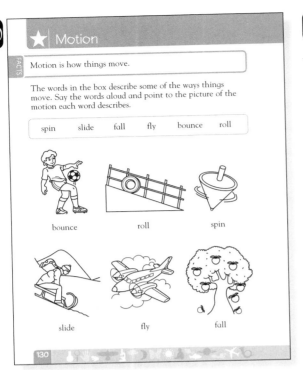

bounce   roll   spin

slide   fly   fall

In addition to the examples given in the exercise, ask your child to name other things that move in the same ways. For example: What else can fly? What other objects roll? Can children spin? Collect items from around the house to demonstrate each action.

131

Pushing and Pulling ★

When you move something away from you, you push it. When you move something closer to you, you pull it.

Look at each picture. Put an **X** in the box to say if the movement shows pushing or pulling.

pull [X] push [ ]   pull [X] push [ ]

pull [ ] push [X]   pull [ ] push [X]

An object won't move unless something pushes or pulls on it (a force). A moving object will keep going in a straight line unless something pushes or pulls on it. Have your child push around a ball to demonstrate this concept in a concrete way.

132

★ Light

Light helps us to see.

Circle the things that generate light.

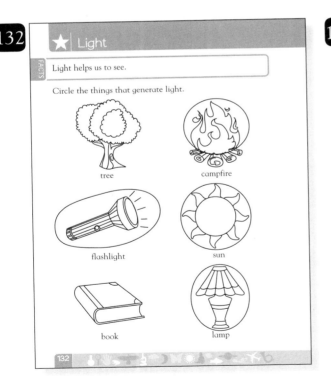

tree   campfire

flashlight   sun

book   lamp

Your child understands that we need light to see. Brainstorm with them and see how many other light sources you can come up with. For example, the moon, the stars, light bulbs, fireflies, matches, fireworks, and lasers. Draw these on a poster.

133

Making Shadow Puppets ★

A shadow is a dark patch that forms where an object blocks out light.

TEST

What You Need:

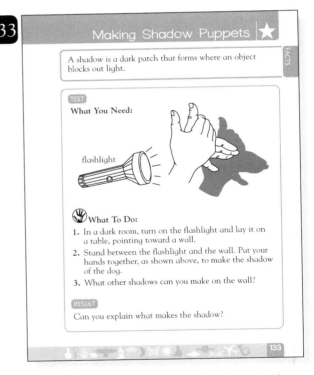

flashlight

What To Do:

1. In a dark room, turn on the flashlight and lay it on a table, pointing toward a wall.
2. Stand between the flashlight and the wall. Put your hands together, as shown above, to make the shadow of the dog.
3. What other shadows can you make on the wall?

RESULT

Can you explain what makes the shadow?

Play outside on a sunny day to show how shadows are made in the sun. Measure your child's shadows at different times of the day—morning, noon, and late afternoon—and discuss how his or her shadow changes. Have your child stand outside on a sunny day and use sidewalk chalk to draw around the shadow they make.

★ A Rainbow

A rainbow is an arch of colors that appears when the sun shines through rain.

Color the rainbow.

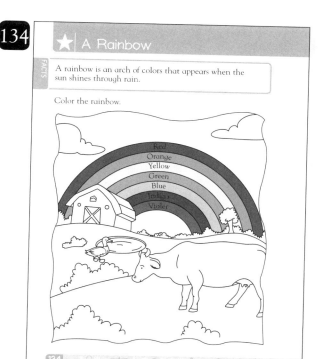

Red
Orange
Yellow
Green
Blue
Indigo
Violet

Try another tactile exercise to illustrate the colors of a rainbow. Use colored candies or colored cereal to create a 3-D rainbow. Glue the candies

Making a Rainbow ★

You can make a rainbow by shining a light through water.

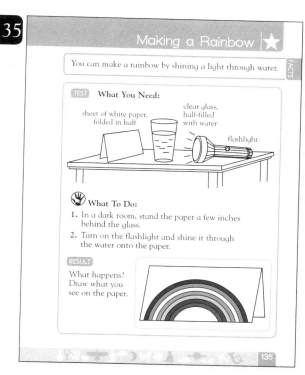

TEST **What You Need:**

sheet of white paper, folded in half

clear glass, half-filled with water

flashlight

✋ **What To Do:**

1. In a dark room, stand the paper a few inches behind the glass.
2. Turn on the flashlight and shine it through the water onto the paper.

RESULT

What happens? Draw what you see on the paper.

or cereal to a sheet of blue construction paper and have your child say the colors aloud. Here's a trick for remembering the rainbow color order: Roy. G. Biv.

★ Solids, Liquids, and Gases

The things around you are solids, liquids, or gases.

Solid things keep their shape. Liquid things take the shape of the container they are in. Gases get bigger to fill the space they are in. Circle all the liquids. Point to the solids.

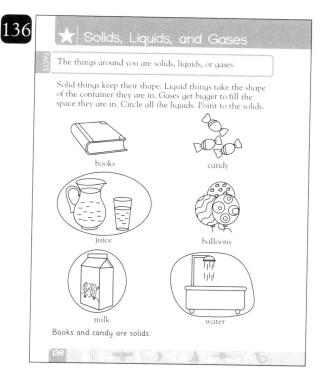

books

candy

juice

balloons

milk

water

Books and candy are solids.

Children of this age find it difficult to understand the abstract properties of matter. They will, however, be able to group materials into states like solids and liquids.

Gas ★

Air is a gas. Air is invisible but you can feel it and see that it is there by blowing bubbles.

TEST

What You Need:

drinking straw

glass of water

RESULT

Draw what you see happening when you blow through the straw in the water. Why does this happen?

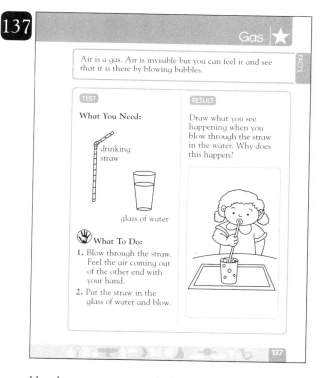

✋ **What To Do:**

1. Blow through the straw. Feel the air coming out of the other end with your hand.
2. Put the straw in the glass of water and blow.

Hands-on experiments help them identify different forms of matter. Concentrate on shapes and teach them to differentiate forms of matter based on shape. Reinforce the concepts they have already learned.

★ Balloons

FACTS

You can fill a balloon with air.

TEST

What You Need:

balloon

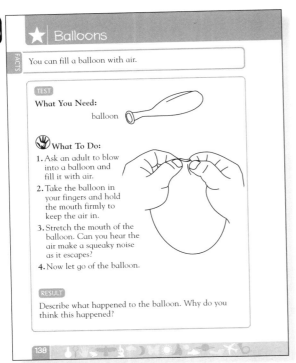

✋ **What To Do:**

1. Ask an adult to blow into a balloon and fill it with air.
2. Take the balloon in your fingers and hold the mouth firmly to keep the air in.
3. Stretch the mouth of the balloon. Can you hear the air make a squeaky noise as it escapes?
4. Now let go of the balloon.

RESULT

Describe what happened to the balloon. Why do you think this happened?

138

This exercise illustrates that gases such as air will fill the space that they are in. Children will also also learn that gases are present but often invisible.

Wind ★

Wind is moving air.

Draw a circle around the things that use the wind. Color the picture. **Colors may vary**

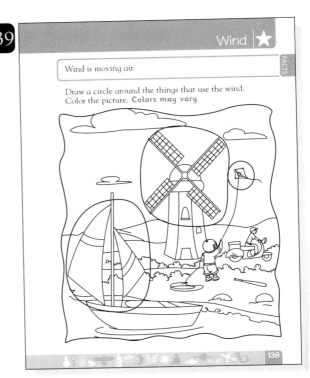

139

Here, the child learns that wind is moving air and that wind has force, as it did when it moved the balloon across the room in the previous exercise. These are not necessarily easy concepts for children of this age, so you may need to discuss.

★ Liquid

Liquid takes the shape of the container it is in.

TEST

What You Need:

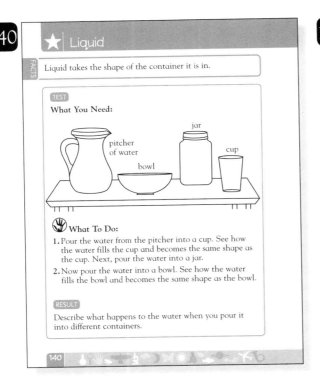

pitcher of water
jar
bowl
cup

✋ **What To Do:**

1. Pour the water from the pitcher into a cup. See how the water fills the cup and becomes the same shape as the cup. Next, pour the water into a jar.
2. Now pour the water into a bowl. See how the water fills the bowl and becomes the same shape as the bowl.

RESULT

Describe what happens to the water when you pour it into different containers.

140

As they experiment with the water, your child will learn in a concrete way that liquids take the shapes of their containers. They will also discover that liquids are visible and can be seen.

Bubbles ★

Bubbles are liquid filled with air.

TEST

What You Need:

2 tablespoons of dish soap

water

pipe cleaner

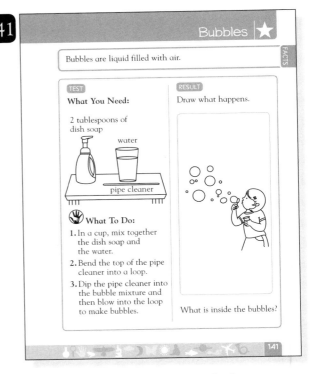

RESULT

Draw what happens.

✋ **What To Do:**

1. In a cup, mix together the dish soap and the water.
2. Bend the top of the pipe cleaner into a loop.
3. Dip the pipe cleaner into the bubble mixture and then blow into the loop to make bubbles.

What is inside the bubbles?

141

Reinforcing scientific concepts with play makes learning fun for children. This activity demonstrates that bubbles are a liquid filled with air, and it's the air that makes them float.

★ Solids

Solids keep their shape.

Draw a line between each object and the shape it matches.

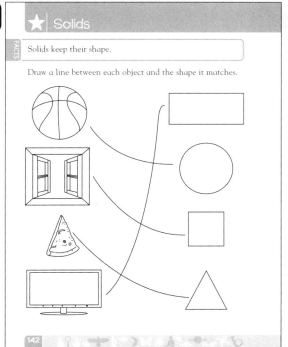

In addition to demonstrating how solids keep their form, this exercise shows how drawing lines to match up the objects to their shapes help kids practice their shapes. Line drawing also helps develop fine motor skills.

Changing Matter ★

Water can be liquid or solid.

TEST

What You Need:

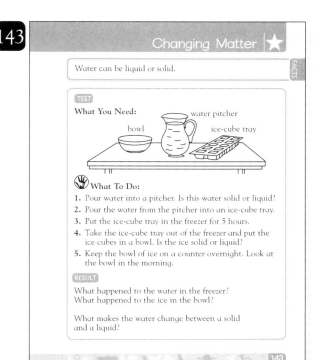

bowl   water pitcher   ice-cube tray

What To Do:

1. Pour water into a pitcher. Is this water solid or liquid?
2. Pour the water from the pitcher into an ice-cube tray.
3. Put the ice-cube tray in the freezer for 5 hours.
4. Take the ice-cube tray out of the freezer and put the ice cubes in a bowl. Is the ice solid or liquid?
5. Keep the bowl of ice on a counter overnight. Look at the bowl in the morning.

RESULT

What happened to the water in the freezer?
What happened to the ice in the bowl?

What makes the water change between a solid and a liquid?

Here, your child sees that water can change from one state to another. For an added element to the experiment, leave the water out long enough for it to evaporate and become a gas. Discuss the results.

★ Freezing

Freezing is when a liquid changes into a solid.
Freezing happens when it is very cold.

Look at the pictures. Circle the thing that will freeze in the cold.

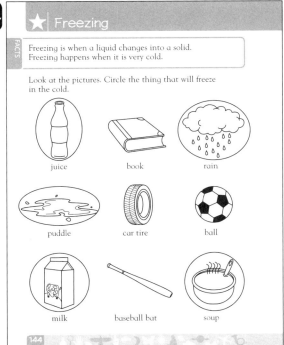

juice   book   rain

puddle   car tire   ball

milk   baseball bat   soup

This activity illustrates how matter can change shape by freezing and melting and how temperature is vital in this change.

Melting ★

Melting is when a solid turns into a liquid.
Melting happens when it is very warm.

Draw a circle around the objects that melt when it is hot.

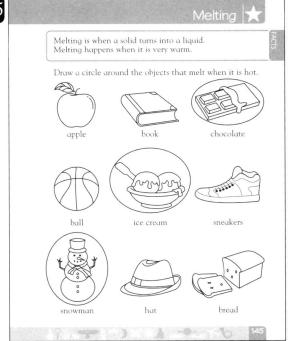

apple   book   chocolate

ball   ice cream   sneakers

snowman   hat   bread

When liquids are cooled enough they freeze. When solids are heated enough they become liquid.

★ Geography

Geography is about the world around you. The people who study geography are called geographers. Geographers study nature. They study things such as the mountains, rivers, and forests. Geographers also study the way humans use and change nature when they make things like cities, parks, and bridges.

Circle the things that a geographer might study.

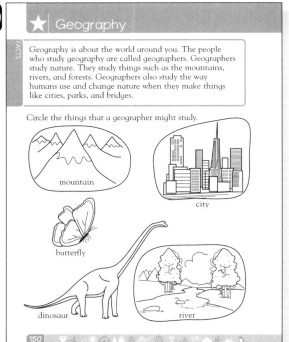

mountain

city

butterfly

dinosaur

river

Ask your child why he or she thinks it might be interesting to learn about the world around them. Encourage your child to share with you questions or thoughts about the subject. This will spark an interest in geography.

Earth ★

You live on a planet called Earth. Earth is one of eight planets in our solar system. All the planets in a solar system share the same sun. Earth travels around the sun once every year. When your part of Earth is tilted toward the sun, it is summer. When your part of Earth is tilted away from the sun, it is winter.

Here is a picture of our solar system. Earth is the third planet from the sun. Circle the planet Earth.

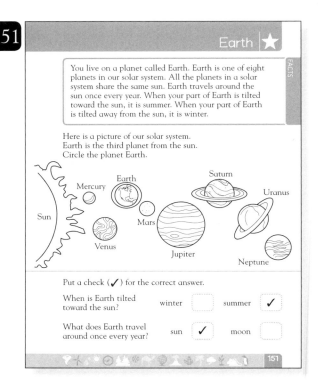

Sun
Mercury
Earth
Saturn
Uranus
Venus
Mars
Jupiter
Neptune

Put a check (✔) for the correct answer.

When is Earth tilted toward the sun?   winter [ ]   summer [✔]

What does Earth travel around once every year?   sun [✔]   moon [ ]

Explain that Earth is the only planet in our solar system people can live on. It is just the right distance from the sun to allow us to live at comfortable temperatures. Let your child point to planets that would be too hot and too cold for us.

★ The Globe

A globe is a map of planet Earth. It is shaped like a ball, just like planet Earth. A globe shows all the land and water on Earth. Most globes are small enough for a person to hold.

Look at the globe below, and then read the list at the side of it. Circle the things in the list that you can find on the globe.

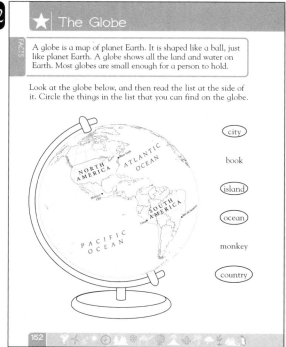

NORTH AMERICA
ATLANTIC OCEAN
SOUTH AMERICA
PACIFIC OCEAN

city
book
island
ocean
monkey
country

If you have a globe at home, encourage your child to spend time exploring it. Ask your child to point out features on the globe that he or she notices. Point out where you live. If you do not have a globe at home, try your local library.

What is a Map? ★

There are many different kinds of maps. A globe is shaped like a ball. Other maps are flat. They may be printed on paper, as charts, or in books. You can also see maps on the screens of computers, tablets, or phones. Flat maps can show the whole Earth or a part of it in a lot of detail.

Look at the different kinds of maps below. Write a **P** in the box under a map if the map is on paper. Write an **S** if the map is on a screen. Write a **G** if the map is a globe.

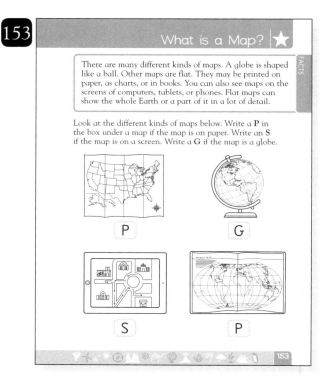

P

G

S

P

Conduct a treasure hunt at home to find maps! Find road maps, transit maps, travel books with maps, or maps on mobile devices. Help your child identify what each type of map shows, and how it is useful.

154

★ Types of Maps

Different maps are used to show and explain different kinds of places. A park map shows you what is in a park. A street map shows you the streets you can travel along. A map of a room shows you the things in that room.

Below are pictures of three different places: a city, a park, and a bedroom. Draw a line to connect each place with its map.

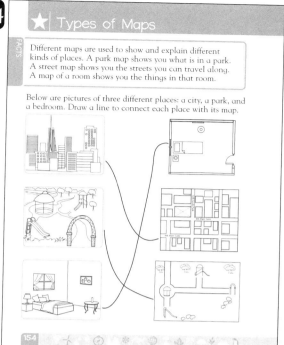

Encourage your child to use crayons or markers to draw a colorful map of his or her bedroom. Brainstorm the important features that should be included on the map. Mention that some maps are actually considered works of art!

155

Types of Maps ★

People use different maps for different reasons. A person driving a car may use a street map. Hikers may need a park map. Students and teachers may need a map of their school. There are many other kinds of maps as well.

Look at the different types of maps below. Who would use each kind of map? Draw a line to connect each map with the people who may need it.

Tell your child how and when you use maps in your daily life. Give examples of common maps you use and their types—paper maps, electronic maps, or both. The next time you use a map, invite your child to read it with you.

156

★ Directions

There are four directions that you need to know about to be able to read a map. Those directions are "north," "south," "east," and "west." No matter where you are, these directions can help you reach the place that you want to go to.

Look at the globe of Earth below.
Then place your finger in the middle of Earth.
Move your finger north, up to the **N**.
Now, move your finger south, down to the **S**.

North

West   **E**ast

South

Explain to your child that since early times, people have used the sun and stars to find their way. Tell him or her that the sun rises in the east and sets in the west. Watch a sunrise or sunset to determine relative directions from your home.

157

Compass Rose ★

Most maps have a tool called a compass rose. It lets you know which direction the top of the map is pointing toward. Most maps have north at the top and south at the bottom. On such maps, west is on the left and east is on the right.

This is the compass rose you will see on a map.
Color the compass rose. Trace in the letters **N**, **S**, **E**, and **W**.

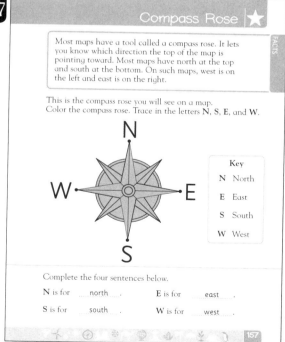

Key	
N	North
E	East
S	South
W	West

Complete the four sentences below.

N is for ___north___.   **E** is for ___east___.

S is for ___south___.   **W** is for ___west___.

Find a map that you commonly use and ask your child to point out the compass rose on the map. Encourage him or her to name the four directions on the rose.

158

★ North

FACTS

The direction "north" is usually found at the top of a map. When you are going north, you are moving toward the top of Earth. You may know about the frozen North Pole. That is where you will end up if you keep going north!

Find the word "north" on the compass rose, and then circle it.

Now, look at the map of an amusement park below. Imagine you are standing at the **X** (**✗**). Which two rides are to the north of you? Circle them on the map.

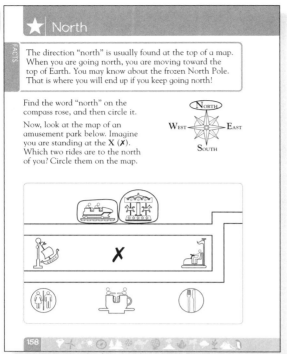

Determine where north is in relation to your home. Challenge your child to point out things and places that are north of your home.

159

South ★

The direction "south" is usually found at the bottom of a map. When you are going south, you are moving toward the bottom of Earth. Have you heard about the freezing South Pole? That is where you will find yourself if you keep going south!

Find the word "south" on the compass rose, and then circle it. Now look at the map of North America. Find the country of Canada. Then color the country directly south of Canada.

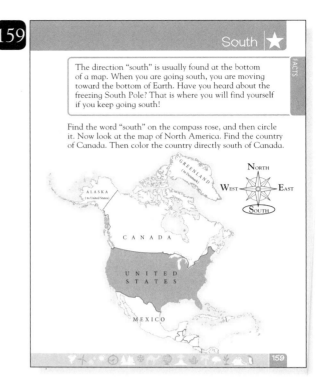

After having figured out which direction is north, stand in the center of the area where you are. Then ask your child to stand south of your position. Remind him or her that south is the opposite of north.

160

★ East

The direction "east" is usually found at the right side of a map. When you are going east, you are moving sideways across Earth from left to right. Did you know that the sun rises in the east?

Look at the town map below. Imagine you are standing at the **X** (**✗**). Which two buildings are to the east of you? Circle them on the map.

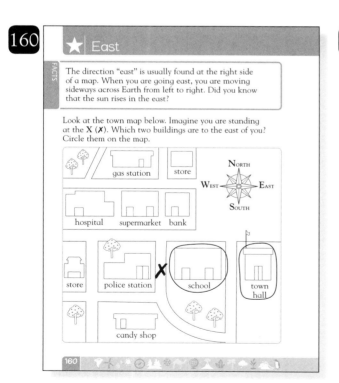

Find a map of your city or town. Find street names or areas that contain the word "East." Together, talk about why the street or area may be called "East."

161

West ★

The direction "west" is usually at the left side of a map. When you are going west, you are moving across Earth from right to left. The sun sets in the west. If you can see the sun setting, you are facing west, and it is time for bed!

Look at the map of Australia below. It shows where some animals are found. Imagine you are standing at the **X** (**✗**). Circle the animal that can be found to the west of you.

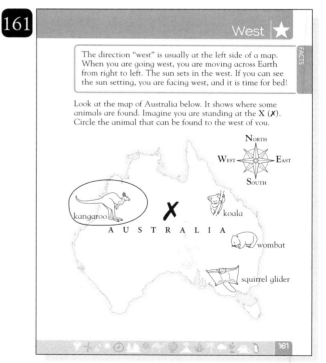

Having determined the four directions around your area, reinforce them by directing your child to walk north, south, east, and then west. Have fun with directions by making quick, silly turns!

⭐ The Natural World

FACTS

In geography, you study both the natural world and the human world. Think about a road on a mountain. The mountain is part of the natural world. It was part of our world long before there was a road. The road is part of the human world. People built the road. Geography is about understanding both the natural and the human world, and how they work together.

Use the words "natural" and "human" to complete the sentences below.

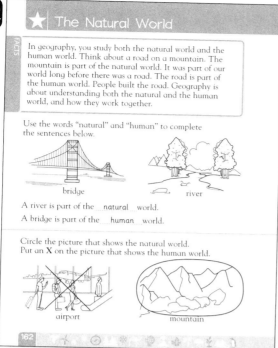

bridge   river

A river is part of the __natural__ world.

A bridge is part of the __human__ world.

Circle the picture that shows the natural world.
Put an **X** on the picture that shows the human world.

airport   mountain

Help your child make a collage of the natural world, using pictures found in magazines and newspapers. Selecting the pictures will help reinforce the concept of the natural world versus the human world.

Your World ⭐

FACTS

Your world has things from the natural world and things from the human world. The flowers and trees in a park are part of the natural world. The house you live in and your school are part of the human world.

Look around you. Draw something that is part of the natural world. Then draw something that is part of the human world.
Answers may vary

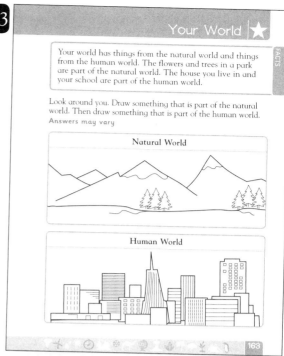

Natural World

Human World

As you travel around town with your child, encourage him or her to point out examples of the human world and the natural world. Then you can explain the ways in which the human world and the natural world work together.

⭐ Natural World Maps

FACTS

Maps of the natural world can help people understand it better. These maps can show mountains, rivers, lakes, types of trees, and even the weather. This information can help people plan a trip as well as pack the right clothes and equipment for it.

Draw lines connecting each natural place with its map.

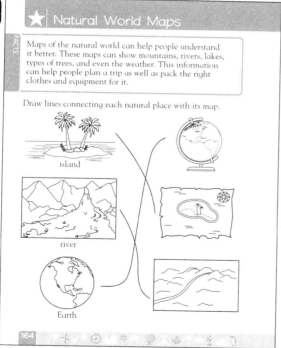

island

river

Earth

Maps help people plan what they need for a trip, so they can dress for the weather or carry the right equipment for different conditions. Ask your child to imagine a visitor to your home today. What would your child suggest the visitor pack?

Continents ⭐

FACTS

There are seven very large areas of land on Earth. These huge areas are called continents. When you look at a globe or a flat map of Earth, you will see the seven continents. The largest continent is Asia. The smallest continent is Australia.

Look at this map of the world. It shows all seven continents. Then follow the instructions below the map.

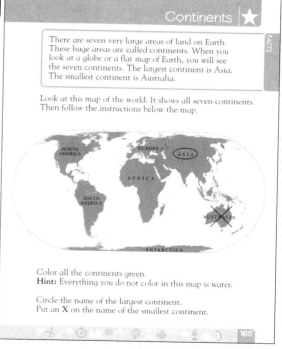

Color all the continents green.
Hint: Everything you do not color in this map is water.

Circle the name of the largest continent.
Put an **X** on the name of the smallest continent.

Together, find the continent you live on and point to it on the map. Explain to your child that no one lives permanently on the continent of Antarctica. Scientists work there, but they go home after a few weeks or months.

★ Mountains and Hills

FACTS

Mountains and hills are high areas of land. Hills are not as high as mountains. Some mountains are so tall that their tops reach the clouds. The tallest mountains have snow on top, even in summer.

Look at the two pictures below. Color the mountains brown. Color the hills green. Then answer the questions.

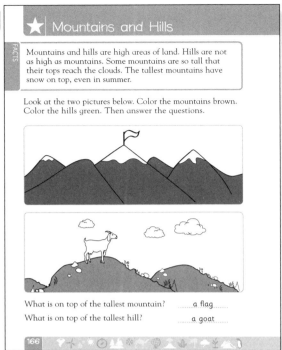

What is on top of the tallest mountain? .... a flag

What is on top of the tallest hill? .... a goat

Look up pictures of some famous mountains and mountain ranges, such as Mt. Everest or the Rocky Mountains, on the internet. To point out the difference between mountains and hills, also look up hill ranges, such as the North Downs or South Downs in England.

Forests ★

FACTS

Forests are large areas of land that are covered with trees. There are many forests on Earth. Many different kinds of animals live inside a forest. Some are large and others are small.

Look at the picture of a forest below. There are many different kinds of animals living in this forest. Circle the animals that you can find.

Tell your child that forests are often shown in green on maps. Point out a forest on a map. If you live near a forest, take your child on a walk through it to experience it firsthand.

★ Deserts

FACTS

The driest places on Earth are called deserts. Many are very hot in the daytime and cold at night, but some are always cold. Deserts get very little rain. Most people do not like to live in such dry places. However, a number of plants and animals have learned to live in the desert.

Look at the picture of a desert below. Circle the different kinds of animals and plants that you can find in the picture.

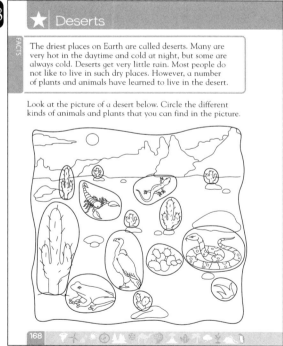

With your child, explore more about how different animals and plants have adapted to live well in the dry desert. Look online or go to the library to find books about desert plants and animals.

Islands ★

FACTS

An island is a piece of land that is completely surrounded by water. Islands can be very large, or they can be very small.

Look at the islands of Hawaii below. Then complete the activities.

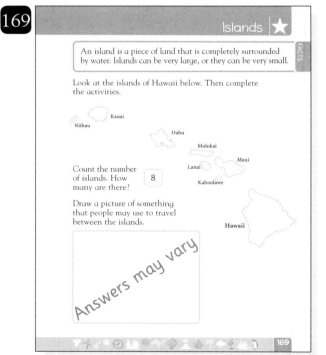

Count the number of islands. How many are there? **8**

Draw a picture of something that people may use to travel between the islands.

Answers may vary

Reinforce the idea that islands can be of different sizes. Greenland, in the Atlantic Ocean, is one of the world's largest islands. Nauru, in the Pacific Ocean, is the world's smallest island nation.

170

★ Oceans

An ocean is a very, very large body of water. There are five oceans on Earth, and they cover most of the planet. They are home to many different kinds of animals, such as whales, sea turtles, and fish. In fact, there are more animals in the oceans than there are on land.

Look at the map of the world below. It shows the continents surrounded by oceans. Color the oceans.

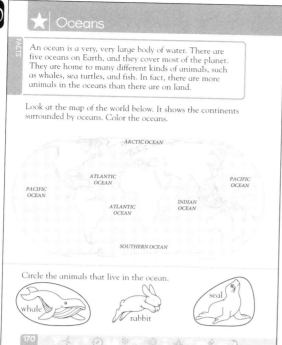

Circle the animals that live in the ocean.

whale   rabbit   seal

Ask your child if he or she can name the ocean that is closest to home. Look on a map together to check his or her answer or to find the answer.

171

Lakes ★

A lake is a large body of water surrounded by land. Some lakes are very big. People would need a large boat to go across a big lake. Other lakes are much smaller. People can cross them in a small boat.

Circle the things made by humans that you might see at a lake. Color the animals that you might also see there.

dinosaur   sailboat

fish   baseball

life jacket   duck

Are lakes part of the natural world or the human world? It depends on the lake! Explain to your child that some lakes are natural, and some were made by people.

172

★ Rivers

Water flows from high places to low places. A small amount of flowing water is called a stream. A large amount of flowing water is called a river. Many towns and cities are built along rivers. Rivers can be long and wide and may move very quickly. You might need a bridge or a boat to get across a river.

Circle the three things you can use to get across a river.

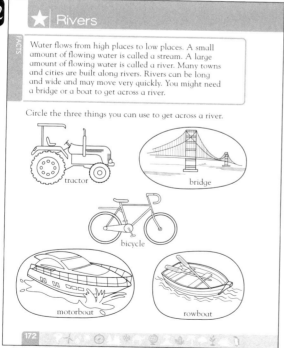

tractor   bridge

bicycle

motorboat   rowboat

Explain to your child that many animals, such as ducks, geese, otters, beavers, and alligators, make their homes in or near rivers. Rivers provide food and shelter that the animals need to live. Find out what animals live in or near rivers in your area.

The Human World ★

The places humans make are part of the human world. We build roads, bridges, and tunnels to help us go places. We make cities, towns, and villages to live in. We create parks and playgrounds so we can enjoy them. All of these things can be found on a map.

Circle the pictures of things that belong to the human world.

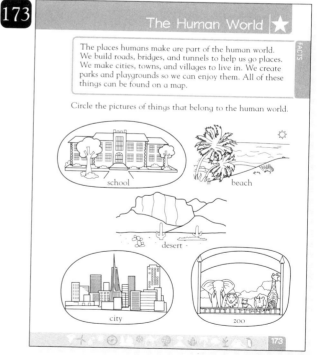

school   beach

desert

city   zoo

Play an "I Spy" game with your child where you take turns to guess whether the items you see around you are from the human world or the natural world. Start with "I spy something from the human world." That is the first clue!

FACTS

A country is an area of Earth that people identify as one place.

Look at the map of the world. Then follow the instructions below. You can ask an adult for help.

Circle the country you live in.
Answers may vary

Write the name of your country.
Answers may vary

Write the name of the leader of your country.
Answers may vary

What language do most people speak in your country?
Answers may vary

Talk to your child about what other countries people in your family have come from or lived in. Point them out on the map.

FACTS

All the people in a country share the same leader, such as a president or a queen. They usually speak the same language. Every country has its own flag, too.

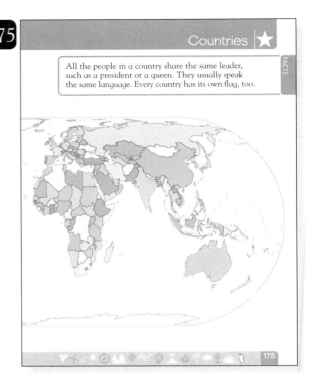

Your child might be curious to know how many countries there are in the world. There are about 200. If he or she is curious to learn more about another country, together find information about its geography, flag, language, and food.

FACTS

Many countries are divided into smaller regions. In some countries, like the United States (US), these smaller regions are called states.

Here is a map of the United States, which is one large country.

If you live in the US, color in your state. If you don't live in the US, color in a state you would like to visit.
Answers may vary

What is the name of the state you colored?
Answers may vary

Name a state that is next to the state you colored.
Answers may vary

Name a state that is far away from the state you colored.
Answers may vary

Point out states you have lived in or visited, or those you would like to visit. Count how many states you and your child have each been to. If you do not live in the United States, share facts that you know about any of the states.

FACTS

The United States is divided into 50 states. A few of these states are small, but some are very large and are filled with many towns and cities.

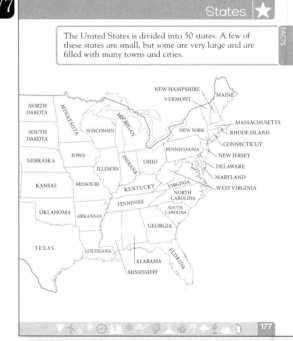

Use the map of the states to review and reinforce the four directions. Ask your child to point to the states in the north, east, south, and west. Let him or her find states that have a direction in their name, for example, North Carolina.

★ Provinces

Some countries are divided into smaller regions known as provinces, rather than states. Canada has ten provinces (and three other regions called territories).

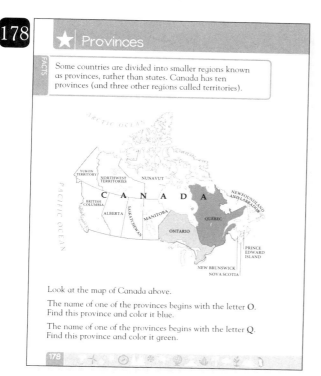

Look at the map of Canada above.

The name of one of the provinces begins with the letter **O**. Find this province and color it blue.

The name of one of the provinces begins with the letter **Q**. Find this province and color it green.

Some of the names of the provinces are long! Help your child learn the names of the provinces by pointing to each province and reading the name aloud to him or her.

Cities ★

A city is a busy place filled with people. There are many roads, houses, and buildings close together in a city. A big city may also have museums, parks, theaters, sports stadiums, and airports.

Look at this map showing a part of a city. Then follow the instructions given below.

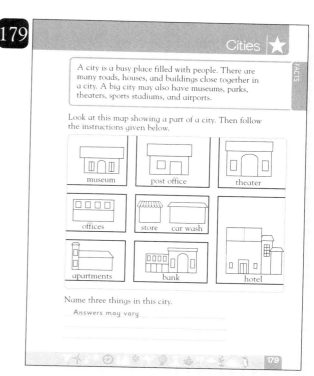

Name three things in this city.

Answers may vary

What is the biggest city near you? Or do you live in the biggest city in your area? Point out your city on a map. Then name the cities around you, pointing to each location, to help your child understand more about the geography of your area.

★ Which is Bigger?

Our Earth is a very big planet. The land on Earth is divided into seven large continents. These continents are further divided into countries.

Look at the shaded areas in each pair of globes below. Which is bigger? Circle the correct globe.

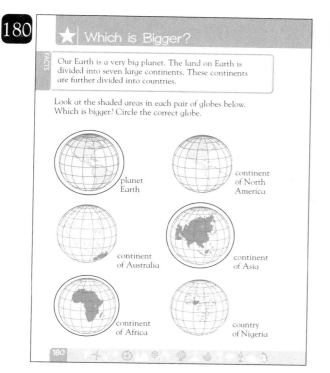

Extend the activity by having your child point out two sections on a globe or map and asking you which is bigger. He or she will gain confidence by being the "teacher" who knows the answer!

Which is Bigger? ★

Some countries are divided into states, as we learned on pages 176 and 177. Some states are very big, while others are very small. States have cities, which can be big or small.

Look at the shaded areas in each pair of maps below. Which is bigger? Circle the correct map.

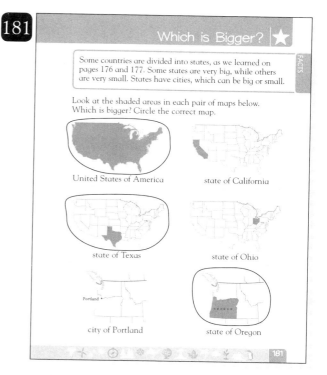

Look at the map of the United States together. Invite your child to find two states that are about the same size and shape.

★ Map Keys

FACTS

Maps tell us about a place using symbols, sometimes shown as pictures. The symbols are explained in what is known as a key. A map's key is a list of the different symbols that the map uses. It helps you read the map.

Match each map symbol to the thing you think it stands for. Ask a grown up for help.

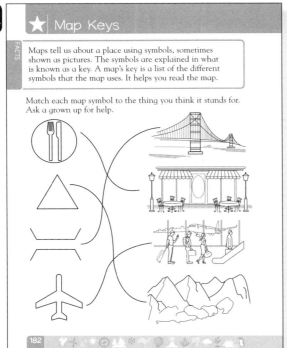

Reinforce the activity on map keys with a real-world example. Show your child maps that you have and ask him or her to point out their keys. Together, identify the different items on a key and find the symbols on the map.

Nature Map Key ★

FACTS

It can be hard for people to find their way around the natural world without a map. Nature maps tell you what you will find in an area of the natural world. Each symbol in the key stands for a different part of the natural world.

Look at this nature map. Then follow the instructions given below.

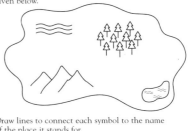

Draw lines to connect each symbol to the name of the place it stands for.

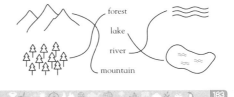

forest
lake
river
mountain

Invite your child to think of one more symbol to add to the nature map. Have him or her look around outside for ideas.

★ City Map Key

FACTS

A city is a big place. Maps can help you find your way around a city. They show you which roads you can take. A city map also shows you where to find the places you want to visit. Without a map, it is easy to get lost.

Look at this map of a part of a city. Draw a line to connect each symbol on the map to the name of the place you think it stands for.

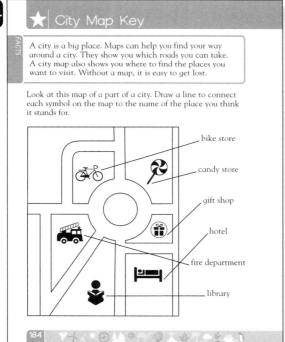

bike store
candy store
gift shop
hotel
fire department
library

Show your child a map of the city or town you live in. Point out important places that are known to your child: your home, school, friend's house, library, and so on. Which important place is closest to home? Which place is the farthest away?

Park Map Key ★

FACTS

A map of a park can show you the activities you can do there. It can also show you how to get to the places you want to visit. The map also shows you where to get help.

Look at the map of a park below. Then, read the list of activities you can do in the park. Draw a line to connect each activity to the symbol on the map that it stands for.

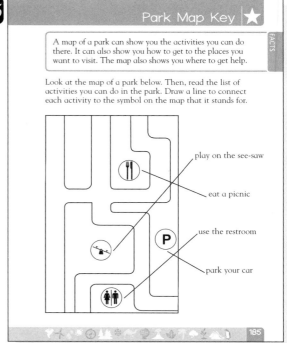

play on the see-saw
eat a picnic
use the restroom
park your car

Tell your child that park maps are often located at the entrance to a park, and in different spots around a park, depending on the park's size. Park maps can sometimes show the spot where the map reader is standing.

★ School Map Key

FACTS

Some map keys use symbols that are not pictures. Instead, they use letters as symbols to tell you what to find there.

Look at this map of a school and its key. The key uses letters to represent different places in the school.

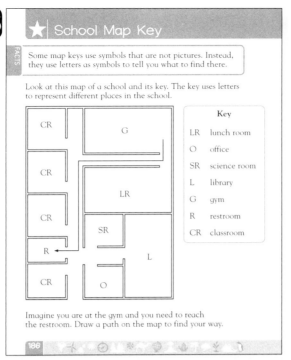

Key	
LR	lunch room
O	office
SR	science room
L	library
G	gym
R	restroom
CR	classroom

Imagine you are at the gym and you need to reach the restroom. Draw a path on the map to find your way.

Have your child think about his or her school. If you were to draw a map of the school, how would it be similar to or different from the school map shown on this page?

Zoo Map Key ★

FACTS

Some map keys do not use words at all. They have symbols that are small pictures of the places or things that are shown on the map.

Look at this map of a zoo. It has small pictures of animals as symbols to show where each can be found in the zoo.

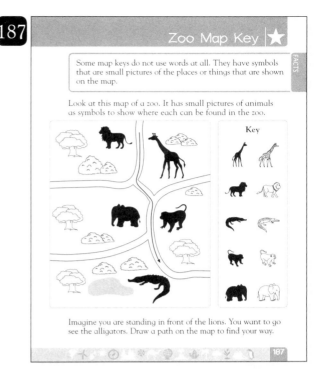

Imagine you are standing in front of the lions. You want to go see the alligators. Draw a path on the map to find your way.

Invite your child to create an imaginary zoo map on a separate piece of paper. He or she might create a zoo of fantastical creatures, or one filled entirely with his or her favorite animals. Have your child include a map key.

★ Using a Road Map

FACTS

Road maps are some of the most commonly used maps. They can show you the roads in a town or a city, or roads that cross much larger areas, such as the highways running from state to state across the whole country.

Here is a map of three states in the US. The states are Washington, Oregon, and California. Use the compass rose to help you answer the questions below.

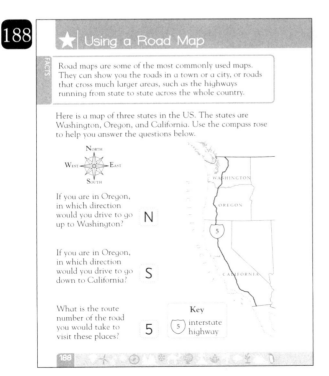

If you are in Oregon, in which direction would you drive to go up to Washington? **N**

If you are in Oregon, in which direction would you drive to go down to California? **S**

What is the route number of the road you would take to visit these places? **5**

Key	
5	interstate highway

Explain to your child that many highways in the US have numbers for names. Interstate highways that travel east and west use even numbers. Interstate highways that travel north and south have odd numbers.

Using a Neighborhood Map ★

FACTS

A map of your neighborhood can help you find your way around the area close to your home. It can also show you the different kinds of places you will find there.

Imagine the map below is of your neighborhood. Answer the questions that follow, using the map, its key, and the compass rose.

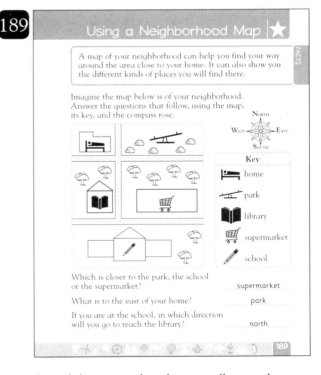

Key	
home	home
park	park
library	library
supermarket	supermarket
school	school

Which is closer to the park, the school or the supermarket? **supermarket**

What is to the east of your home? **park**

If you are at the school, in which direction will you go to reach the library? **north**

Extend the activity by taking a walk around your neighborhood with your child. Take turns pointing out the things you would include if you were making a map of the neighborhood.

★ Using a Park Map

Some maps tell you the choices you have when you visit a place. A park map, for example, helps you plan what you might do when you visit that park.

Look at this park map. Use direction words such as "left," "right," "next to," "in front of," and similar words to describe the path you would take to enjoy the activities given below. Trace your path on the map using your finger.

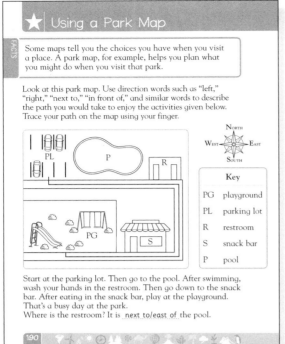

Key

PG   playground
PL   parking lot
R   restroom
S   snack bar
P   pool

Start at the parking lot. Then go to the pool. After swimming, wash your hands in the restroom. Then go down to the snack bar. After eating in the snack bar, play at the playground. That's a busy day at the park.
Where is the restroom? It is __next to/east of__ the pool.

Have your child practice giving directions to others. Ask him or her to give you directions from where you are to another room, such as a bathroom. Reinforce their use of direction words, such as left, right, and straight ahead.

Using a School Map ★

A map can also help you to find your way when you are inside a building. You can still use a compass rose with this type of map.

Look at this map of a school. Answer the questions below, using only the map and the compass rose to help you.

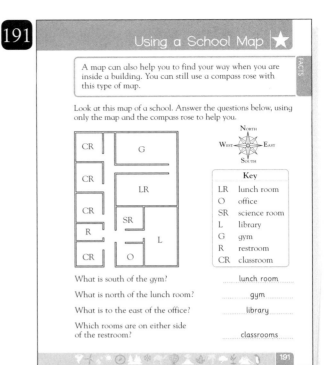

Key

LR   lunch room
O   office
SR   science room
L   library
G   gym
R   restroom
CR   classroom

What is south of the gym?   __lunch room__

What is north of the lunch room?   __gym__

What is to the east of the office?   __library__

Which rooms are on either side of the restroom?   __classrooms__

A museum is another type of building that might have a map. Go online to find maps for the museums that are near you or of interest to you and your child. Have your child describe what they see in each map.

★ Which Map?

Where do you want to go? What do you want to do? When you want to answer these questions, you use a map.

Jess and Miguel need different kinds of maps. Read about their trips below. Then put a check (✓) next to the map that each child needs.

Jess and her mother are driving across the United States to see Grandma and Grandpa.

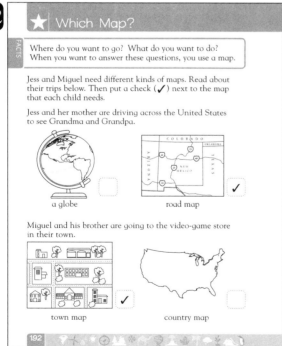

a globe   road map ✓

Miguel and his brother are going to the video-game store in their town.

town map ✓   country map

Ask your child to describe scenarios when someone might need the park map and the country map. Let your child take the lead and you can fill in details if necessary.

Which Map? ★

There are different kinds of maps. Each map is useful at a different time. Which map do you need?

Tanya and Leon also need maps. Below, read about what they need them for. Then put a check (✓) next to the map that each child needs.

Tanya and her parents are planning to buy furniture for their house.

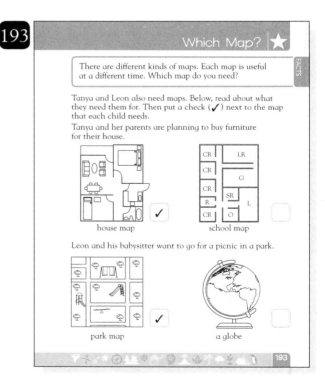

house map ✓   school map

Leon and his babysitter want to go for a picnic in a park.

park map ✓   a globe

Ask your child to describe scenarios when someone might need the school map and the globe. Let your child take the lead and you can fill in details if necessary.

★ The Lowercase Alphabet

FACTS

Lowercase letters are the small letters.
The first letters of the alphabet are **a** through **n**.

Trace lowercase letters **a** through **n**.
Then write these letters in lowercase on your own.

a a a a a a a art	h h h h h h h ham
b b b b b b b bad	i i i i i i i ill
c c c c c c c cat	j j j j j j j jet
d d d d d d dot	k k k k k k k kit
e e e e e e e egg	l l l l l l l lot
f f f f f f f fit	m m m m m mad
g g g g g g g get	n n n n n n n not

Children can also practice writing other simple three-letter words in lowercase letters. Help them think of words that begin with **a** through **n**.

The Lowercase Alphabet ★

FACTS

The letters in most words are in lowercase.
The last letters of the alphabet are **o** through **z**.

Trace lowercase letters **o** through **z**.
Then write these letters in lowercase on your own.

o o o o o o o odd	u u u u u u u up
p p p p p p p pat	v v v v v v v vet
q q q q q q q quit	w w w w w wet
r r r r r r r rag	x x x x x x-ray
s s s s s s s sit	y y y y y y y yes
t t t t t t t tap	z z z z z z z zip

Can you think of some words beginning with
the letters **a** through **z**?

Have your child look in books for short, simple words starting with **o** through **z** and set in lowercase. Children can copy the words and name the letters as they write. Read the words with your child.

★ The Uppercase Alphabet

FACTS

Uppercase letters are used in the names of people, places, or events. These are the letters **A** through **N** in uppercase.

Practice writing the uppercase letters. First trace the letters.
Then write uppercase letters **A** through **N** on your own.

A A A A A April	H H H H Hannah
B B B B B Brad	I I I I I I I Ivan
C C C C C C Cody	J J J J J J Joe
D D D D D D Dan	K K K K K K Kim
E E E E E Easter	L L L L L Logan
F F F F F F Fred	M M M Morgan
G G G G Grace	N N N N N Nora

Invite children to write their first, middle, and last names with correct capitalization.

The Uppercase Alphabet ★

FACTS

Uppercase letters are used at the beginning of a sentence and in titles. Here are the letters **O** through **Z** in uppercase.

Practice writing the uppercase letters. First trace the letters.
Then write uppercase letters **O** through **Z** on your own.

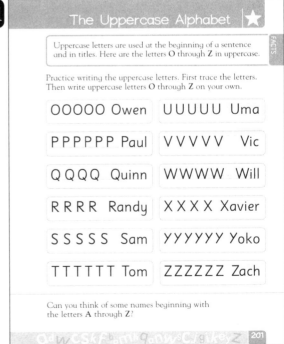

O O O O O Owen	U U U U U Uma
P P P P P P Paul	V V V V V Vic
Q Q Q Q Quinn	W W W W Will
R R R R Randy	X X X X Xavier
S S S S S Sam	Y Y Y Y Y Y Yoko
T T T T T Tom	Z Z Z Z Z Z Zach

Can you think of some names beginning with
the letters **A** through **Z**?

Continue to practice uppercase writing by writing the name of your street and city.

★ Book Time

FACTS Books have covers. Covers give information about books.

Description	Instruction
The title is the name of the book.	Look at the book's cover. Draw a box around the title.
The author is the person who wrote the book.	Draw a line under the author's name.
A book title uses uppercase letters. People's names also start with uppercase letters.	Circle all the uppercase letters.
The title and picture on a book's cover can give you a clue as to what the book will be about.	What do you think you would read in this book? Finally, color the book cover.

Silly Skunk Stories

Rosy Sniffin

When you read books with your children, point out the features on the cover: title, author, and illustrator. Invite children to make predictions about the story based on the information on the cover. If the book is a familiar one, talk about why the cover illustration is (or is not) a good choice for the book.

Telling a Story ★

Stories have a beginning, a middle, and an end.

Look at the pictures below. Then tell the story they show aloud. What happens first? What happens next? What happens last? When you have told the story, color the pictures.
Answers may vary

1. A skunk picked some flowers in the forest.
2. A dog wandered into the forest.
3. The skunk was afraid of the dog.
4. The skunk offered the dog flowers. They became friends.

After reading books to children, invite them to retell what happens first, next, and at the end.

★ Short "a"

 The letter a can sound like the a in "apple" (short "a") or the a in "ape" (long "a").

Each word is missing its short "a." Write the letter to complete the word. Then read each word aloud.

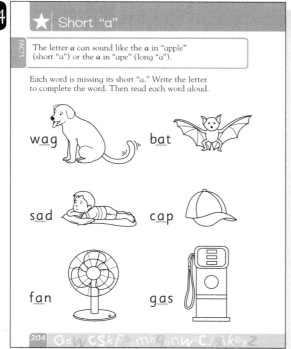

wag   bat

sad   cap

fan   gas

Find simple words in books that have an **a**. Read them with your child and ask if the word has a short "a" or long "a."

Rhyming Words ★

Two words that end in the same sound are called rhyming words. Rhyming words begin with different sounds.

Read the sentences aloud. Draw a line under the rhyming words.

My <u>dad</u> was <u>mad</u>.

A <u>mat</u> is <u>flat</u>.

Put the <u>rag</u> in the <u>bag</u>.

The <u>rat</u> <u>sat</u> on the cap.

Encourage your child to think of other short "a" rhymes. Offer help in writing them down.

★ Rhyming Match

Rhyming words often have similar spellings. Sometimes rhyming words can have completely different spellings.

Read each word aloud. Find the pairs of rhyming words in the balloons. Color each pair the same color.

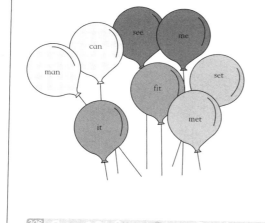

Invite your child to name other words that rhyme with the words in the balloons. Write them on the page.

Nursery Rhymes ★

A nursery rhyme is a poem or song for children. Nursery rhymes are passed down through the years.

Read the nursery rhyme aloud. Underline the rhyming words. Draw a picture that illustrates the nursery rhyme.

Hey, <u>diddle</u>, <u>diddle</u>,
The cat and the <u>fiddle</u>,
The cow jumped over the <u>Moon</u>.
The little dog laughed
To see such sport,
And the dish ran away with the <u>spoon</u>.
Drawings may vary

What other nursery rhymes do you know? Repeat this activity with other favorites.

★ Spotting the Rhymes

Saying words aloud can make it easier to figure out if they rhyme. Here are some more rhyming words to practice.

Find the rhyming words to practice. Draw a line between each pair.

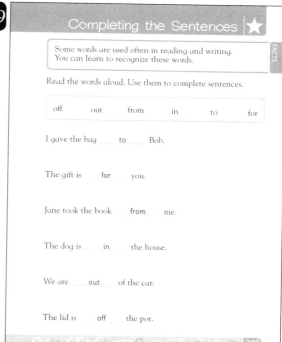

book
corn
clock
hook
horn
socks
fox
block

Point out that although "fox" and "socks" rhyme, they do not end with the same letters.

Completing the Sentences ★

Some words are used often in reading and writing. You can learn to recognize these words.

Read the words aloud. Use them to complete sentences.

off	out	from	in	to	for

I gave the bag ___to___ Bob.

The gift is ___for___ you.

June took the book ___from___ me.

The dog is ___in___ the house.

We are ___out___ of the car.

The lid is ___off___ the pot.

Look online for your school or district's list of kindergarten high-frequency words (or sight words).

★ Story Characters

A character is a person or animal in a story.

Read the story aloud.

A wolf liked to look at the stars. One night,
he walked along looking up at the stars.
He didn't see a hole in the ground and fell into it.
Another wolf passing by said, "You see the stars far
away. Why don't you see the ground under your feet?"

Below, circle the character that this story is about.

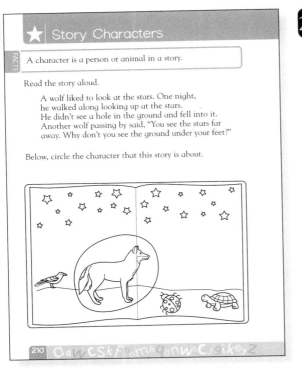

Invite your child to name and describe favorite
characters from well-known stories.

Story Setting ★

A setting is where and when a story takes place.

Read the story aloud.

Jenny and Jack climbed on a sled. They zoomed
down a hill. The winter air turned their cheeks cold.
The sled stopped at the bottom of the hill.
Jack said, "Let's ride again!"

Circle the picture that shows the setting of the story.

As you read books to your child, point out details
about the setting. Talk about how the setting
adds to the story.

★ Short "e"

The letter **e** can sound like the **e** in "egg"
(short "e") or the **e** in "eel" (long "e").

Each word is missing its short "e." Write the letter
to complete the word. Then read each word aloud.

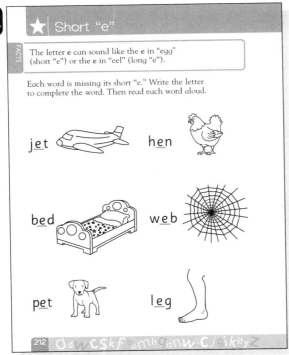

jet   hen

bed   web

pet   leg

Find simple words in books that have an **e**.
Read them with your child and ask if the word
has a short "e" or a long "e."

Rhyming Words ★

Rhyming words in a sentence make it more fun
to read. Here are some more rhyming words.

Read the sentences aloud. Draw lines under
the rhyming words.

I <u>led</u> the <u>red</u> hen.

She fed the <u>wet</u> <u>pet</u>.

A bird can <u>rest</u> in a <u>nest</u>.

Ten <u>men</u> saw the <u>pen</u>.

Encourage your child to think of other short "e"
rhymes. Help your child write them.

★ Information

People read for different reasons.
Sometimes they read to learn.

Read the text below.

A map helps you find your way. A map can show your home. It can show your school. A map can show you how to go from your home to your school.

Circle the picture that shows what the text is about.

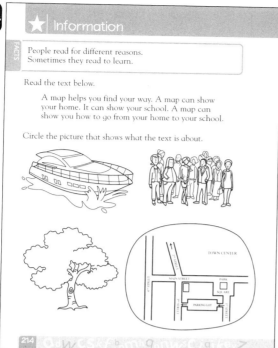

Describe examples of things you read to learn: for example, newspapers, cookbooks, and instructions.

Labels ★

Labels are a text feature.
They give information about a picture.

Write labels naming the parts of the tiger.
Use the words from the word bank.

| back | ear | eye | leg | nose | tail |

Look for examples of labels in texts around your home. Point them out to your child.

★ Spotting the Nouns

A noun names a person, a place, or a thing.

Circle the words that are nouns.

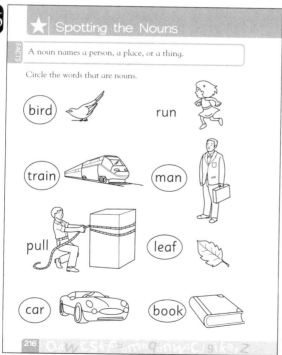

bird   run

train   man

pull   leaf

car   book

Ask your child to name other nouns. Search for things that are nouns in the place where you are sitting.

Spotting the Verbs ★

A verb is an action word. It names anything one can do or be.

Circle the words that are verbs.

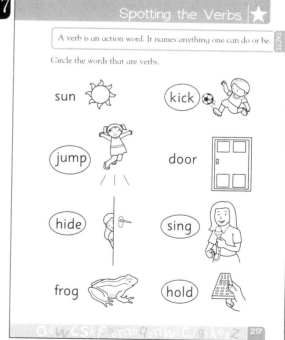

sun   kick

jump   door

hide   sing

frog   hold

Invite your child to name other verbs. Your child can act out different verbs and name them, for instance, "dance," "skip," and "wiggle."

218

★ Short "i"

FACTS The letter **i** can sound like the **i** in "big" (short "i") or the **i** in "ripe" (long "i").

Each word is missing its short "i." Write the letter to complete the word. Then read each word aloud.

d i g   k i d

s i t   r i p

b i b   p i n

Find simple words in books that have an **i**. Read them with your child and ask your child if the word has a short "i" or long "i."

219

Rhyming Words ★

FACTS One way to create a word that rhymes with another word is to change the first letter of the word.

Make rhyming words using letters from the letter bank.
Answers may vary

r	d	w	p	f	t

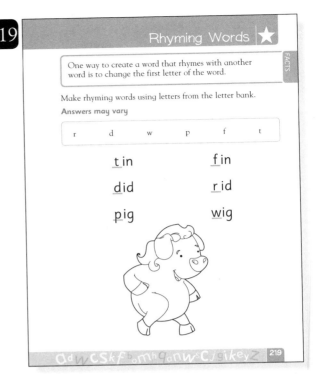

t in   f in
d id   r id
p ig   w ig

Encourage your child to think of other short "i" rhyming words. Offer help when writing the words.

220

★ Spotting the Adjectives

FACTS Adjectives are words that describe people, places, or things.

Draw a line between the picture and the word that describes it.

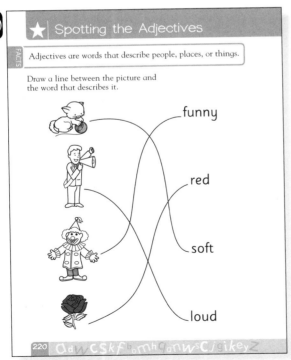

funny

red

soft

loud

Ask your child to name other adjectives. Use adjectives to describe the things you see around you.

221

First, Next, Last ★

FACTS Telling or writing information in order helps it make sense.

This story is out of order. What happens first, next, and last? Write 1, 2, and 3 by the pictures to put them in the correct order.

Words that convey time and order are called temporal words. Ask your child to retell other stories using words such as "first," "second," "next," "then," "finally," and "last."

★ Ordering Events

Make sense of information by telling or writing it in order.

Read the text below. Then look at the pictures. Number the pictures 1, 2, 3, and 4 to show the order in which the story happened.

Meg wanted to sell lemonade. First, she made the lemonade. Next, she set up her stand. Then, she hung up a sign. Finally, Meg sold lots of lemonade to her friends!

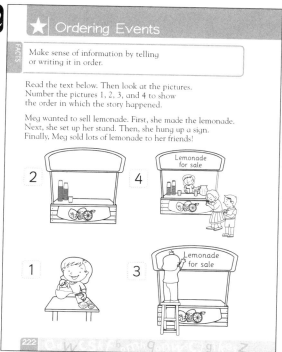

Have your child retell the story in order using temporal words.

Short "o" ★

The letter o can sound like the o in "dog" (short "o") or the o in "rope" (long "o").

Each word is missing its short "o." Write the letter to complete the word. Then read each word aloud.

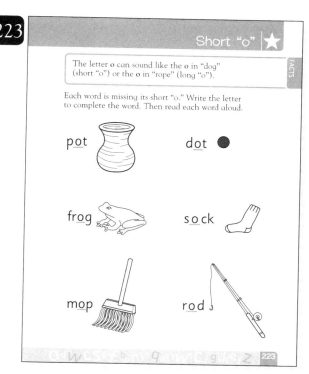

p_o_t   d_o_t

frog   s_o_ck

mop   rod

Find simple words in books that have an o. Read them with your child and ask your child if the word has a short "o" or long "o."

★ Rhyming Words

If words end with the same sound, they are rhyming words.

Read the sentences aloud. Circle the rhyming words.

The (cat) sits on the (mat).

(Bob) likes corn on the (cob).

Lots of (dogs) sit on (logs).

The (pot) is (not) too (hot).

While you read the sentences aloud, invite your child to point to other words that have a short "o" sound, even if they don't rhyme. For instance, "on," "lots," and "of."

Sorting ★

Words can name a general idea or topic, such as "place" or "job." Other words are more specific, such as "city" or "teacher."

Find the words that name foods in the spaces. Color those spaces red. Find the words that name animals in the spaces. Color those spaces green.

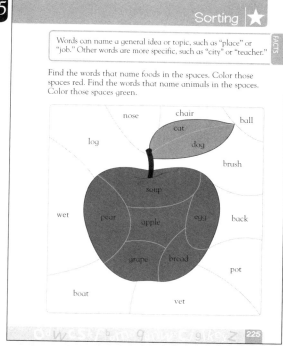

Collect some objects from around the house that have a similar theme: for example, toys and tools. Have your child sort and group the items and name the word that describes each group.

★ Plurals: Adding s

Singular means one. Plural means more than one. To make some words plural, add an **s** at the end of the word.

Make these words plural.

bat_s_

pig_s_

cane_s_

pan_s_

Brainstorm other words that can be made plural with an -**s**.

Plurals: Adding es ★

Add **es** to make a plural of words that end in **ch**, **sh**, **s**, or **x**.

Make these words plural.

fox_es_

dishe_s_

matche_s_

dresse_s_

Brainstorm other words that can be made plural with an -**es**.

★ My Favorite Storybook

A story has a title, or name. Stories are made up by authors. Stories also have characters and a setting.

Write down the title, author, characters, and setting of your favorite storybook. Write down why you like it.

My Favorite Storybook

Title: **Answers may vary**

Author: **Answers may vary**

Characters: **Answers may vary**

Setting: **Answers may vary**

Why I like this book: **Answers may vary**

Draw a picture of something that happens in your favorite storybook.

Answers may vary

If your child has several favorite books, repeat the activity on separate pieces of paper.

My Favorite True Book ★

Books about true events are called nonfiction books. Nonfiction books can inform us about a subject.

Write down the title, author, and subject of your favorite true book. Write down why you like it.

My Favorite True Book

Title: **Answers may vary**

Author: **Answers may vary**

Subject: **Answers may vary**

Why I like this book: **Answers may vary**

Draw a picture of what your favorite true book is about.

Answers may vary

If your child has several favorite books, repeat the activity on separate pieces of paper.

★ Short "u"

FACTS

The letter **u** can sound like the **u** in "up" (short "u") or the **u** in "use" (long "u").

Each word is missing its short "u." Write the letter to complete the word. Then read each word aloud.

r u g

bud

hut

cub

bus

p u p

Find simple words in books that have a **u**. Read them with your child and ask your child if the word has a short "u" or long "u."

Rhyming Words ★

FACTS

Using a rhyme in a sentence can make it easier to remember.

Read the sentences aloud. Draw lines under the rhyming words.

It is <u>fun</u> to <u>run</u>.

Can you <u>cut</u> a <u>nut</u>?

A <u>bug</u> is on the <u>mug</u>.

The <u>fox</u> is in the <u>box</u>.

Encourage your child to think of other short "u" rhymes. Offer help in writing them. Also encourage your child to point out other short vowel sounds, such as the short "a" in "can" or the short "o" in "on."

★ Sound-alike Words

FACTS

Some words sound alike but are spelled differently. These are called homophones.

Read each pair of words aloud. They sound alike! Trace the letters that change the spelling of the words.

tea   tee

son   sun

toe   tow

tail   tale

hair   hare

blew   blue

Words that sound alike are called homophones. "Homo" means "same" and "phone" means "sound." What other homophones can you and your child think of?

Action Song ★

FACTS

This popular song names different parts of the body.

Sing or say the song. As you sing, point to the parts named. Then use words from the song to label the parts of the body.

Head, shoulders, knees and toes, knees and toes.
Head, shoulders, knees and toes, knees and toes.
And eyes, and ears and mouth and nose.
Head, shoulders, knees and toes, knees and toes.

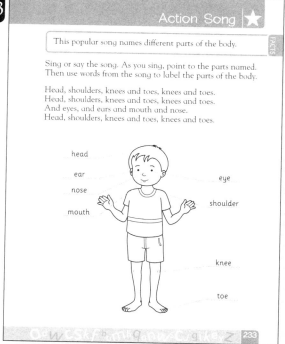

head
ear
nose
mouth
eye
shoulder
knee
toe

If you can, teach your child the movements that go with this song. This will make the song easier to remember.

★ Question Words

FACTS

Question words help people think about and understand what they read, do, or see.

The animals are running a race in the park. Look at the picture. Then answer the questions.

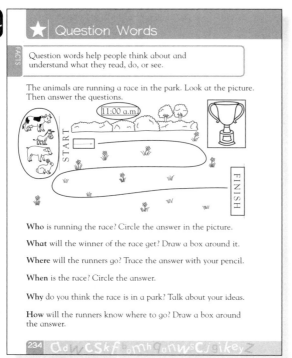

Who is running the race? Circle the answer in the picture.

What will the winner of the race get? Draw a box around it.

Where will the runners go? Trace the answer with your pencil.

When is the race? Circle the answer.

Why do you think the race is in a park? Talk about your ideas.

How will the runners know where to go? Draw a box around the answer.

Here, children are invited to explain why they think the race is in a park. Answers will vary; there are no wrong answers. This is a good opportunity for children to think critically. For example, is running in a park safer than running in the streets? Maybe traffic would have been tied up if roads were closed for a run.

Question Words ★

FACTS

Question words are words that help people ask for information.

Select question words from the word bank to best complete each question. **Answers may vary**

| Who | What | Where | When | Why | How |

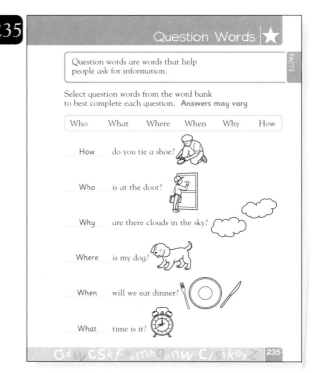

How   do you tie a shoe?

Who   is at the door?

Why   are there clouds in the sky?

Where   is my dog?

When   will we eat dinner?

What   time is it?

Be sure to encourage your child to write the letters with correct capitalization. Words that begin a sentence start with an uppercase letter.

★ Consonant Blends

FACTS

Letters are used together to make new sounds. These letters are called blends.

Use the letters from the letter bank to complete each word. Say the words aloud.

| bl | br | cl | cr | gl | gr |

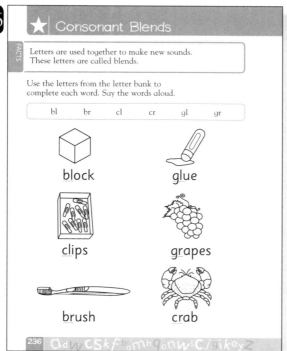

block

glue

clips

grapes

brush

crab

Encourage your child to think of other words with the **bl**, **br**, **cl**, **cr**, **gl**, and **gr** consonant blends.

Consonant Blends ★

FACTS

Certain letters make special sounds when they are used together.

C + H makes the sound that starts the word "chip."
S + H makes the sound that starts the word "sheep."
T + H makes the sound that starts the word "thin."
Draw a line to connect each word to its sound.

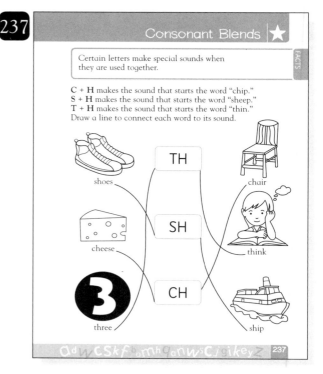

shoes   TH   chair

cheese   SH   think

three   CH   ship

Have your child keep an eye out for signs around town that have the **ch**, **sh**, and **th** consonant blends. Point them out as you see them and read them aloud.

★ Nouns and Verbs

Sometimes one word has more than one meaning.
Some words are both nouns and verbs.

Use the words in the word bank to write
the names of the pictures.

box	duck	fall	train

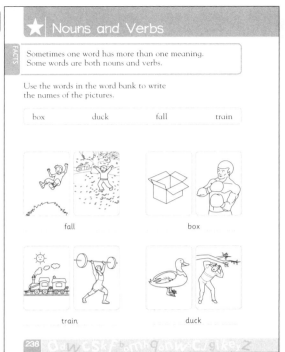

fall   box

train   duck

As you read or converse with your children, keep
eyes and ears open for other words that work as
nouns and verbs (for example, "walk," "shower,"
and "hook").

Handwriting Letters ★

Every letter has an uppercase and a lowercase form.

For each letter, fill in the missing uppercase
or lowercase letter.

A a   B b   C c   D d

E e   F f   G g   H h

I i   J j   K k   L l

M m   N n   O o   P p

Q q   R r   S s   T t

U u   V v   W w   X x

Y y   Z z

For extra practice, have children write
their names and complete address.

★ Handwriting Words

Some words are easy to recognize.
Others need to be sounded out.

Say the words describing these pictures aloud.
Then write the words.

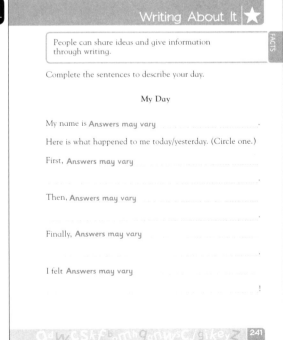

cat   fan   bed

nut   sit   pig

rug   cut   bat

For extra practice, invite children to write
a note to a grandparent or have them help
write a grocery list.

Writing About It ★

People can share ideas and give information
through writing.

Complete the sentences to describe your day.

My Day

My name is **Answers may vary**

Here is what happened to me today/yesterday. (Circle one.)

First, **Answers may vary**

Then, **Answers may vary**

Finally, **Answers may vary**

I felt **Answers may vary**

This activity can be repeated regularly on
separate pieces of paper. Tell your child that
writing daily about one's thoughts and experiences
is called keeping a journal. At this age, children
may not want to take on a daily journal, but using
this activity as a template for regular practice can
build writing skills.

★ Letters of the Alphabet

We spell words with letters. A set of these letters is called the alphabet. Each letter has a different shape and sound.

Read the letters of the alphabet aloud or sing them.

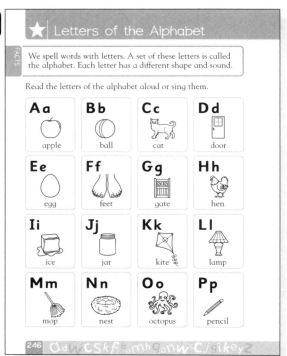

Aa apple	**Bb** ball	**Cc** cat	**Dd** door
Ee egg	**Ff** feet	**Gg** gate	**Hh** hen
Ii ice	**Jj** jar	**Kk** kite	**Ll** lamp
Mm mop	**Nn** nest	**Oo** octopus	**Pp** pencil

You can make a set of reusable cards from pages 246 and 247. Photocopy the pages, laminate them, and then cut out the individual letter cards. You may want to glue cord onto the letters before laminating them so that your child can touch and feel each letter.

Letters of the Alphabet ★

The alphabet has 26 letters. Each letter has an uppercase and a lowercase form.

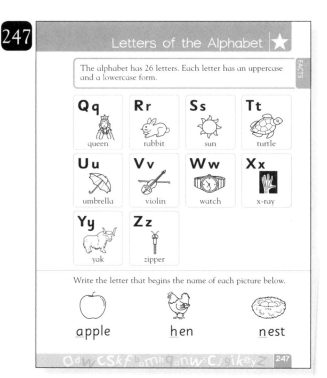

Qq queen	**Rr** rabbit	**Ss** sun	**Tt** turtle
Uu umbrella	**Vv** violin	**Ww** watch	**Xx** x-ray
Yy yak	**Zz** zipper		

Write the letter that begins the name of each picture below.

apple   hen   nest

Review each letter with your child and work together to come up with places where he or she has seen the letter—perhaps in a name, on a sign, or in his or her city, town, or street address.

★ Uppercase and Lowercase

Activities using the alphabet help children identify, read, and write uppercase and lowercase letters.

Trace the uppercase and lowercase letters of the alphabet wherever they are missing.

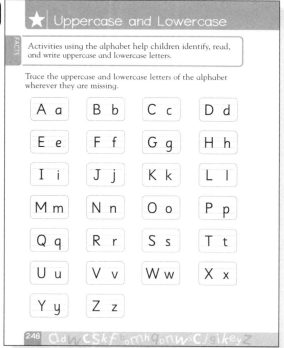

A a	B b	C c	D d
E e	F f	G g	H h
I i	J j	K k	L l
M m	N n	O o	P p
Q q	R r	S s	T t
U u	V v	W w	X x
Y y	Z z		

This activity gives your child practice in writing uppercase and lowercase letters and forming them correctly. Ask your child to say the name of each letter aloud as he or she traces it.

Matching Letters ★

Matching the uppercase and lowercase letters of the alphabet helps children with reading and writing.

Draw a line from each sock on the top clothesline to the sock with the matching lowercase letter on the bottom clothesline.

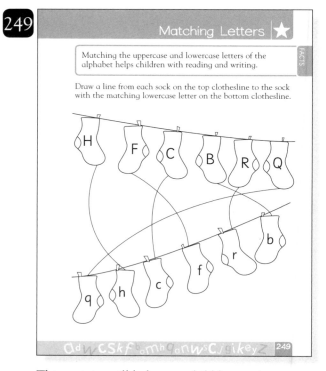

This activity will help your child have a better understanding of corresponding uppercase and lowercase letters. Use pages 246 and 247, or the cards you made, to review other corresponding uppercase and lowercase letters.

★ Vowels and Consonants

FACTS Words are spelled with letters. Some letters are consonants and some are vowels. The letters **a**, **e**, **i**, **o**, and **u** are vowels. The letter **y** is sometimes a vowel and sometimes a consonant. The other letters of the alphabet are consonants.

Read each picture's name aloud. Circle the vowel you hear in the middle of each word.

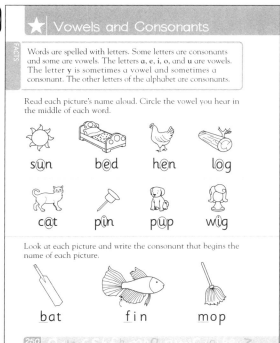

s(u)n b(e)d h(e)n l(o)g

c(a)t p(i)n p(u)p w(i)g

Look at each picture and write the consonant that begins the name of each picture.

bat fin mop

Teach your child to distinguish vowels from consonants. Let him or her sort letter blocks or cards into vowels and consonants while saying each letter. Say some simple words and ask your child to identify the middle vowel. For example, "What's the middle letter in the word 'hat'?"

Letter Sounds ★

FACTS Each letter has a different sound. For example, the letters **b-a-t** spell "bat." The letters **b-u-g** spell "bug."

Look at each picture and say its name aloud. Then write the letters of its name in the boxes in the correct order.

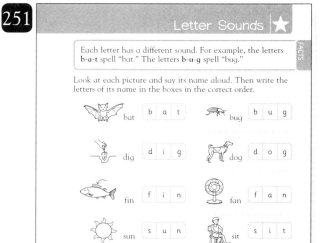

bat b a t   bug b u g

dig d i g   dog d o g

fin f i n   fan f a n

sun s u n   sit s i t

cup c u p   cat c a t

mat m a t   mop m o p

Help your child connect sounds to printed text. This provides a way for your child to approach new words. Help him or her say the sound of each letter in the words above. Practice this often when you talk about new words.

★ Consonants b, c, d, and f

FACTS The letter **b** begins the word "book." The letter **c** begins the word "cat." The letter **d** begins the word "duck." The letter **f** begins the word "fun."

Trace the uppercase and lowercase letters in each row. Circle the picture in each row whose name begins with the same letter.

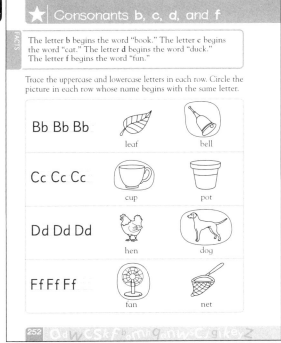

Bb Bb Bb   leaf   bell

Cc Cc Cc   cup   pot

Dd Dd Dd   hen   dog

Ff Ff Ff   fan   net

Find pictures of things that begin with **b**, **c**, **d**, and **f**. Label small boxes with the letters. Play a sorting game. Let your child say the name of each picture and then place it in the correct box.

Consonants g, h, j, and k ★

FACTS The letter **g** begins the word "gift." The letter **h** begins the word "hut." The letter **j** begins the word "jump." The letter **k** begins the word "kite."

Trace the uppercase and lowercase letters in each row. Circle the picture in each row whose name begins with the same letter.

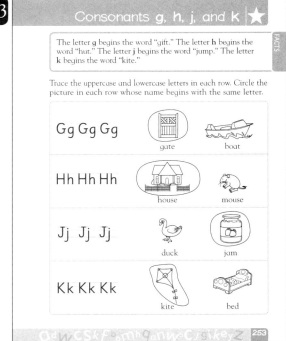

Gg Gg Gg   gate   boat

Hh Hh Hh   house   mouse

Jj Jj Jj   duck   jam

Kk Kk Kk   kite   bed

Ask your child to think of five words that begin with **g**, five words that begin with **h**, five that begin with **j**, and five that begin with **k**. Offer help if your child needs it. You could also add that **g** sometimes has a **j** sound, as in the word "gentle."

★ Consonants l, m, n, and p

FACTS

The letter **l** begins the word "lamp." The letter **m** begins the word "mop." The letter **n** begins the word "net." The letter **p** begins the word "pan."

Trace the uppercase and lowercase letters at the beginning of each row. Circle the two words in each row that begin with the same letter.

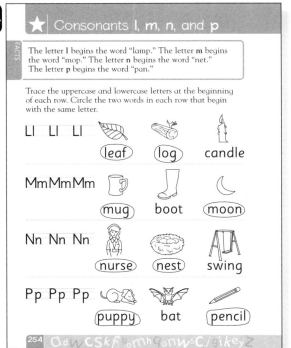

Ll Ll Ll — (leaf) (log) candle

MmMmMm — (mug) boot (moon)

Nn Nn Nn — (nurse) (nest) swing

Pp Pp Pp — (puppy) bat (pencil)

Play the sorting game again. Find pictures of things that begin with **l**, **m**, **n**, and **p**. Label small boxes with the letters. Let your child say the name of each picture and then place it in the correct box.

Consonants q, r, s, and t ★

FACTS

The letter **q** begins the word "quilt." The letter **r** begins the word "rabbit." The letter **s** begins the word "sock." The letter **t** begins the word "top."

Trace the uppercase and lowercase letters at the beginning of each row. Circle the two words in each row that begin with the same letter.

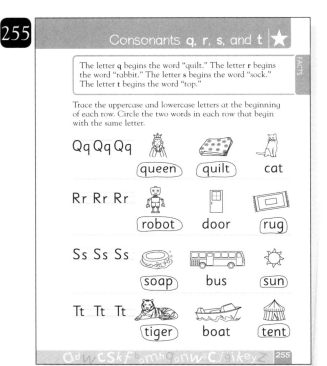

Qq Qq Qq — (queen) (quilt) cat

Rr Rr Rr — (robot) door (rug)

Ss Ss Ss — (soap) bus (sun)

Tt Tt Tt — (tiger) boat (tent)

Reinforce how to pronounce the letters **q**, **r**, **s**, and **t**. Say words beginning with these letters and let your child repeat each word aloud. Words could include "quarter," "round," "super," and "tongue."

★ Consonants v, w, x, y, and z

FACTS

The letter **v** begins the word "van." The letter **w** begins the word "window." The letter **x** begins the word "x-ray." The letter **y** begins the word "yard." The letter **z** begins the word "zebra."

Trace the uppercase and lowercase letters at the beginning of each row. Circle the word or words in each row that begin with the same letter.

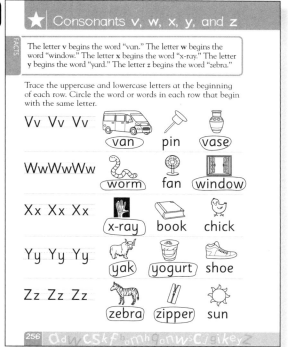

Vv Vv Vv — (van) pin (vase)

WwWwWw — (worm) fan (window)

Xx Xx Xx — (x-ray) book chick

Yy Yy Yy — (yak) (yogurt) shoe

Zz Zz Zz — (zebra) (zipper) sun

Ask your child to think of more words that begin with or contain these less commonly used consonants. Examples include "voice," "wand," "fox," "you," and "pizza." Don't forget to remind your child that the letter **y** is sometimes used as a vowel, too.

Letter Sounds ★

FACTS

Words have different sounds based on the order of the letters they contain. If the beginning, middle, or final letters of a word change, a new word with a different sound is made.

Read each pair of words below. Then underline the letters that are different in each pair.

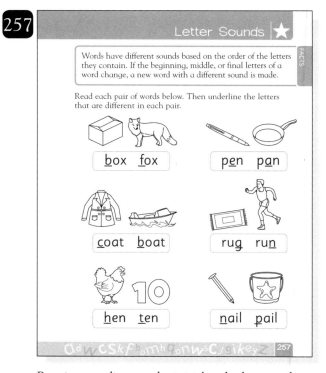

box fox

pen pan

coat boat

rug run

hen ten

nail pail

Practice sounding out the initial and other sounds of words. Make sure your child understands the terms beginning, or initial, middle, and ending sounds. Use the word "hen," for example, and exaggerate the sound of each letter.

★ Beginning Sounds

FACTS Each letter in a word has a different sound. Identifying the initial sound of a word helps you to say it.

Read each picture's name on the left. Using a letter from the box, complete the rhyming picture's name on the right.

h	p	f

can   fan

bat   hat

cup   pup

fin   pin

pen   hen

258

Write rhyming words on index cards, using specific-colored markers for each group of words. For example, red for words ending in "-up," blue for words ending in "-at," and green for words ending in "-ad." Let your child identify the rhyme and sort the cards into groups.

Middle Vowel Sounds ★

FACTS Recognizing simple consonant-vowel-consonant words builds knowledge of words, their sounds, and spellings.

Read each picture's name on the left. Using a vowel from the box, complete the picture's name on the right.

o	a	u

leg   log

hut   hat

pin   pan

cap   cup

map   mop

259

Reinforce sounds and letters. Use a dark marker to write the five vowels at the bottom of five small paper cups. After working on the page, review the 10 words and ask your child to identify the paper cup with the correct vowel for each word.

★ Final Sounds

FACTS The ending sounds of words can be short or extended. Some letters produce short, or stop, sounds, such as the **t** in "bat." Other words end with extended, or continuous, letter sounds. For example, the letter **r** can be extended in "far."

Look at the first picture in each row. Read its name aloud. Look at the other two pictures in the row. Find the picture's name that ends in the same sound as the first picture's name. Circle that picture and its name.

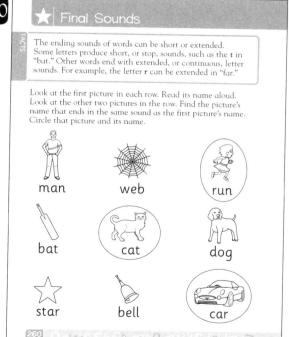

man   web   run

bat   cat   dog

star   bell   car

260

Read the words "sun" and "moon." Ask your child if they end with the same sound. Then say the words "door" and "book." Ask if they end with the same sound. Explore saying and writing words with the same ending sounds as "door." Examples are "floor," "car," and "your."

Different Letter Sounds ★

FACTS Words can be broken up into letters and the sounds of the letters.

Read the words aloud and write each letter in a separate box.

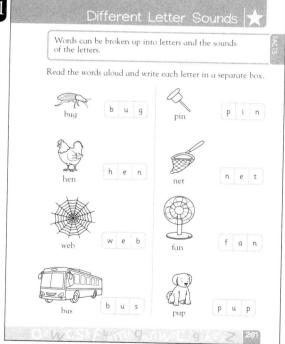

bug | b | u | g | pin | p | i | n |

hen | h | e | n | net | n | e | t |

web | w | e | b | fan | f | a | n |

bus | b | u | s | pup | p | u | p |

261

As an extension to this activity, find some more simple consonant-vowel-consonant words and practice breaking these words up into sounds with your child.

★ | The Long "a" Sound

FACTS
The long sound of the vowel **a** says its name. You hear the long "a" sound in the word "snake."

Read each picture's name aloud. Circle the names of the six pictures that have the long "a" sound. Make an **X** on the names of the two pictures that have the short "a" sound, as heard in "cat."

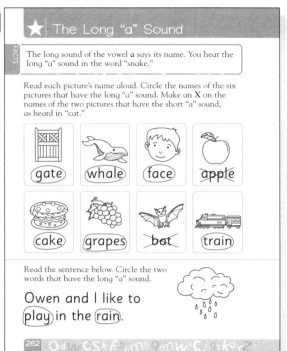

gate whale face apple
cake grapes bat train

Read the sentence below. Circle the two words that have the long "a" sound.

Owen and I like to play in the rain.

Reinforce that long vowel sounds say the name of the vowel. Use a set of cards or magnetic letters and say each vowel. With your child, write a list of words with the long "a" sound.

The Long "e" Sound | ★

FACTS
The long sound of the vowel **e** says its name. You hear the long "e" sound in the word "cheese."

Read each picture's name aloud. Circle the names of the six pictures that have the long "e" sound. Make an **X** on the names of the two pictures that have the short "e" sound, as heard in "pen."

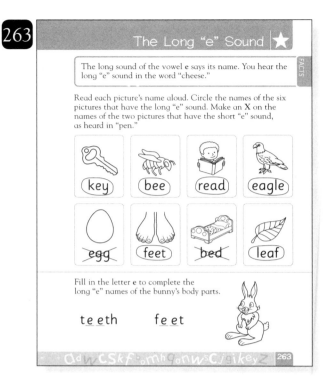

key bee read eagle
egg feet bed leaf

Fill in the letter **e** to complete the long "e" names of the bunny's body parts.

te e th   fe e t

Help your child distinguish the long vowel sound of the letter **e** from the short "e" sound. Find pictures of things with both sounds. Engage him or her in sorting the pictures into two containers, one labeled "short vowel" and the other "long vowel."

★ | The Long "i" Sound

FACTS
The long sound of the vowel **i** says its name. You hear the long "i" sound in the word "lion."

Read each picture's name aloud. Circle the names of the six pictures that have the long "i" sound. Make an **X** on the names of the two pictures that have the short "i" sound, as heard in "tin."

ice mice pin pipe
fish kite dice iron

Read the sentence below. Circle the two words that have the long "i" sound.

The tiger is a big cat that has stripes.

Cut a large piece of construction paper into the shape of a kite and attach a tail with a piece of string. With your child, find and write the long "i" words on small cards. Tape the cards to the tail. Use these words to write a poem with your child.

The Long "o" Sound | ★

FACTS
The long sound of the vowel **o** says its name. You hear the long "o" sound in the word "boat."

Read each picture's name aloud. Circle the names of the six pictures that have the long "o" sound. Make an **X** on the names of the two pictures that have the short "o" sound, as heard in "pot."

oval open goat mop
yogurt log toast soap

Read the sentence below. Circle the two words that have the long "o" sound.

Jenny likes to eat yogurt and toast.

Draw an oval on a large sheet of paper. Write some long "o" and short "o" words on small cards. Guide your child to identify and then tape the cards with long "o" words onto the oval.

★ The Long "u" Sound

The long sound of the vowel **u** says its name. You hear the long "u" sound in the word "cube."

Read the words on the balloons aloud. Color the five balloons that have words with the long "u" sound. Make an **X** on the two balloons that have words with the short "u" sound, as heard in "fun."

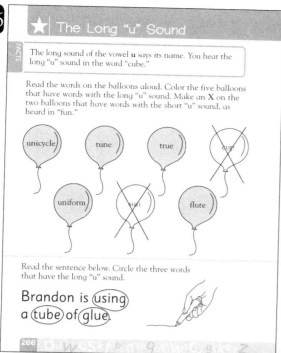

Read the sentence below. Circle the three words that have the long "u" sound.

Brandon is (using) a (tube) of (glue).

Review the long "u" sound by writing a short rhyme with your child. For example, "Does the boy in blue have the glue?" or "The unicorn wore a uniform."

The Tricky Letter y ★

The letter **y** can be tricky. Sometimes, it makes the long "e" vowel sound, as in the word "funny." Sometimes, it makes the long "i" vowel sound, as in the word "sky."

Circle the letter **y** in each word below. Read the word aloud. Listen to the "e" sound y makes in each word.

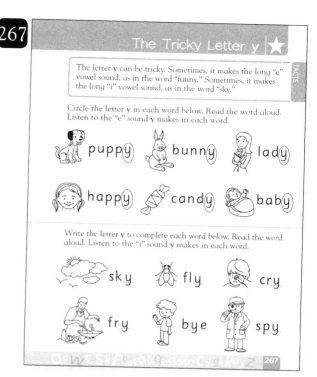

pupp(y)   bunn(y)   lad(y)

happ(y)   cand(y)   bab(y)

Write the letter **y** to complete each word below. Read the word aloud. Listen to the "i" sound y makes in each word.

sky   fly   cry

fry   bye   spy

Say words that end in the letter **y**, emphasizing the final sound, such as "carry," "silly," "sly," "spy," "lucky," "hungry," "why," and "dry." Ask your child to hold up a card showing the letter **e** or **i**, depending on the sound of **y** in each word.

★ The Short "a" Sound

The word "apple" begins with the short sound of the vowel **a**. Some other words with the short "a" sound are "ax," "bag," and "rat."

Circle the names of the four pictures that have the short "a" sound. Make an **X** on the names of the two pictures that have the long "a" sound.

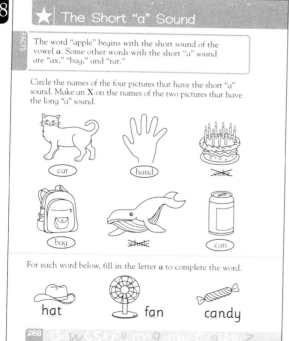

cat   hand   cake

bag   whale   can

For each word below, fill in the letter **a** to complete the word.

hat   fan   candy

Give your child a card with the letter **a**. Then give him or her a card with a consonant and ask your child to place the consonant before the **a**. Ask him or her to think of words that begin with those two letters. Finally, ask whether each word has a long or short "a" sound.

The Short "e" Sound ★

The word "egg" begins with the short sound of the vowel **e**. You also hear the short "e" sound in the words "elbow," "desk," and "hen."

Read each picture's name in the word wheel aloud. Color each section of the wheel in which the picture's name has the short "e" sound.

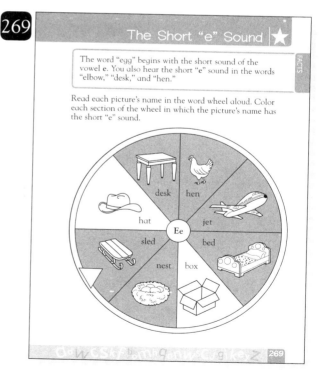

desk   hen
hat   jet
Ee
sled   bed
nest   box

Reinforce the sounds of the letter **e**. List words with both long and short "e" sounds. Read them randomly. Let your child show an index card labeled "long" or "short" based on the letter sound he or she hears in each word. Examples include "pet," "bean," "met," "meet," "red," and "bead."

★ The Short "i" Sound

FACTS
The word "pin" has the short sound of the vowel i. You also hear the short "i" sound in the words "pig," "fin," and "fish."

Read each picture's name in the word wheel aloud. If the word has the short "i" sound, underline the letter i. Make an **X** on the words that have the long "i" sound.

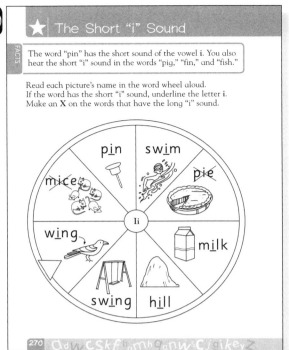

Help your child see words in context. Write sentences with short "i" words. Read them aloud, emphasizing the short "i" words. Then ask which words have the short "i" sound. An example of a sentence could be "The *little pig* had a curly tail."

The Short "o" Sound ★

FACTS
The word "dog" has the short sound of the vowel o. You also hear the short "o" sound in the words "top" and "mop."

Read each picture's name aloud. Circle the six names that have the short "o" sound. Make an **X** on the two names that have the long "o" sound.

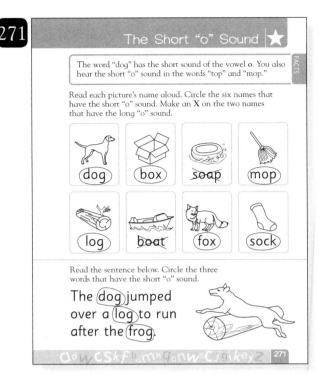

Read the sentence below. Circle the three words that have the short "o" sound.

The dog jumped over a log to run after the frog.

Record your voice reading words with the short "o" sound. Let your child read some words and record his or her voice. Listen to the recording as you view a list of words that includes those recorded. Help your child identify and highlight the words he or she hears.

★ The Short "u" Sound

FACTS
The word "umbrella" has the short sound of the vowel **u**. You also hear the short "u" sound in the words "drum," "pup," and "sun."

Read each picture's name aloud. Circle the six names that have the short "u" sound. Make an **X** on the two names that have the long "u" sound.

Read the sentence below. Circle the three words that have the short "u" sound.

The bug is snug in the rug.

Read pairs of words, such as "run fun," "pan can," and "bump jump." Some words should have the short sound of the letter **u**, and the others should not. Let your child show a thumbs-up for the pairs with the short "u" sound and a thumbs-down for the others.

Letters and Words ★

FACTS
The individual letter sounds in simple words can be changed to make new words.

Read each picture's name on the left. Fill in the letter to complete the picture's name on the right.

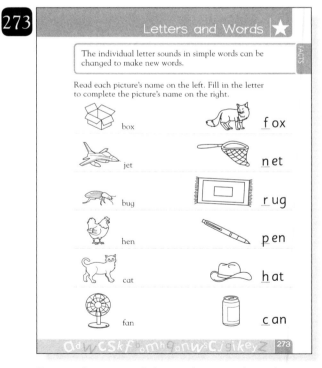

Practice letter sounds by emphasizing those that your child may find challenging to hear and identify. Examples are "n" and "m," "b" and "p," and "d" and "t." Have your child show a letter card when he or she hears a particular sound.

★ Beginning Sounds

To identify spoken words, let your child listen to the beginning sounds of the words.

Look at the picture of each animal. Say the letter on the animal aloud. Then draw a line to match each animal to its name.

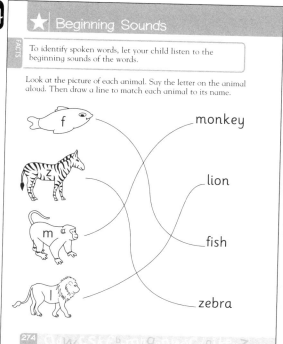

monkey

lion

fish

zebra

After your child works on this page, encourage him or her to think of more animal names. Ask your child to tell you the beginning letter of each name.

Rhyming Words ★

Rhyming words have the same ending sound. For example, "cap" and "nap" end with the same letter sound.

Read the pictures' names in each box aloud. Circle "yes" if the words rhyme and "no" if the words do not rhyme.

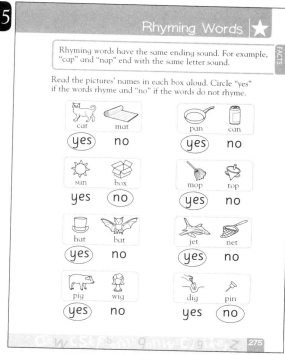

Read nursery rhymes aloud with your child. Emphasize the rhyming words. Let your child see the words and guide him or her to point to the words that rhyme.

★ Syllables

Every word has one or more syllables, or beats. For example, the word "boat" has one syllable, the word "butter" has two syllables, and the word "dinosaur" has three syllables.

Read each animal's name aloud. As you say the word, count the number of its syllables. Circle the correct number.

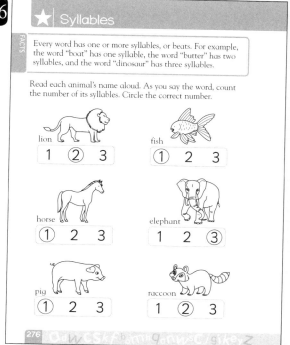

While you are working through this page, bang on a toy drum or a metal pot to emphasize the number of syllables in each word. After that, encourage your child to say names of family members and friends and count the number of syllables in each name.

More Syllables ★

Every syllable has one vowel sound. For example, the word "tomato" has three vowel sounds and three syllables.

Read each sentence aloud. Circle the number of syllables in each underlined word.

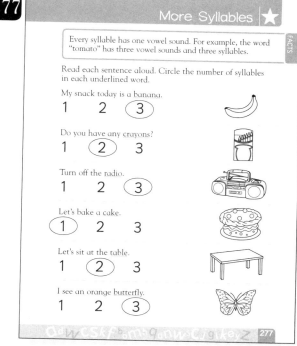

Guide your child to create a few sentences and help him or her write them down. In each sentence, examine the words and in each word, the syllables. Encourage him or her to count the syllables. Dinosaur names, such as "stegosaurus," can be particularly exciting examples.

★ Sight Words

FACTS

Sight words, or high-frequency words, are words commonly used in speaking and writing. The spelling of some of these words does not follow the usual letter-sound pattern.

Practice reading and using the sight words listed below.

all	four	on	too
am	get	please	under
are	good	ran	was
at	have	say	what
be	he	she	who
but	into	so	will
came	like	that	with
did	no	there	yes
do	now	they	you
eat	of	this	your

Write these words on cards. With your child, practice using them to create sentences. The next time you are reading a story with your child, encourage him or her to identify sight words in the text.

Using Sight Words ★

FACTS

Learning to spell and use sight words improves fluency in reading.

Read each sentence below. Circle the correct sight word to complete the sentence.

I know the days (of) has the week.

Do (you) your have a red crayon?

Does (she) her have a brother?

That girl be (is) my friend.

Kate went (to) am the zoo.

A cat is in so (the) tree.

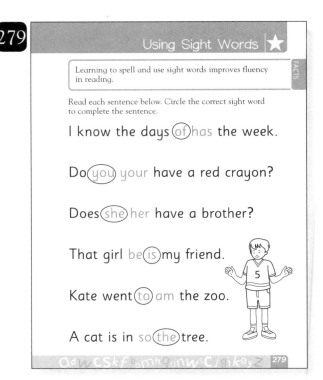

Your child learns sight words, or high-frequency words, by repeatedly seeing and using them. Write sentences with the sight words missing. Let your child choose the word that makes the most sense.

★ Letters Make Words

FACTS

Words are made with letters that are placed in order from left to right.

Find the words from the word box in the rectangles below. Each rectangle has three words hidden in it. Circle the words and read them aloud.

bat	cat	milk	rat	horse
drum	doll	kiwi	pear	

Food Words

p e a r g o j k i w i q v m i l k

Toy Words

d o l l r j h i b a t x d r u m x

Animal Words

c a t j z p r a t g u l h o r s e

This activity will help your child distinguish words from random groups of letters. By seeing groups of concept words, he or she will see that words convey ideas and meanings. Introduce your child to simple word searches that contain three-letter words.

Reading Print ★

FACTS

Print, or written text, is made up of letters and words that are read from left to right.

Read the words in each sentence aloud. Circle the word at the end of each line.

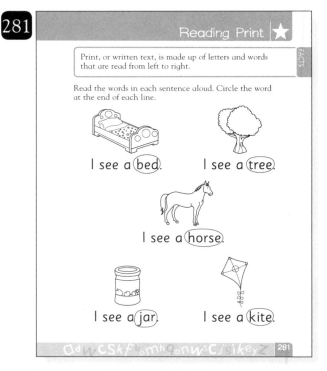

I see a (bed).   I see a (tree).

I see a (horse).

I see a (jar).   I see a (kite).

If necessary, help your child follow the pattern of reading word by word. Place a small card under each word as you read from left to right to reinforce the reading process.

★ Reading from Left to Right

FACTS
Words in a sentence are read from left to right. At the end of a line, you return to the left side of the next line to continue reading.

Draw a line from the word in the box to the same word on the right.

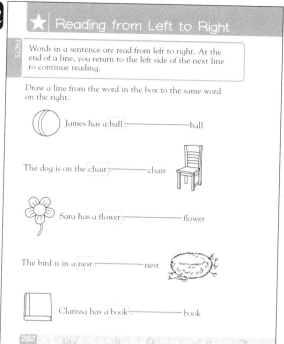

James has a ball ———— ball

The dog is on the chair ———— chair

Sara has a flower ———— flower

The bird is in a nest ———— nest

Clarissa has a book ———— book

While working through this page, reinforce the fact that each sentence conveys an idea or a thought. After reading, you could test your child on the spelling of some of the words on this page, such as "book," "nest," and "chair."

Reading and Counting Words ★

FACTS
Words are combined to form sentences. The words in a sentence are separated by a single space between each word.

The sentences below tell a story. Count the words in each sentence. Circle the number of words each sentence contains.

I have a bear.

1 2 3 ④ 5 6 7

It is a brown bear.

1 2 3 4 ⑤ 6 7

It is not a big bear.

1 2 3 4 5 ⑥ 7

The little bear sits in a chair.

1 2 3 4 5 6 ⑦

My little bear is a teddy bear.

1 2 3 4 5 6 ⑦

Help your child gain confidence as a reader as he or she counts the words in a sentence successfully. Point out the use of uppercase letters to begin sentences and punctuation, such as periods, to end sentences.

★ Words Make Sentences

FACTS
Each sentence ends with a punctuation mark, such as a period (.).

Look at each sentence below. The spaces between words are missing. Draw a line between the letters where each space should be. Add a period at the end of each sentence.

I|can|jump.

I|like|swings.

My|cat|is|asleep.

I|can|fly|a|kite.

Ask your child to look around him or her to think of some small sentences. Help your child to write them, and then draw attention to each word and its meaning. Encourage your child to use finger spaces between each word when writing.

Words Make Sentences ★

FACTS
A sentence is a group of words that expresses a complete thought. Sentences can be long or short.

Read each sentence aloud. Count the words in each sentence and circle the correct number.

I like ice cream.

1 2 3 ④ 5 6

I like vanilla ice cream.

1 2 3 4 ⑤ 6

I like vanilla ice-cream cones.

1 2 3 4 5 ⑥

I like rainbow sprinkles, too.

1 2 3 4 ⑤ 6

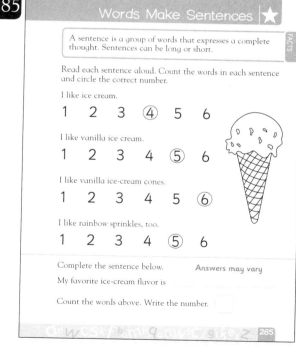

Complete the sentence below.   Answers may vary

My favorite ice-cream flavor is

Count the words above. Write the number.

After completing this page, ask questions and guide your child to write simple sentences about one of his or her favorite things. Count the words in each sentence to show your child how he or she is forming ideas with words.

★ Rhyming Sentences

FACTS Sentences that end with rhyming words are called rhyming sentences. Some poems have rhyming sentences.

Read each sentence aloud. Look at each picture and pick the correct word to complete the rhyme.

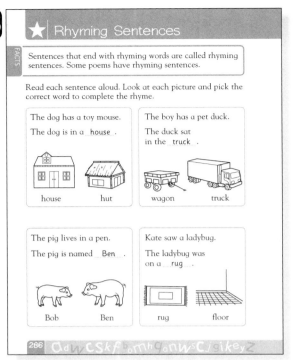

The dog has a toy mouse.
The dog is in a __house__ .

house   hut

The boy has a pet duck.
The duck sat in the __truck__ .

wagon   truck

The pig lives in a pen.
The pig is named __Ben__ .

Bob   Ben

Kate saw a ladybug.
The ladybug was on a __rug__ .

rug   floor

Your child will gain confidence as a reader as he or she reads each rhyme. Follow up this activity by reading simple poems from a book or from a website. Leave out some of the rhyming words and let your child fill them in.

Reading a Story ★

FACTS You read words from left to right, top to bottom, and then page by page.

The pictures in the boxes below tell a story. Follow the numbers to read the story and answer the questions.

1   The puppy barks.

2   The puppy is given food.

3   The puppy eats her food.

4   Finally, the puppy sleeps.

In which picture does the puppy bark?   **1**

In which picture does the puppy eat?   **3**

In which picture does the puppy sleep?   **4**

In which picture is the puppy given food?   **2**

To check comprehension of the picture story on this page, ask questions such as "Why does the puppy bark?" Point out the numbers on each picture and reinforce that there is a sequence of events in the story.

★ Reading a Story

FACTS Knowing the sounds that letters make helps children recognize words and builds reading skills.

Read the story aloud. Circle the correct word to answer each question.

A Puppy Named Pooky

Joey has a little puppy.
She is a funny puppy.
The puppy is named Pooky.
One day, Pooky went to hide.
Where are you, Pooky?
Pooky was under the table.

What is the story about?
a cat   (a puppy)

Is the puppy big or little?
big   (little)

What is the name of the puppy?
Joey   (Pooky)

Where was Pooky hiding?
(under the table)   under the bed

Reading words and listening to their sounds carefully is a step toward comprehending text. As your child listens to a story, he or she begins to see that words have meaning. Check his or her understanding of text. Read the text slowly, then repeat it. Review it before asking questions.

Reading to Understand ★

FACTS Children should be able to read with purpose and understanding. Regular reading reinforces fluency so that children read accurately, quickly, and with expression.

Read all about the life of a frog in the four boxes. Pick the correct word to complete each sentence below.

The Life of a Frog

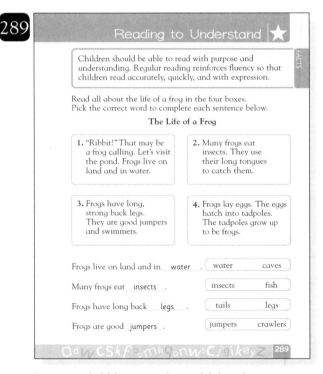

1. "Ribbit!" That may be a frog calling. Let's visit the pond. Frogs live on land and in water.

2. Many frogs eat insects. They use their long tongues to catch them.

3. Frogs have long, strong back legs. They are good jumpers and swimmers.

4. Frogs lay eggs. The eggs hatch into tadpoles. The tadpoles grow up to be frogs.

Frogs live on land and in __water__ .   water   caves

Many frogs eat __insects__ .   insects   fish

Frogs have long back __legs__ .   tails   legs

Frogs are good __jumpers__ .   jumpers   crawlers

Let your child listen to the real-life information on this page one or two times before he or she answers the questions. If your child does not recall the information, show him or her how to look back at the text to find answers.

Practice Page

Practice Page